MOST
requested
RECIPES

160

Taste *of* Home
RDA ENTHUSIAST BRANDS, LLC • MILWAUKEE, WI

364 RECIPES TO WIN YOU RAVES!

Taste of Home readers have created one of the best recipe swaps ever! Home cooks just like you share their most popular dishes, and each is evaluated by cooking experts to assure you it is easy to follow, tastes great and will cook up wonderfully in your kitchen. *Taste of Home Most Requested Recipes* contains 364 of our best-loved recipes.

This outstanding collection has everything you need...from weeknight dinners to company fare, including appetizers, brunch, soups, salads, sides and a scrumptious assortment of cookies and desserts. A bonus chapter, Seasonal Specialties, has memorable treats for year-round entertaining.

Inside you'll find quotes sprinkled throughout the pages from our TasteofHome.com community. These quotes let you know how much members enjoyed a particular recipe.

Two at-a-glance icons are a quick way for you to find the most popular recipe features:

FAST FIX ▶ These recipes are ready in 30 minutes or less.

(5) INGREDIENTS These recipes require no more than five items (not counting water, oil, salt and pepper) to create a delicious dish.

As always, the recipes give clear, concise directions and use readily available ingredients. The bounty of color food photos make it delightful to flip through the pages. Prep and cook times allow you to accurately plan your time in the kitchen.

With the delectable recipes featured in *Most Requested Recipes,* you're sure to place a winner on the dinner table each and every time.

MOST requested RECIPES

EDITORIAL

Editor-In-Chief	Catherine Cassidy
Creative Director	Howard Greenberg
Editorial Operations Director	Kerri Balliet
Managing Editor/Print & Digital Books	Mark Hagen
Associate Creative Director	Edwin Robles Jr.
Editor	Janet Briggs
Art Director	Raeann Sundholm
Layout Designer	Courtney Lovetere
Editorial Production Manager	Dena Ahlers
Copy Chief	Deb Warlaumont Mulvey
Copy Editors	Dulcie Shoener, Kaitlin Stainbrook, Mary-Liz Shaw
Chief Food Editor	Karen Berner
Food Editors	James Schend; Peggy Woodward, RD
Recipe Editors	Mary King; Jenni Sharp, RD; Irene Yeh
Content Operations Manager	Colleen King
Content Operations Assistant	Shannon Stroud
Executive Assistant	Marie Brannon
Test Kitchen & Food Styling Manager	Sarah Thompson
Test Cooks	Nicholas Iverson (Lead), Matthew Hass, Lauren Knoelke
Food Stylists	Kathryn Conrad (Senior), Shannon Roum, Leah Rekau
Prep Cooks	Megumi Garcia, Melissa Hansen, Bethany Van Jacobson, Sara Wirtz
Photography Director	Stephanie Marchese
Photographers	Dan Roberts, Jim Wieland
Photographer/Set Stylist	Grace Natoli Sheldon
Set Stylists	Stacey Genaw, Melissa Haberman, Dee Dee Jacq
Editorial Business Manager	Kristy Martin
Editorial Business Associate	Samantha Lea Stoeger
Editor, Taste of Home	Jeanne Ambrose
Associate Creative Director, Taste of Home	Erin Burns
Art Director, Taste of Home	Kristin Bowker

BUSINESS

Vice President, Chief Sales Officer	Mark S. Josephson
General Manager, Taste Of Home Cooking School	Erin Puariea

THE READER'S DIGEST ASSOCIATION, INC.

President and Chief Executive Officer	Bonnie Kintzer
Chief Financial Officer	Colette Chestnut
Vice President, Chief Operating Officer, North America	Howard Halligan
Vice President, Enthusiast Brands, Books & Retail	Harold Clarke
Vice President, North American Operations	Philippe Cloutier
Chief Marketing Officer	Leslie Dukker Doty
Vice President, North American Human Resources	Phyllis E. Gebhardt, SPHR
Vice President, Brand Marketing	Beth Gorry
Vice President, Global Communications	Susan Russ
Vice President, North American Technology	Aneel Tejwaney
Vice President, Consumer Marketing Planning	Jim Woods
Cover Photography	Jim Wieland
Set Stylist	Melissa Haberman
Food Stylist	Kathryn Conrad

International Standard Book Number: 978-1-61765-393-3
International Standard Serial Number: 2166-5022
Component Number: 119200013H00

Pictured on the front cover: Slow Cooker Beef Vegetable Stew (p. 136); Coconut-Pecan German Chocolate Pie (p. 169); Hero Pasta Salad (p. 115)

Pictured on the back cover: Tex-Mex Sloppy Joes (p. 52); Cranberry-Orange Trifle (p. 171)

TABLE OF CONTENTS

106

118

152

FETA BRUSCHETTA, PAGE 15

CHILLY COFFEE PUNCH, 14

LOADED BAKED POTATO DIP, 7

WHITE CHOCOLATE PARTY MIX, 11

APPETIZERS, SNACKS & BEVERAGES

Everyone loves to nibble on scrumptious little bites! Whether enjoyed at a party, served before dinner or devoured while watching the big game, the full-flavored snacks are popular no matter what the occasion. In fact, the faves on the following pages were rated absolutely delicious by home cooks just like you. Looking for a tasty dip, refreshing beverage or party contribution? Turn the page and start noshing!

SAVORY PEAR TARTS

Tiny pear tarts are a quick, easy and elegant addition to a party. Sprinkle the tops with a bit of candied pecans or walnuts for a slight crunch that complements the tender pears and flaky pastry.
—**LEE BELL** HOUSTON, TX

PREP: 30 MIN. • **BAKE:** 10 MIN./BATCH • **MAKES:** 50 APPETIZERS

- 2 **shallots, thinly sliced**
- ¼ **cup orange juice**
- ¼ **cup balsamic vinegar**
- ¼ **cup honey**
- 2 **tablespoons sugar**
- 1 **tablespoon lemon juice**
- 1 **garlic clove, minced**
- ⅛ **teaspoon salt**
- ⅛ **teaspoon pepper**
- 2 **Bosc pears, halved and sliced**
- 1 **package (17.3 ounces) frozen puff pastry, thawed**
- ⅓ **cup crumbled blue cheese**
    Chopped glazed pecans, optional

1. Combine the first nine ingredients in a small saucepan. Bring to a boil over medium heat; cook until liquid is reduced by half. Add pears; cook and stir 6-8 minutes or until pears are tender.
2. Meanwhile, preheat oven to 400°. Unfold puff pastry. Roll each pastry into a 10-in. square. Using a 2-in. round cookie cutter, cut out 25 circles from each square. Transfer to a greased baking sheet. Bake for 7-9 minutes or until golden brown.
3. Spoon pear mixture over pastries; sprinkle with cheese and, if desired, pecans.

PEANUT BUTTER & JELLY BITES

My friend is an avid runner. After I heard that she craved a peanut butter and jelly sandwich during a race, I whipped up these easy-to-carry bites for her.
—**JENNIFER HEASLEY** YORK, PA

PREP: 25 MIN. • **BAKE:** 15 MIN. + COOLING • **MAKES:** 2 DOZEN

- 4 **ounces cream cheese, softened**
- ½ **cup strawberry jelly, divided**
- 2 **tubes (8 ounces each) refrigerated seamless crescent dough sheets**
- ½ **cup creamy peanut butter**
- 1 **cup confectioners' sugar**
- 5 **tablespoons 2% milk**

1. Preheat oven to 350°. In a small bowl, beat cream cheese and ¼ cup jelly until smooth. Unroll each sheet of crescent dough into a rectangle. Spread each with half of the filling to within ½ in. of edges. Roll up jelly-roll style, starting with a long side; pinch seam to seal. Cut each roll widthwise into 12 slices; place on parchment paper-lined baking sheets, cut side down.
2. Bake 12-15 minutes or until golden brown. Cool on pans 2 minutes. Remove to wire racks to cool.
3. In a small bowl, beat the peanut butter, confectioners' sugar and milk until smooth. Drizzle over rolls; top with the remaining jelly.

FAST FIX ▶

LOADED BAKED POTATO DIP

I never thought of using waffle-cut fries as a scoop for dip until a friend of mine did at a baby shower. They're ideal for my cheesy bacon and chive dip, which tastes just like a baked potato topper.
—**ELIZABETH KING** DULUTH, MN

START TO FINISH: 10 MIN. • **MAKES:** 2½ CUPS

- 2 **cups (16 ounces) reduced-fat sour cream**
- 2 **cups (8 ounces) shredded reduced-fat cheddar cheese**
- 8 **center-cut bacon or turkey bacon strips, chopped and cooked**
- ⅓ **cup minced fresh chives**
- 2 **teaspoons Louisiana-style hot sauce**
  Hot cooked waffle-cut fries

In a small bowl, mix the first five ingredients until blended; refrigerate until serving. Serve with waffle fries.

❝ This dip was awesome with some oven fries—my hungry fireman devoured it! ❞
—**LAUREN HANAKO** TASTEOFHOME.COM

⑤ INGREDIENTS

ITALIAN MEATBALL BUNS

One of the greatest gifts I love to share with my six grandkids is making special recipes just for them. The meatballs tucked inside the rolls are a savory surprise.
—**TRINA LINDER-MOBLEY** CLOVER, SC

PREP: 30 MIN. + RISING • **BAKE:** 15 MIN. • **MAKES:** 2 DOZEN

- 12 **frozen bread dough dinner rolls**
- 1 **package (12 ounces) frozen fully cooked Italian meatballs, thawed**
- 2 **tablespoons olive oil**
- ¼ **cup grated Parmesan cheese**
- ¼ **cup minced fresh basil**
- 1½ **cups marinara sauce, warmed**

1. Let dough stand at room temperature 25-30 minutes or until softened.
2. Cut each roll in half. Wrap each portion around a meatball, enclosing meatball completely; pinch dough firmly to seal. Place on greased baking sheets, seam side down. Cover with kitchen towels; let rise in a warm place until almost doubled, about 1½ to 2 hours.
3. Preheat oven to 350°. Bake buns 12-15 minutes or until golden brown. Brush tops with oil; sprinkle with cheese and basil. Serve with marinara sauce.

(5) INGREDIENTS

SUMMERTIME TEA

You can't have a summer gathering around here without this sweet tea to cool you down. It's wonderful for sipping while basking by the pool.

—ANGELA LIVELY SPRING, TX

PREP: 15 MIN. + CHILLING
MAKES: 18 SERVINGS (¾ CUP EACH)

- 14 **cups water, divided**
- 6 **individual black tea bags**
- 1½ **cups sugar**
- ¾ **cup thawed frozen orange juice concentrate**
- ¾ **cup thawed frozen lemonade concentrate**
- 1 **cup tequila, optional**
  Fresh mint leaves and lemon or lime slices, optional

1. In a large saucepan, bring 4 cups water to a boil. Remove from heat; add tea bags. Cover and steep 3-5 minutes. Discard tea bags.

2. Stir in the sugar, concentrates and remaining water. If desired, add tequila. Refrigerate until chilled. If desired, garnish with mint and lemon.

TOP TIP

Storing Tea

Tea bags and loose tea may be stored at room temperature in an airtight container and out of direct sunlight for up to 2 years. If you're a fan of specialty or flavored teas, keep each kind or flavor of tea in a separate storage container.

PEPPERONI EXTREME DIP

With just 10 minutes of prep time and assistance from a slow cooker, this truly is a no-fuss dip.

—**LAURA STONESIFER** HOULTON, WI

PREP: 10 MIN. • **COOK:** 3 HOURS
MAKES: 2¼ QUARTS

- 4 cups (16 ounces) shredded cheddar cheese
- 3½ cups spaghetti sauce
- 2 cups mayonnaise
- 1 package (8 ounces) sliced pepperoni, chopped
- 1 can (6 ounces) pitted ripe olives, chopped
- 1 jar (5¾ ounces) sliced green olives with pimientos, drained and chopped
  Tortilla chips

Combine the first six ingredients in a 4-qt. slow cooker coated with cooking spray. Cover and cook on low 1½ hours; stir. Cover and cook 1½ hours longer or until cheese is melted. Serve with the tortilla chips.

---

⑤ INGREDIENTS FAST FIX

RANCH SNACK MIX

This fast-to-fix munchie has become a favorite. The recipe makes a generous 24 cups and doesn't involve any cooking!

—**LINDA MURPHY** PULASKI, WI

START TO FINISH: 15 MIN.
MAKES: 6 QUARTS

- 1 package (12 ounces) miniature pretzels
- 2 packages (6 ounces each) Bugles
- 1 can (10 ounces) salted cashews
- 1 package (6 ounces) miniature cheddar cheese fish-shaped crackers
- 1 envelope ranch salad dressing mix
- ¾ cup canola oil

In two large bowls, combine pretzels, Bugles, cashews and crackers. Sprinkle with the dressing mix; toss gently to combine. Drizzle with oil; toss until well coated. Store the snack mix in airtight containers.

---

⑤ INGREDIENTS

S'MORES-DIPPED APPLES

For me, the flavor combination of marshmallows, graham crackers and apples can't be beat. Others must think the same thing: Anytime I take the apples to a bake sale, they sell out in a flash.

—**MARIA REGAKIS** SAUGUS, MA

PREP: 20 MIN. • **COOK:** 10 MIN. + CHILLING
MAKES: 8 SERVINGS

- 8 large Granny Smith apples
- 8 wooden pop sticks
- 2 tablespoons butter
- 2 packages (16 ounces each) large marshmallows
- 2 cups coarsely crushed graham crackers
- 1 package (11½ ounces) milk chocolate chips

1. Line a baking sheet with waxed paper; generously coat waxed paper with cooking spray. Wash and dry apples; remove stems. Insert pop sticks into apples.

2. In a large heavy saucepan, melt the butter over medium heat. Add marshmallows; stir until melted. Dip apples, one at a time, into warm marshmallow mixture, allowing excess to drip off. Place on prepared baking sheet and refrigerate until set, about 15 minutes.

3. Place graham cracker crumbs in a shallow dish. In top of a double boiler or a metal bowl over barely simmering water, melt chocolate chips; stir until smooth. Dip bottom half of apples in chocolate; dip bottoms in cracker crumbs. Place on baking sheet. Refrigerate until set.

STUFFED BABY RED POTATOES

This recipe just says "party!" The ingredients are basic, but the finished appetizer makes it seem that you worked a lot harder than you did.

—**CAROLE BESS WHITE** PORTLAND, OR

PREP: 45 MIN. • **BAKE:** 15 MIN.
MAKES: 2 DOZEN

- 24 small red potatoes (about 2½ pounds)
- ¼ cup butter, cubed
- ½ cup shredded Parmesan cheese, divided
- ½ cup crumbled cooked bacon, divided
- ⅔ cup sour cream
- 1 egg, beaten
- ½ teaspoon salt
- ⅛ teaspoon pepper
- ⅛ teaspoon paprika

1. Scrub potatoes; place in a large saucepan and cover with water. Bring to a boil. Reduce heat; cover and cook 15-20 minutes or until tender. Drain.
2. Preheat oven to 375°. When potatoes are cool enough to handle, cut a thin slice off the top of each. Scoop out the pulp, leaving a thin shell. (Cut thin slices from potato bottoms to level if necessary.)
3. In a large bowl, mash the potato tops and pulp with butter. Set aside 2 tablespoons each of cheese and bacon for garnish; add remaining cheese and bacon to potatoes. Stir in the sour cream, egg, salt and pepper. Spoon mixture into potato shells. Top with remaining cheese and bacon; sprinkle with paprika.
4. Place in an ungreased 15x10x1-in. baking pan. Bake 12-18 minutes or until a thermometer reads 160°.

ANTIPASTO BRAID

We're big fans of Mediterranean food, so bread stuffed with a tasty antipasto was bound to be a favorite in my family. Meat and cheese make it a hearty appetizer.

—**PATRICIA HARMON** BADEN, PA

PREP: 25 MIN. • **BAKE:** 30 MIN. + STANDING
MAKES: 12 SERVINGS

- ⅓ cup pitted Greek olives, chopped
- ¼ cup marinated quartered artichoke hearts, drained and chopped
- ¼ cup julienned oil-packed sun-dried tomatoes
- 2 tablespoons plus 2 teaspoons grated Parmesan cheese, divided
- 3 tablespoons olive oil, divided
- 1 tablespoon chopped fresh basil or 1 teaspoon dried basil
- 1 tube (11 ounces) refrigerated crusty French loaf
- 6 thin slices prosciutto or deli ham
- 4 slices provolone cheese
- ¾ cup julienned roasted sweet red peppers

1. Preheat oven to 350°. In a small bowl, toss the olives, artichokes, tomatoes, 2 tablespoons Parmesan cheese, 2 tablespoons oil and basil until combined.
2. On a lightly floured surface, carefully unroll French loaf dough; roll into a 15x10-in. rectangle. Transfer to a greased 15x10x1-in. baking pan. Layer prosciutto, provolone cheese and red peppers lengthwise down center third of rectangle. Top with olive mixture.

3. On each long side, cut 10 strips about 3½ in. into the center. Starting at one end, fold alternating strips at an angle across filling, pinching ends to seal. Brush with remaining oil and sprinkle with remaining Parmesan cheese.
4. Bake 30-35 minutes or until golden brown. Let stand 10 minutes before cutting. Serve warm.

⑤INGREDIENTS FAST FIX

BACON-WRAPPED TATER TOTS

Indulge in one of these scrumptious bacon-wrapped treats and you'll taste why they're a hit with kids of all ages. They'll go fast—you may want to double the recipe!

—**JONI HILTON** ROCKLIN, CA

START TO FINISH: 25 MIN.
MAKES: 32 APPETIZERS

- 16 bacon strips, cut in half
- ½ cup maple syrup
- 1 teaspoon crushed red pepper flakes
- 32 frozen Tater Tots

1. Preheat oven to 400°. Cook bacon in a large skillet over medium heat until partially cooked but not crisp. Remove bacon to paper towels to drain; keep warm.
2. Combine syrup and pepper flakes. Dip each bacon piece in syrup mixture, then wrap around a Tater Tot. Secure with toothpicks.
3. Place on a greased rack in a 15x10x1-in. baking pan. Bake 12-15 minutes or until bacon is crisp.

WHITE CHOCOLATE PARTY MIX

You'll appreciate this microwave recipe when your oven is tied up with holiday baking. But don't reserve this snack only for Christmas—it's a perfect treat anytime. To color-coordinate to the season, buy red and green M&M's for Christmas, red and white for Valentine's Day, pastels for Easter and spring, or orange and black for Halloween.

—NORENE WRIGHT MANILLA, IN

START TO FINISH: 30 MIN.
MAKES: 5 QUARTS

- **5 cups Cheerios**
- **5 cups Corn Chex**
- **2 cups salted peanuts**
- **1 pound chocolate M&M's**
- **1 package (10 ounces) mini pretzels**
- **2 packages (12 ounces each) white baking chips**
- **3 tablespoons canola oil**

1. In a large bowl, combine the first five ingredients; set aside. In a microwave-safe bowl, heat chips and oil at 70% power for 1 minute, stirring once. Microwave on high for 5 seconds; stir until smooth.

2. Pour over cereal mixture and mix well. Spread onto three waxed paper-lined baking sheets. Cool; break apart. Store in an airtight container.

NOTE *This recipe was tested in a 1,100-watt microwave.*

HOLIDAY SALSA

You can tell that the recipe is a success when guests hover around the serving dish until it's scraped clean. The longer this salsa marinates in the refrigerator, the better it tastes.
—**SHELLY PATTISON** LUBBOCK, TX

PREP: 20 MIN. + CHILLING • **MAKES:** 12 SERVINGS

- 1 **package (12 ounces) fresh or frozen cranberries**
- 1 **cup sugar**
- 6 **green onions, chopped**
- ½ **cup fresh cilantro leaves, chopped**
- 1 **jalapeno pepper, seeded and finely chopped**
- 1 **package (8 ounces) cream cheese, softened**
  Assorted crackers or tortilla chips

1. Place cranberries and sugar in a food processor; cover and pulse until coarsely chopped. Transfer to a small bowl. Stir in the onions, cilantro and pepper. Cover and refrigerate for several hours or overnight.
2. To serve, place cream cheese on a serving plate. Drain salsa and spoon over cream cheese. Serve with crackers or chips.
NOTE *Wear disposable gloves when cutting hot peppers; the oils can burn skin. Avoid touching your face.*

FAST FIX ▶
HERBED CHEESE STICKS

We love the breadsticks at our local pizza parlor when they're hot and gooey right from the oven. Now I can get that same wonderful goody, but I never have to leave the house.
—**HEATHER BATES** ATHENS, ME

START TO FINISH: 30 MIN. • **MAKES:** 16 CHEESE STICKS

- 1 **package (6½ ounces) pizza crust mix**
- 1½ **teaspoons garlic powder**
- 1 **tablespoon olive oil**
- 1 **cup (4 ounces) shredded part-skim mozzarella cheese**
- ¼ **cup shredded Parmesan cheese**
- 1 **teaspoon Italian seasoning**
  Pizza sauce

1. Preheat oven to 450°. Mix pizza dough according to package directions, adding garlic powder to dry mix. Cover; let rest 5 minutes.
2. Knead dough 4-5 times or until easy to handle. On a greased baking sheet, press dough into an 8-in. square. Brush top with oil; sprinkle with cheeses and Italian seasoning.
3. Bake 6-8 minutes or until cheese is lightly browned. Cut in half; cut each half crosswise into eight strips. Serve with pizza sauce.

MUSHROOM & ONION CRESCENTS

I knew these stuffed crescents were keepers when my husband ate most of the filling before I could roll it up in the dough. Now I've had to get sneaky when I make them.

—**CARRIE POMMIER** FARMINGTON, MN

PREP: 25 MIN. • **BAKE:** 10 MIN. • **MAKES:** 8 ROLLS

- 3 **tablespoons butter, divided**
- 1 **cup sliced baby portobello mushrooms**
- 1 **medium onion, halved and sliced**
- 3 **garlic cloves, minced**
- ⅓ **cup grated Parmesan cheese**
- 1 **tablespoon minced fresh parsley**
- 1 **tube (8 ounces) refrigerated reduced-fat crescent rolls**
- ½ **cup shredded part-skim mozzarella cheese**

1. Preheat oven to 375°. In a large skillet, heat 2 tablespoons butter over medium-high heat. Add mushrooms and onion; cook and stir 2-3 minutes or until softened. Reduce heat to medium-low; cook and stir 10-12 minutes or until onion is golden. Add garlic; cook 1 minute longer. Remove from heat; stir in Parmesan cheese and parsley.

2. Unroll crescent dough; separate into triangles. Place 1 tablespoon mushroom mixture at the wide end of each triangle; top with 1 tablespoon mozzarella cheese and roll up. Place 2 in. apart on an ungreased baking sheet, point side down; curve ends to form a crescent. Melt remaining butter; brush over tops.

3. Bake 10-12 minutes or until golden brown. Refrigerate any leftovers.

❝ Delicious! Even my 6-year-old loved it! Of course I had to chop up the mushrooms to fool him! ❞
—**BRANDSAN** TASTEOFHOME.COM

FAST FIX ▸

MINI CRAB TARTS

Crisp phyllo tart shells are heavenly with this warm, rich, creamy crab filling. They're always a hit at get-togethers.

—**LINDA STEMEN** MONROEVILLE, IN

START TO FINISH: 25 MIN. • **MAKES:** 30 APPETIZERS

- 2 **packages (1.9 ounces each) frozen miniature phyllo tart shells**
- 1 **egg**
- ¼ **cup 2% milk**
- ¼ **cup mayonnaise**
- 1 **tablespoon all-purpose flour**
- ⅛ **teaspoon salt**
- 1 **can (6 ounces) lump crabmeat, drained**
- 2 **tablespoons shredded Monterey Jack cheese**
- 1 **tablespoon chopped green onion**
  Thinly sliced green onions, optional

1. Preheat oven to 375°. Place tart shells in an ungreased 15x10x1-in. baking pan. In a small bowl, whisk egg, milk, mayonnaise, flour and salt until smooth. Stir in crab, cheese and chopped onion. Spoon into tart shells.

2. Bake 9-11 minutes or until set. Garnish with sliced onions if desired. Serve warm.

CREAMY JALAPENO POPPER DIP

This recipe will remind you of a jalapeno popper without all the messiness. If my husband had his way, he would have me make this for him every weekend.

—**DEBORAH PEIRCE** VIRGINIA BEACH, VA

PREP: 15 MIN. • **BAKE:** 30 MIN.
MAKES: 2 CUPS

- 4 **bacon strips, chopped**
- 1 **package (8 ounces) cream cheese, softened**
- 2 **cups (8 ounces) shredded cheddar cheese**
- ½ **cup sour cream**
- ¼ **cup 2% milk**
- 3 **jalapeno peppers, seeded and chopped**
- 1 **teaspoon white wine vinegar**
- ⅓ **cup panko (Japanese) bread crumbs**
- 2 **tablespoons butter**
  Tortilla chips

1. Preheat oven to 350°. In a small skillet, cook bacon over medium heat until crisp, stirring occasionally. Remove with a slotted spoon; drain on paper towels. Discard drippings, reserving 1 tablespoon.

2. In a large bowl, mix the cream cheese, cheddar cheese, sour cream, milk, jalapenos, vinegar, cooked bacon and reserved drippings. Transfer to a greased 8-in.-square baking dish. Sprinkle with bread crumbs; dot with butter.

3. Bake 30-35 minutes or until bubbly and topping is golden brown. Serve with chips.

NOTE *Wear disposable gloves when cutting hot peppers; the oils can burn skin. Avoid touching your face.*

⑤INGREDIENTS

CHILLY COFFEE PUNCH

For a twist on the usual fruit punch, try a flavored coffee with ice cream. Make the base the day before for easy prep the day of serving.

—**JUDY WILSON** SUN CITY WEST, AZ

PREP: 10 MIN. + CHILLING
MAKES: 24 SERVINGS

- 6 **cups hot strong brewed coffee**
- ¼ **cup sugar**
- ½ **cup coffee liqueur**
- 1 **carton (1½ quarts) vanilla ice cream, softened**
- 1 **carton (1½ quarts) chocolate ice cream, softened**
  Optional toppings: whipped cream, chocolate syrup and chocolate shavings

1. In a pitcher, combine the coffee and sugar, stirring to dissolve sugar. Refrigerate, covered, until cold, about 45 minutes.

2. Stir liqueur into coffee. Just before serving, spoon the ice cream into a punch bowl. Stir in coffee mixture. If desired, serve with toppings.

FETA BRUSCHETTA

You won't believe the compliments you'll receive when you greet guests with these warm appetizers. Each crispy bite offers the savory tastes of feta cheese, basil, garlic and tomatoes. They're terrific for holiday parties or most any gathering.

—STACEY RINEHART EUGENE, OR

START TO FINISH: 30 MIN.
MAKES: 10 APPETIZERS

- ¼ **cup butter, melted**
- ¼ **cup olive oil**
- 10 **slices French bread (1 inch thick)**
- 1 **package (4 ounces) crumbled feta cheese**
- 2 **to 3 garlic cloves, minced**
- 1 **tablespoon minced fresh basil or 1 teaspoon dried basil**
- 1 **large tomato, seeded and chopped**

1. Preheat oven to 350°. In a small bowl, combine butter and oil; brush onto both sides of bread. Place on a baking sheet. Bake 8-10 minutes or until lightly browned on top.
2. Combine the feta cheese, garlic and basil; sprinkle over toast. Top with tomato. Bake 8-10 minutes longer or until heated through. Serve warm.

TOP TIP

Seeding Tomatoes

To seed a tomato, cut it in half and gently squeeze each tomato half. Seeding a tomato this way not only removes the seeds, but also eliminates some of the juice that can make a dish too watery. If you don't want to lose as much juice, use a small spoon to scoop out the seeds.

QUESO FUNDIDO

Dig in to this hot one-skillet dip and enjoy gooey cheese and the spicy kick from chorizo and pepper jack.

—JULIE MERRIMAN SEATTLE, WA

PREP: 20 MIN. • **BAKE:** 15 MIN. • **MAKES:** 6 CUPS

- 1 **pound uncooked chorizo**
- 2 **cups fresh or frozen corn, thawed**
- 1 **large red onion, chopped**
- 1 **poblano pepper, chopped**
- 8 **ounces fresh goat cheese, crumbled**
- 2 **cups cubed Monterey Jack cheese**
- 1 **cup cubed pepper jack cheese**
- 1 **large tomato, seeded and chopped**
- 3 **green onions, thinly sliced**
  Blue corn tortilla chips

1. Preheat oven to 350°. Crumble chorizo into a 10-in. ovenproof skillet; add corn, red onion and pepper. Cook over medium heat 6-8 minutes or until meat is fully cooked; drain. Stir in the cheeses.

2. Bake 14-16 minutes or until bubbly. Sprinkle with tomato and green onions. Serve with chips.

TOP TIP

Keeping Dips Warm

Warm dips may be prepared ahead and then heated in a slow cooker instead of the oven. During a party, a slow cooker can keep the dip warm. The dip will also stay warm in a chafing dish or fondue pot or on a hot plate.

BAKED CREAMY SPINACH DIP

I'm a fan of classic dishes, but I frequently tweak them a bit to suit my family's tastes. My cheesy spinach dip is a little lighter than other versions I've seen and pairs well with bagel chips.

—JENNIFER TIDWELL FAIR OAKS, CA

PREP: 25 MIN. • **BAKE:** 30 MIN. • **MAKES:** 14 SERVINGS (¼ CUP EACH)

- 2 **packages (10 ounces each) frozen chopped spinach, thawed**
- 1 **tablespoon butter**
- 2 **garlic cloves, minced**
- 1 **tablespoon all-purpose flour**
- 1 **can (12 ounces) evaporated milk**
- ½ **cup grated Parmesan cheese, divided**
- ¼ **cup cream cheese**
- ¼ **cup ricotta cheese**
- ¼ **teaspoon ground nutmeg**
- ½ **teaspoon salt**
- ¼ **teaspoon pepper**
  Bagel chips

1. Preheat oven to 350°. Place spinach in a colander over a bowl; squeeze dry, reserving 1 cup spinach liquid.

2. In a large saucepan, heat butter over medium heat. Add garlic; cook 1 minute. Stir in flour until blended; gradually whisk in milk and reserved spinach liquid. Bring to a boil, stirring constantly; cook and stir 2-3 minutes or until the sauce is thickened. Stir in ¼ cup Parmesan cheese, cream cheese, ricotta cheese, seasonings and spinach; cook and stir until blended.

3. Transfer to a 1½-qt. baking dish. Bake 25-30 minutes or until bubbly and top is lightly browned. Remove from oven; top with remaining Parmesan cheese. Bake 4-5 minutes longer or until cheese is melted. Serve with bagel chips.

FAST FIX ▶
SHRIMP AND GOAT CHEESE STUFFED MUSHROOMS

Here's a fast, easy recipe that makes a delicious appetizer for all your holiday parties.
—**MARY ANN LEE** CLIFTON PARK, NY

START TO FINISH: 30 MIN. • **MAKES:** ABOUT 2 DOZEN

- ½ **pound uncooked shrimp, peeled, deveined and finely chopped**
- 1 **log (4 ounces) herbed fresh goat cheese, crumbled**
- ⅓ **cup chopped green onions**
- ¼ **cup panko (Japanese) bread crumbs**
- 1 **teaspoon minced fresh gingerroot**
- ½ **teaspoon crushed red pepper flakes**
- ½ **teaspoon salt**
- ¼ **teaspoon pepper**
- ½ **pound whole baby portobello mushrooms, stems removed**
- 2 **tablespoons sesame oil**
  Thinly sliced green onions, optional

1. Preheat oven to 350°. In a small bowl, mix shrimp, goat cheese, onions, bread crumbs, ginger, pepper flakes, salt and pepper. Mound shrimp mixture into mushroom caps and place on an ungreased baking sheet. Drizzle with sesame oil.
2. Bake 10-15 minutes or until shrimp turns pink. If desired, garnish with green onions. Serve warm.

FAST FIX ▶
SMOKED SALMON BITES WITH SHALLOT SAUCE

Tangy Dijon-mayo sauce adds zip to layers of crisp arugula, smoked salmon and shaved Asiago cheese. I make these a couple of times a year.
—**JAMIE BROWN-MILLER** NAPA, CA

START TO FINISH: 30 MIN. • **MAKES:** 25 APPETIZERS

- 1 **sheet frozen puff pastry, thawed**
- **SAUCE**
- 2 **shallots**
- 2 **tablespoons Dijon mustard**
- 1 **tablespoon mayonnaise**
- 1 **tablespoon red wine vinegar**
- ¼ **cup olive oil**
- **FINISHING**
- 1 **cup fresh arugula or baby spinach, coarsely chopped**
- 4½ **ounces smoked salmon or lox, thinly sliced**
- ½ **cup shaved Asiago cheese**

1. Preheat oven to 400°. Unfold puff pastry; cut into 25 squares. Transfer to greased baking sheets. Bake 11-13 minutes or until golden brown.
2. Meanwhile, grate one shallot and finely chop the other. In a small bowl, combine shallots, mustard, mayonnaise and vinegar. While whisking, gradually add oil in a steady stream. Spoon a small amount of sauce onto each pastry; layer with arugula and salmon. Drizzle with remaining sauce and sprinkle with cheese.

❝These were tasty and looked great.❞
—**WILLIAMSEGRAVES** TASTEOFHOME.COM

HOT BACON CHEESE DIP

I've tried several warm dip recipes before, but this one is a surefire people-pleaser. It's thick, with lots of bacon and cheese flavors that always keep my friends happily munching.

—SUZANNE WHITAKER KNOXVILLE, TN

PREP: 15 MIN. • **COOK:** 2 HOURS
MAKES: 4 CUPS

- 2 **packages (8 ounces each) cream cheese, cubed**
- 4 **cups (16 ounces) shredded cheddar cheese**
- 1 **cup half-and-half cream**
- 2 **teaspoons Worcestershire sauce**
- 1 **teaspoon dried minced onion**
- 1 **teaspoon prepared mustard**
- 16 **bacon strips, cooked and crumbled**
   Tortilla chips or French bread slices

1. In a 1½-qt. slow cooker, combine the first six ingredients. Cover and cook on low 2-3 hours or until cheeses are melted, stirring occasionally.
2. Just before serving, stir in the bacon. Serve warm with tortilla chips or bread.

MIXED BERRY SANGRIA

My light, tasty beverage is so refreshing. I like to serve it with spoons so everyone can enjoy the fresh berries once the sangria is gone.

—LINDA CIFUENTES MAHOMET, IL

PREP: 10 MIN. + CHILLING
MAKES: 10 SERVINGS (¾ CUP EACH)

- 1 **bottle (750 milliliters) sparkling white wine**
- 2½ **cups white cranberry juice**
- ⅔ **cup light or coconut rum**
- ⅓ **cup each fresh blackberries, blueberries and raspberries**
- ⅓ **cup chopped fresh strawberries Ice cubes**

In a large pitcher, mix wine, juice and rum; add fruit. Cover and refrigerate at least 2 hours; serve over ice.

NACHO SCOOPS

Serve your group a big platter of these fun and crazy-tasty nacho bites as you cheer for your team. You'll score big with the cute and savory cups.
—**RAINE D GOTTESS** OAK HILL, FL

PREP: 40 MIN. • **BAKE:** 5 MIN./BATCH
MAKES: 12 DOZEN

- ¾ pound ground beef
- 1 medium onion, finely chopped
- 1 medium sweet red pepper, finely chopped
- 1 envelope taco seasoning
- 1 can (14½ ounces) diced tomatoes and green chilies, undrained
- 1 can (4 ounces) chopped green chilies
- 8 ounces pepper jack cheese, cubed
- 4 ounces process cheese (Velveeta), cubed
- 4 ounces cream cheese, softened, cubed
- 1 package (12 ounces) tortilla chip scoops
- 2 cups (8 ounces) shredded Mexican cheese blend
  Sour cream and pickled jalapeno slices

1. In a large skillet, cook the beef, onion and red pepper over medium heat until meat is no longer pink; drain. Stir in the taco seasoning, tomatoes and green chilies. Cook and stir 5-7 minutes or until thickened.
2. Reduce heat to low. Stir in pepper jack cheese, process cheese and cream cheese until melted.
3. Preheat the oven to 375°. Place 4 dozen tortilla chip scoops on an ungreased baking sheet. Add a rounded teaspoon of beef mixture to each. Sprinkle with the Mexican cheese blend.
4. Bake about 5 minutes or until heated through. Garnish each with sour cream and a jalapeno pepper slice. Repeat with remaining tortilla chip scoops.

APPLE-MUSTARD GLAZED MEATBALLS

Convenient frozen meatballs simplify prep in this couldn't-be-easier appetizer. Apple jelly and spicy brown mustard play starring roles in the sweet and savory sauce that glazes the meatballs beautifully.
—**PAM CORDER** MONROE, LOUISIANA

PREP: 10 MIN. • **BAKE:** 30 MIN.
MAKES: 32 MEATBALLS

- 32 frozen fully cooked homestyle meatballs (½ ounce each)
- ⅓ cup apple jelly
- 3 tablespoons unsweetened apple juice
- 3 tablespoons spicy brown mustard
- ½ teaspoon Worcestershire sauce
- ¼ teaspoon hot pepper sauce

1. Place meatballs in a single layer in a greased 15x10x1-in. baking pan. Bake according to package directions.
2. Meanwhile, combine the remaining ingredients in a large saucepan. Bring to a boil over medium heat.
3. Transfer meatballs to sauce; stir gently to coat. Return to a boil. Reduce heat; simmer, uncovered, 3-5 minutes or until sauce is thickened, stirring occasionally.

(5) INGREDIENTS

HAWAIIAN CHEESE BREAD

This bread is absolutely scrumptious. My mother's friend brought it to a party at work, and after one bite, Mom knew she had to have the recipe. Simple and fast, the loaf is a hit with everybody and at every kind of function.
—**AMY MCILVAIN** WILMINGTON, DE

PREP: 15 MIN. • **BAKE:** 25 MIN.
MAKES: 16 SERVINGS

- 1 loaf (1 pound) Hawaiian sweet bread
- 1 block (8 ounces) Swiss cheese
- 3 slices red onion, chopped
- ½ cup butter, melted
- 3 garlic cloves, minced
- 1 teaspoon salt

1. Preheat oven to 350°. Cut bread diagonally into 1-in. slices to within 1 in. of bottom. Repeat cuts in opposite direction. Cut Swiss cheese into ¼-in. slices; cut slices into small pieces. Insert into bread. Mix onion, butter, garlic and salt; spoon over bread.
2. Wrap loaf in foil. Bake 25-30 minutes or until cheese is melted. Serve warm.

GREEK BREADSTICKS

Get ready for rave reviews with my crispy Greek-inspired appetizers. They're best served hot and fresh from the oven with your favorite tzatziki sauce.

—JANE WHITTAKER PENSACOLA, FL

PREP: 20 MIN. • **BAKE:** 15 MIN. • **MAKES:** 32 BREADSTICKS

- ¼ **cup marinated quartered artichoke hearts, drained**
- 2 **tablespoons pitted Greek olives**
- 1 **package (17.3 ounces) frozen puff pastry, thawed**
- 1 **carton (6½ ounces) spreadable spinach and artichoke cream cheese**
- 2 **tablespoons grated Parmesan cheese**
- 1 **egg**
- 1 **tablespoon water**
- 2 **teaspoons sesame seeds**
  Refrigerated tzatziki sauce, optional

1. Preheat oven to 400°. Place artichokes and olives in a food processor; cover and pulse until finely chopped. Unfold one pastry sheet on a lightly floured surface; spread half of the cream cheese over half of pastry. Top with half of the artichoke mixture. Sprinkle with half of the Parmesan cheese. Fold plain half over filling; press gently to seal.

2. Repeat with remaining pastry, cream cheese, artichoke mixture and Parmesan cheese. Whisk egg and water; brush over tops. Sprinkle with sesame seeds. Cut each rectangle into sixteen ¾-in.-wide strips. Twist strips several times; place 2 in. apart on greased baking sheets.

3. Bake 12-14 minutes or until golden brown. Serve warm, with tzatziki sauce if desired.

COCONUT CASHEW CRUNCH

This crunch is always a hit for Christmas snacking. It's one of my husband's favorites, even though he says he doesn't like coconut! It's incredible on ice cream.

—DANA NEMECEK SKIATOOK, OK

PREP: 20 MIN. • **BAKE:** 50 MIN. • **MAKES:** 3 QUARTS

- 9 **cups Rice Krispies**
- 2 **cups flaked coconut**
- 1 **can (8 ounces) salted cashew pieces**
- 1 **cup packed brown sugar**
- ½ **cup butter, cubed**
- ½ **cup light corn syrup**
- 1 **teaspoon vanilla extract**
- ½ **teaspoon baking soda**

1. Preheat oven to 250°. In a large bowl, combine the cereal, coconut and cashews.

2. In a large saucepan, combine the brown sugar, butter and corn syrup; bring to a boil over medium heat, stirring constantly. Cook and stir 5 minutes. Remove from heat; stir in vanilla and baking soda. Pour over cereal mixture; toss to coat.

3. Transfer to two foil-lined 15x10x1-in. baking pans. Bake 50-60 minutes or until golden brown, stirring every 15 minutes. Cool completely in pan on a wire rack. Serve as is or use as a topping for ice cream, fruit or yogurt. Store in airtight containers.

> ❝ So nice for gifting at Christmas! Very easy to make and delicious. ❞
>
> **—PRICELESS** TASTEOFHOME.COM

GINGERED SWEET & SPICY HOT WINGS

My hot wings are a foolproof way to curry a little favor with the men in my life. Thanks to tons of sweet (orange marmalade) and hot (Sriracha) flavors bursting through with every bite, these wings are a winner on game day or any day of the week.

—JENNIFER LOCKLIN CYPRESS, TX

PREP: 15 MIN. + MARINATING • **BAKE:** 35 MIN.
MAKES: ABOUT 3 DOZEN

- 1 **cup orange marmalade**
- ½ **cup minced fresh cilantro**
- ½ **cup Sriracha Asian hot chili sauce**
- ½ **cup reduced-sodium soy sauce**
- ¼ **cup lime juice**
- ¼ **cup rice vinegar**
- ¼ **cup ketchup**
- ¼ **cup honey**
- 4 **garlic cloves, minced**
- 1 **tablespoon minced fresh gingerroot**
- 1 **tablespoon grated lime peel**
- 1 **tablespoon sesame oil**
- 1 **teaspoon salt**
- 1 **teaspoon pepper**
- 4 **pounds chicken wingettes and drumettes**

1. In a large resealable plastic bag, combine the first 14 ingredients. Add chicken; seal bag and turn to coat. Refrigerate 8 hours or overnight.
2. Preheat oven to 375°. Drain chicken, discarding marinade. Transfer chicken to two greased 15x10x1-in. baking pans. Bake 35-45 minutes or until juices run clear.

(5) INGREDIENTS FAST FIX

STRAWBERRY LEMONADE SMOOTHIE

We love the perfect blend of sweetness and citrus in this refreshing smoothie. It's so easy to throw together, I often find myself making one for breakfast or a midday snack.
—JAMIE KING DULUTH, MN

START TO FINISH: 5 MIN. • **MAKES:** 4 SERVINGS

- 2 **cups lemonade**
- ¾ **cup (6 ounces) lemon yogurt**
- ½ **teaspoon vanilla extract**
- 2 **cups frozen unsweetened strawberries**

Place all ingredients in a blender; cover and process 15 seconds or until blended. Serve immediately.

ORANGE RICOTTA PANCAKES, PAGE 26

FARMER'S CASSEROLE, 27

MAPLE-GLAZED SAUSAGES, 40

PEANUT BUTTER & JELLY WAFFLES, 37

Breakfast & Brunch

Wake up sleepyheads with the tantalizing aromas of breakfast, and you'll be surprised at how quickly they come to the table. From flapjacks and savory egg bakes to luscious overnight French toast and delicious sausage, you'll find the ideal eye-opening meal to get your family's day off to a fabulous start.

FAST FIX

SCRAMBLED EGG MUFFINS

After enjoying scrambled egg muffins at a local restaurant, I came up with a savory version that my husband likes even better. Freeze the extras to reheat on busy mornings.

—**CATHY LARKINS** MARSHFIELD, MO

START TO FINISH: 30 MIN. • **MAKES:** 1 DOZEN

- ½ **pound bulk pork sausage**
- 12 **eggs**
- ½ **cup chopped onion**
- ¼ **cup chopped green pepper**
- ½ **teaspoon salt**
- ¼ **teaspoon garlic powder**
- ¼ **teaspoon pepper**
- ½ **cup shredded cheddar cheese**

1. Preheat oven to 350°. In a large skillet, cook sausage over medium heat until no longer pink; drain.

2. In a large bowl, beat eggs. Add onion, green pepper, salt, garlic powder and pepper. Stir in sausage and cheese.

3. Spoon by ⅓ cupfuls into muffin cups coated with cooking spray. Bake 20-25 minutes or until a knife inserted near the center comes out clean.

FREEZE OPTION *Cool baked egg muffins. Cover and place on waxed paper-lined baking sheets and freeze until firm. Transfer to resealable plastic freezer bags; return to freezer. To use, place in greased muffin pan, cover loosely with foil and reheat in a preheated 350° oven until heated through. Or, microwave each muffin on high 30-60 seconds or until heated.*

HOT FRUIT COMPOTE

Pair the sweet and colorful fruit compote with an egg casserole for a delightful brunch. It can bake right alongside the eggs, so everything is conveniently done at the same time.

—**JOYCE MOYNIHAN** LAKEVILLE, MN

PREP: 15 MIN. • **BAKE:** 40 MIN. • **MAKES:** 20 SERVINGS

- 2 **cans (15¼ ounces each) sliced pears, drained**
- 1 **can (29 ounces) sliced peaches, drained**
- 1 **can (20 ounces) unsweetened pineapple chunks, drained**
- 1 **package (20 ounces) pitted dried plums**
- 1 **jar (16 ounces) unsweetened applesauce**
- 1 **can (21 ounces) cherry pie filling**
- ¼ **cup packed brown sugar**

1. Preheat oven to 350°. In a large bowl, combine the first five ingredients. Pour into a 13 x 9-in. baking dish coated with cooking spray. Spread pie filling over fruit mixture; sprinkle with brown sugar.

2. Cover and bake 40-45 minutes or until bubbly. Serve the compote warm.

FARM FRESH QUICHE

Going to the farmers market and talking with people who work on the farm inspires me to make recipes like this one, a quiche loaded with fresh veggies.

—**HEATHER KING** FROSTBURG, MD

PREP: 35 MIN. • **BAKE:** 30 MIN. + STANDING • **MAKES:** 6 SERVINGS

- ¼ **cup olive oil**
- 1 **bunch broccoli, cut into florets**
- 1 **small onion, finely chopped**
- 3 **cups chopped fresh mustard greens or spinach**
- 3 **garlic cloves, minced**
- 1 **sheet refrigerated pie pastry**
- 4 **eggs**
- 1 **cup 2% milk**
- 1 **tablespoon minced fresh rosemary or 1 teaspoon dried rosemary, crushed**
- ½ **teaspoon salt**
- ½ **teaspoon pepper**
- ½ **cup shredded smoked cheddar cheese, divided**
- ½ **cup shredded Swiss cheese, divided**

1. Preheat oven to 375°. In a large skillet, heat oil over medium-high heat. Add broccoli and onion; cook and stir until broccoli is crisp-tender. Stir in greens and garlic; cook and stir 4-5 minutes longer or until greens are wilted.

2. Unroll pastry sheet into a 9-in. pie plate; flute edge. Fill with broccoli mixture. In a small bowl, whisk eggs, milk, rosemary, salt and pepper. Stir in ¼ cup cheddar cheese and ¼ cup Swiss cheese; pour over vegetables. Sprinkle with remaining cheeses.

3. Bake 30-35 minutes or until a knife inserted near the center comes out clean. Let stand 15 minutes before cutting.

FAST FIX ►

ORANGE RICOTTA PANCAKES

These popular pancakes are likely to spark a desire to have hotcakes for breakfast as often as possible.

—**BREHAN KOHL** ANCHORAGE, AK

START TO FINISH: 30 MIN. • **MAKES:** 12 PANCAKES

- 1½ cups all-purpose flour
- 3 tablespoons sugar
- 1½ teaspoons baking powder
- ½ teaspoon baking soda
- ¼ teaspoon salt
- 1 egg
- 1 cup part-skim ricotta cheese
- ¾ cup 2% milk
- ½ teaspoon grated orange peel
- ½ cup orange juice
- ¼ cup butter, melted
- ½ teaspoon vanilla extract
  Maple syrup and confectioners' sugar

1. In a bowl, whisk the first five ingredients. In another bowl, whisk egg, cheese, milk, orange peel, orange juice, melted butter and vanilla until blended. Add to the dry ingredients; stir just until moistened.

2. Lightly grease a griddle; heat over medium heat. Pour batter by ¼ cupfuls onto griddle. Cook until bubbles on top begin to pop and bottoms are golden brown. Turn; cook until second side is golden brown. Serve with maple syrup and confectioners' sugar.

DELECTABLE GRANOLA

Be sure to remove the granola from the cookie sheets within 20 minutes or the granola may stick to the sheets.

—**LORI STEVENS** RIVERTON, UT

PREP: 20 MIN. • **BAKE:** 25 MIN. + COOLING • **MAKES:** 11 CUPS

- 8 cups old-fashioned oats
- 1 cup finely chopped almonds
- 1 cup finely chopped pecans
- ½ cup flaked coconut
- ½ cup packed brown sugar
- ½ cup canola oil
- ½ cup honey
- ¼ cup maple syrup
- 2 teaspoons ground cinnamon
- 1½ teaspoons salt
- 2 teaspoons vanilla extract
  Plain yogurt, optional

1. Preheat oven to 350°. In a large bowl, combine the oats, almonds, pecans and coconut. In a small saucepan, combine the brown sugar, oil, honey, maple syrup, cinnamon and salt. Heat 3-4 minutes over medium heat until sugar is dissolved. Remove from heat; stir in vanilla. Pour over the oat mixture; stir to coat.

2. Transfer to two 15x10x1-in. baking pans coated with cooking spray. Bake 25-30 minutes or until crisp, stirring every 10 minutes. Cool in pans on wire racks. Store in an airtight container. Serve with yogurt if desired.

FARMER'S CASSEROLE

Between family and friends, we average 375 visitors a year! This casserole is very handy for overnight guests. You can put it together the night before, let the flavors blend, and then bake it in the a.m.
—**NANCY SCHMIDT** CENTER, CO

PREP: 10 MIN. + CHILLING • **BAKE:** 55 MIN.
MAKES: 6 SERVINGS

- 3 **cups frozen shredded hash brown potatoes**
- ¾ **cup shredded Monterey Jack cheese**
- 1 **cup cubed fully cooked ham**
- ¼ **cup chopped green onions**
- 4 **eggs**
- 1 **can (12 ounces) evaporated milk**
- ¼ **teaspoon pepper**
- ⅛ **teaspoon salt**

1. Place potatoes in an 8-in.-square baking dish. Sprinkle with cheese, ham and onions. Whisk eggs, milk, pepper and salt; pour over all. Cover and refrigerate for several hours or overnight.

2. Remove from the refrigerator 30 minutes before baking. Preheat oven to 350°. Bake, uncovered, 55-60 minutes or until a knife inserted near center comes out clean.

TOP TIP

How Fresh Are the Eggs in Your Refrigerator?

Properly refrigerated, eggs will keep about 3 weeks after you bring them home. You can easily check the freshness of an uncooked egg by placing it in a glass of cold water. If the egg is fresh, it will remain on the bottom of the glass. If the egg floats to the surface of the water, it is not fresh and should not be used. If the egg stands upright and bobs on the bottom of the glass, it is less than fresh but is still all right to use. These eggs are good when you need to prepare hard-cooked eggs because they'll be easier to peel.

FAST FIX

BLUEBERRY FRENCH TOAST

Sit down to hot-off-the-griddle stuffed French toast and fresh blueberry sauce in as little as half an hour. The bread is toasted to a golden brown, and the delectable filling features cream cheese flavored with blueberry preserves and maple syrup. The fast sauce is out of this world!

—*TASTE OF HOME* TEST KITCHEN

START TO FINISH: 30 MIN. • **MAKES:** 8 SERVINGS (1¾ CUPS SAUCE)

- 1 package (8 ounces) cream cheese, softened
- ¼ cup maple syrup, divided
- 2 tablespoons blueberry preserves
- 16 slices French bread (½ inch thick)
- 2 eggs
- 1 cup 2% milk
- 2 tablespoons all-purpose flour
- 2 teaspoons vanilla extract
- ¼ teaspoon salt

SAUCE

- 1 cup sugar
- 1 cup cold water
- 2 tablespoons cornstarch
- 1 cup fresh or frozen blueberries
- 1 tablespoon butter

1. Beat the cream cheese, 2 tablespoons syrup and preserves in a small bowl. Spread over eight slices of bread; top with remaining bread.

2. Whisk the eggs, milk, flour, vanilla, salt and remaining syrup in a shallow bowl. Dip both sides of sandwiches into egg mixture. Cook on a greased hot griddle until golden brown on both sides.

3. Combine the sugar, water and cornstarch until smooth in a small saucepan. Bring to a boil over medium heat; cook and stir 3 minutes or until thickened. Stir in blueberries; bring to a boil. Reduce heat and simmer 8-10 minutes or until berries burst. Remove from heat; stir in the butter. Serve with French toast.

BACON BREAKFAST CUPS

My son joked about adding bacon to cupcakes. I made bacon cups the next morning. The look on his face was priceless.

—**KAREN BURKETT** RESEDA, CA

PREP: 30 MIN. • **BROIL:** 5 MIN. • **MAKES:** 6 SERVINGS

- 18 turkey bacon strips, cut in half
- 1 cup frozen shredded hash brown potatoes
- 2 eggs
- 2 teaspoons 2% milk
  Dash each salt and pepper
- 2 teaspoons butter
- ¼ cup shredded Mexican cheese blend
  Chopped green onion and fresh parsley

1. Preheat oven to 375°. Line 12 alternating cups in a mini-muffin pan with bacon pieces, crisscrossing three strips in each so they resemble spokes of a wheel. Loosely crumple twelve 3-in. strips of aluminum foil into balls; place in cups to keep bacon from sliding. Bake 15-20 minutes or until bacon is crisp.

2. Cook potatoes according to package directions. In a small bowl, whisk eggs, milk, salt and pepper. In a small skillet, heat butter over medium heat. Pour in egg mixture; cook and stir until eggs are thickened and no liquid egg remains.

3. Transfer bacon cups to a baking sheet; remove foil. Spoon hash browns and scrambled eggs into cups; sprinkle with cheese. Broil 3-4 in. from heat 3-5 minutes or until cheese is melted. Sprinkle with green onion and parsley.

> "Took them to a Bible study and everyone loved them. They all were gone but three. Perfect size and tasted amazing. Definitely going to make again."
> —**WAVER** TASTEOFHOME.COM

DUTCH BAKED PANCAKE WITH STRAWBERRY-ALMOND COMPOTE

Pannekoeken, or Dutch baked pancakes, are a treat in my husband's family. You can also try this recipe with vanilla extract, blueberries and lemon peel.

—JENNIFER BECKMAN FALLS CHURCH, VA

PREP: 15 MIN. • **BAKE:** 20 MIN.
MAKES: 6 SERVINGS (3 CUPS TOPPING)

- 2 tablespoons butter
- 4 eggs
- ⅔ cup 2% milk
- 2 tablespoons grated orange peel
- ½ teaspoon almond extract
- ⅔ cup all-purpose flour
- 2 tablespoons sugar
- ½ teaspoon kosher salt

TOPPING

- 1 pound fresh strawberries, hulled and quartered
- ½ cup slivered almonds, toasted
- 2 tablespoons orange juice
- 1 tablespoon sugar

1. Preheat oven to 400°. Place butter in a 9-in. pie plate. Place in oven 4-5 minutes or until butter is melted; carefully swirl to coat evenly.
2. Meanwhile, in a large bowl, whisk eggs, milk, orange peel and extract until blended. Whisk in flour, sugar and salt. Pour into hot pie plate. Bake 20-25 minutes or until puffed and sides are golden brown and crisp.
3. In a small bowl, combine topping ingredients. Remove pancake from oven; serve immediately with topping.
NOTE *To toast nuts, spread in a 15x10x1-in. baking pan. Bake at 350° for 5-10 minutes or until lightly browned, stirring occasionally. Or, spread in a dry nonstick skillet and heat over low heat until lightly browned, stirring occasionally.*

FIRST-PRIZE DOUGHNUTS

One year I entered 18 kinds of baked goods in the county fair, and all of them won ribbons. Here is my favorite prizewinning doughnut recipe. I have been making doughnuts since I was a bride, which was quite some time ago!

—BETTY CLAYCOMB ALVERTON, PA

PREP: 25 MIN. + RISING • **COOK:** 5 MIN./BATCH
MAKES: 20 DOUGHNUTS

- 2 packages (¼ ounce each) active dry yeast
- ½ cup warm water (110° to 115°)
- ½ cup warm 2% milk (110° to 115°)
- ½ cup sugar
- ½ cup shortening
- 2 eggs
- 1 teaspoon salt
- 4½ to 5 cups all-purpose flour
  Oil for deep-fat frying

TOPPINGS

- 1¼ cups confectioners' sugar
- 4 to 6 tablespoons water
  Colored sprinkles and/or assorted breakfast cereals

1. In a large bowl, dissolve yeast in warm water. Add the milk, sugar, shortening, eggs, salt and 2 cups flour; beat until smooth. Stir in enough remaining flour to form a soft dough.
2. Turn onto a floured surface; knead until smooth and elastic, about 6-8 minutes. Place in a greased bowl, turning once to grease the top. Cover and let rise in a warm place until doubled, about 1 hour.
3. Punch dough down. Turn onto a floured surface; roll out to ½-in. thickness. Cut with a floured 2½-in. doughnut cutter. Place on greased baking sheets. Cover and let rise until doubled, about 1 hour.
4. In an electric skillet or deep fryer, heat oil to 375°. Fry doughnuts, a few at a time, until golden brown on both sides. Drain on paper towels.
5. In a shallow bowl, combine confectioners' sugar and water until smooth. Dip warm doughnuts in glaze; decorate as desired with sprinkles and/or cereals.

GRUYERE & PROSCIUTTO STRATA

Prosciutto, sweet onions and Gruyere combine for a perfect make-ahead brunch dish, and there are never any leftovers.
—**PATTI LAVELL** ISLAMORADA, FL

PREP: 15 MIN. + CHILLING • **BAKE:** 35 MIN. • **MAKES:** 9 SERVINGS

- 2 teaspoons canola oil
- 4 ounces thin slices prosciutto, chopped
- 2 large sweet onions, chopped (4 cups)
- 1 carton (8 ounces) egg substitute
- 2½ cups 2% milk
- ¼ teaspoon ground mustard
- ⅛ teaspoon pepper
- 8 cups cubed French bread
- 1½ cups (6 ounces) shredded Gruyere or Swiss cheese, divided

1. In a large skillet, heat oil over medium-high heat. Add prosciutto; cook and stir until crisp. Remove from pan with a slotted spoon. Add onions to the same pan; cook and stir until tender.

2. In a large bowl, whisk egg substitute, milk, mustard and pepper. Stir in bread and onions. Reserve 2 tablespoons cooked prosciutto for topping; stir remaining prosciutto into bread mixture.

3. Transfer half of the mixture to a greased 13x9-in. baking dish; sprinkle with half of the cheese. Top with remaining bread mixture. Separately cover and refrigerate strata and reserved prosciutto overnight.

4. Preheat oven to 350°. Remove strata from refrigerator while oven heats. Bake, uncovered, 20 minutes. Sprinkle with remaining cheese; top with reserved prosciutto. Bake 15-20 minutes longer or until a knife inserted near the center comes out clean. Let stand 5-10 minutes before serving.

FAST FIX

BREAKFAST EGGS IN FOIL BOWLS

Breakfast around the campfire couldn't be easier with these single-serving bowls. Filled with savory bacon, eggs, cheese and more, they'll give your family a hearty start to a day outdoors.
—**JENNIFER MEADOWS** MATTOON, IL

START TO FINISH: 30 MIN. • **MAKES:** 3 SERVINGS

- 6 eggs
- ⅓ cup milk
- ⅛ teaspoon salt
- ⅛ teaspoon garlic powder
- ⅛ teaspoon pepper
- ½ cup shredded cheddar cheese
- ¼ cup chopped green pepper
- 4 frozen fully cooked breakfast sausage links, thawed and chopped
- 4 bacon strips, cooked and crumbled
- 2 green onions, chopped

1. Prepare grill for indirect medium heat.

2. In a small bowl, whisk the first five ingredients. Pour into three 4½-in. disposable foil tart pans coated with cooking spray. Sprinkle with cheese, green pepper, sausage, bacon and onions.

3. Cover each pan with foil. Grill, covered, for 20-22 minutes or until eggs are completely set.

FAST FIX

BROWN SUGAR OATMEAL PANCAKES

My family absolutely loves these pancakes. I make them every Saturday and Sunday; if I don't, my family doesn't believe it's the weekend! My son's friends often spend the night, and I think it's because they like the pancakes so much. Molasses and syrup add extra deliciousness to the hotcakes.
—**SHARON BICKETT** CHESTER, SC

START TO FINISH: 15 MIN. • **MAKES:** ABOUT 10 PANCAKES

- ½ cup plus 2 tablespoons quick-cooking oats
- ½ cup whole wheat flour
- ½ cup all-purpose flour
- ½ teaspoon baking soda
- ½ teaspoon salt
- ⅓ cup packed brown sugar
- 1 egg
- 2 tablespoons canola oil
- 1 cup buttermilk

1. In a small bowl, combine oats, flours, baking soda, salt and sugar. In another small bowl, beat the egg, oil and buttermilk. Stir into dry ingredients just until moistened.

2. Pour batter by ⅓ cupfuls onto a greased hot griddle. Turn when bubbles form on top; cook until the second side is golden brown.

SWEDISH PUFF COFFEE CAKE

Some of my most treasured childhood memories involve waking to the heavenly scent of this almond-glazed coffee cake baking in the oven.

—MARY SHENK DEKALB, IL

PREP: 35 MIN. • **BAKE:** 30 MIN. + COOLING
MAKES: 12 SERVINGS

- 1 **cup all-purpose flour**
- ½ **cup cold butter, cubed**
- 2 **tablespoons ice water**

TOPPING

- 1 **cup water**
- ½ **cup butter**
- 1 **teaspoon almond extract**
- 1 **cup all-purpose flour**
- 3 **eggs**

GLAZE

- 1 **cup confectioners' sugar**
- 2 **tablespoons butter, softened**
- 1 **tablespoon 2% milk**
- 1 **teaspoon almond extract**
- 1 **cup flaked coconut**

1. Preheat oven to 375°. Place the flour in a small bowl; cut in butter until crumbly. Gradually add ice water, tossing with a fork until dough holds together when pressed. On an ungreased baking sheet, press dough into a 10-in. circle.

2. For topping, in a large saucepan, bring water and butter to a rolling boil. Remove from heat; stir in extract. Add the flour all at once and beat until blended. Cook over medium heat until mixture pulls away from sides of pan and forms a ball, stirring vigorously. Remove from heat; let mixture stand 5 minutes.

3. Add eggs, one at a time, beating well after each addition until smooth. Continue beating until mixture is smooth and shiny; spread over pastry.

4. Bake 30-35 minutes or until lightly browned. If needed, cover loosely with foil during the last 5 minutes to prevent overbrowning. Remove from pan to a wire rack to cool completely.

5. For glaze, in a small bowl, beat confectioners' sugar, butter, milk and extract until smooth. Spread over top; sprinkle with coconut.

BROCCOLI-MUSHROOM BUBBLE BAKE

I got bored with the same old breakfast casseroles served at our monthly moms meetings, so I created something new. Judging by the reactions of the other moms, this one's a keeper.

—SHANNON KOENE BLACKSBURG, VA

PREP: 20 MIN. • **BAKE:** 25 MIN. • **MAKES:** 12 SERVINGS

- 1 teaspoon canola oil
- ½ pound sliced fresh mushrooms, finely chopped
- 1 medium onion, finely chopped
- 1 tube (16.3 ounces) large refrigerated flaky biscuits
- 1 package (10 ounces) frozen broccoli with cheese sauce
- 3 eggs
- 1 can (5 ounces) evaporated milk
- 1 teaspoon Italian seasoning
- ½ teaspoon garlic powder
- ½ teaspoon salt
- ¼ teaspoon pepper
- 1½ cups (6 ounces) shredded Colby-Monterey Jack cheese

1. Preheat oven to 350°. In a large skillet, heat oil over medium-high heat. Add mushrooms and onion; cook and stir 4-6 minutes or until tender.

2. Cut each biscuit into eight pieces; place in a greased 13x9-in. baking dish. Top with mushroom mixture.

3. Cook broccoli with cheese sauce according to package directions. Spoon over mushroom mixture.

4. In a large bowl, whisk eggs, milk and seasonings; pour over top. Sprinkle with cheese. Bake 25-30 minutes or until golden brown.

PUFF PANCAKE WITH BLUEBERRY SAUCE

While I was in Texas on vacation, I discovered this pancake recipe. The light and puffy pancake really does melt in your mouth! It's a definite family-pleaser.

—BARBARA MOHR MILLINGTON, MI

START TO FINISH: 30 MIN. • **MAKES:** 4 SERVINGS

- 2 tablespoons butter
- 2 eggs
- ½ cup milk
- ½ cup all-purpose flour
- 2 tablespoons sugar
- ⅛ teaspoon ground cinnamon

BLUEBERRY SAUCE

- ¼ cup packed brown sugar
- 1 tablespoon cornstarch
- ¼ cup orange juice
- 1 cup fresh or frozen blueberries
- ¼ teaspoon vanilla extract

1. Place butter in a 9-in. pie plate; place in a 425° oven for 4-5 minutes or until melted.

2. Meanwhile, in a small bowl, whisk eggs and milk. In another small bowl, combine flour, sugar and cinnamon; whisk in egg mixture until smooth. Pour into prepared pie plate. Bake for 18-22 minutes or until sides are crisp and golden brown.

3. Meanwhile, in a small saucepan, combine the brown sugar and cornstarch. Gradually whisk in orange juice until smooth. Stir in blueberries. Bring to a boil over medium heat, stirring constantly. Cook and stir 1-2 minutes longer or until thickened. Remove from the heat; stir in the vanilla. Serve with pancake.

CROISSANT BREAKFAST CASSEROLE

Turning croissants and marmalade into a classic overnight casserole makes a wonderful treat for family and guests around the breakfast table.

—JOAN HALLFORD FORT WORTH, TX

PREP: 15 MIN. + CHILLING • **BAKE:** 25 MIN.
MAKES: 12 SERVINGS

- 1 jar (18 ounces) orange marmalade
- ½ cup apricot preserves
- ⅓ cup orange juice
- 3 teaspoons grated orange peel
- 6 croissants, split
- 5 eggs
- 1 cup half-and-half cream
- 1 teaspoon almond or vanilla extract
  Quartered fresh strawberries

1. In a small bowl, mix marmalade, preserves, orange juice and peel. Arrange the croissant bottoms in a greased 13x9-in. baking dish. Spread with 1½ cups marmalade mixture. Add croissant tops.
2. In another bowl, whisk the eggs, cream and extract; pour over the croissants. Spoon the remaining marmalade mixture over the tops. Refrigerate, covered, overnight.
3. Preheat oven to 350°. Remove the casserole from the refrigerator while oven heats. Bake, uncovered, 25-30 minutes or until a knife inserted near the center comes out clean. Let stand 5 minutes before serving. Serve with the strawberries.

FAST FIX

BBQ CHICKEN POLENTA WITH FRIED EGG

In college, BBQ chicken with polenta warmed me up before class. Now I cook it for brunch with friends and family.

—EVAN JANNEY LOS ANGELES, CA

START TO FINISH: 25 MIN.
MAKES: 4 SERVINGS

- 2 cups shredded cooked chicken breasts
- ¾ cup barbecue sauce
- 1 tablespoon minced fresh cilantro
- 2 tablespoons olive oil, divided
- 1 tube (1 pound) polenta, cut into 8 slices
- 1 small garlic clove, minced
- 4 eggs

1. In a small saucepan, combine the chicken, barbecue sauce and cilantro; heat through over medium heat, stirring occasionally.
2. In a large skillet, heat 1 tablespoon oil over medium-high heat. Add the polenta; cook 2-3 minutes on each side or until lightly browned. Transfer to a serving plate; keep warm.
3. In same pan, heat remaining oil over medium-high heat. Add garlic; cook and stir 1 minute. Break eggs, one at a time, into pan. Reduce heat to low. Cook until desired doneness, turning after whites are set, if desired. Serve over polenta with chicken mixture.

(5) INGREDIENTS FAST FIX

BREAKFAST PATTIES

When I was looking for lower-fat, high-protein breakfast options, I took an old sausage recipe and made it new again, using ground turkey.

—JO ANN HONEY LONGMONT, CO

START TO FINISH: 30 MIN.
MAKES: 16 PATTIES

- 2 pounds lean ground turkey
- 1½ teaspoons salt
- 1 teaspoon dried sage leaves
- 1 teaspoon pepper
- ½ teaspoon ground ginger
- ½ teaspoon cayenne pepper

1. Crumble turkey into a large bowl. Add the salt, sage, pepper, ginger and cayenne. Shape mixture into sixteen 2½-in. patties.
2. In a large skillet, cook patties over medium heat 4-6 minutes on each side or until no longer pink.

TOP TIP

Breakfast Sausage Your Way

Homemade sausage patties are very easy to make, and you can modify the recipe to suit your tastebuds. They also freeze easily. Place patties in a single layer on a plastic wrap-lined baking sheet and freeze. Once patties are frozen, remove from baking sheet and stack with two squares of waxed paper between each patty. Freeze in a resealable freezer bag.

FAST FIX

MINI-CHIP COCOA PANCAKES

For the chocoholic in you, get your fix early in the day by whipping up a batch of cocoa hotcakes dotted with mini chocolate chips!

—JOYCE MOYNIHAN LAKEVILLE, MN

START TO FINISH: 30 MIN.
MAKES: 12 PANCAKES

- 1¼ cups all-purpose flour
- ¼ cup baking cocoa
- ¼ cup sugar
- 3 teaspoons baking powder
- ½ teaspoon salt
- 2 eggs
- 1 cup 2% milk
- 3 tablespoons butter, melted
- 1½ teaspoons vanilla extract
- ⅔ cup miniature semisweet chocolate chips
  Powdered sugar and whipped cream, optional

1. In a large bowl, whisk the first five ingredients. In another bowl, whisk the eggs, milk, butter and vanilla until blended. Add to the flour mixture; stir just until moistened. Fold in the chocolate chips.

2. Coat a griddle with cooking spray; heat over medium heat. Pour the batter by ¼ cupfuls onto the griddle. Cook until bubbles on top begin to pop. Turn; cook until second side is lightly browned. If desired, dust with powdered sugar and serve with whipped cream.

TOP TIP

Make Cleanup Easy for Pancakes and Waffles

Mix up pancake or waffle batter in a wide-mouthed pitcher or 4-cup liquid measuring cup. Then it's easy to pour the batter onto the griddle. And cleanup's quicker, too.

— **DARLA GERMAUX** SAXTON, PA

“ These were delicious and so easy to make! ”
—ANGEL182009 TASTEOFHOME.COM

SAUSAGE AND EGG CASSEROLE

Try this dish for the perfect combination of eggs, sausage, bread and cheese. My mom and I like it because it bakes up tender and golden, slices beautifully and goes over well whenever we serve it.

—**GAYLE GRIGG** PHOENIX, AZ

PREP: 15 MIN. + CHILLING • **BAKE:** 40 MIN.
MAKES: 8-10 SERVINGS

- 1 **pound bulk pork sausage**
- 6 **eggs**
- 2 **cups milk**
- 1 **teaspoon salt**
- 1 **teaspoon ground mustard**
- 6 **slices white bread, cut into ½-inch cubes**
- 1 **cup (4 ounces) shredded cheddar cheese**

1. In a skillet, brown and crumble sausage; drain and set aside. In a large bowl, beat eggs; add milk, salt and mustard. Stir in bread cubes, cheese and sausage. Pour into a greased 11x7-in. baking dish. Cover and refrigerate 8 hours or overnight.
2. Preheat oven to 350°. Remove casserole from refrigerator while oven heats. Bake, uncovered, 40 minutes or until a knife inserted near center comes out clean.

FAST FIX

HOME-STYLE SAUSAGE GRAVY AND BISCUITS

My mother-in-law introduced me to her hamburger gravy, and I modified it slightly. We have this every weekend.

—**MICHELE BAPST** JACKSONVILLE, NC

START TO FINISH: 30 MIN.
MAKES: 8 SERVINGS

- 1 **tube (16.3 ounces) large refrigerated flaky biscuits**
- 1 **pound bulk pork sausage**
- 1 **cup chopped sweet onion**
- 2 **tablespoons butter**
- 1 **envelope country gravy mix**
- 1 **tablespoon all-purpose flour**
  Dash each garlic powder, Italian seasoning, onion powder and pepper
- 1½ **cups 2% milk**
- 1 **cup reduced-sodium chicken broth**

1. Bake biscuits according to package directions.
2. Meanwhile, in a large skillet, cook sausage and onion over medium heat until sausage is no longer pink; drain. Add butter; cook until melted. Stir in the gravy mix, flour and seasonings until blended. Gradually add milk and broth. Bring to a boil; cook and stir for 1 minute or until thickened. Serve with the biscuits.

OVERNIGHT RAISIN FRENCH TOAST

A colleague gave this recipe to me years ago and it's become a brunch favorite. I love the convenience of good make-ahead dishes, and this is one I turn to all the time. I like to sprinkle it with cinnamon and sugar when removing it from the oven.

—**STEPHANIE WEAVER** SLIGO, PA

PREP: 15 MIN. + CHILLING • **BAKE:** 45 MIN.
MAKES: 12 SERVINGS

- 1 **loaf (1 pound) cinnamon-raisin bread, cubed**
- 1 **package (8 ounces) cream cheese, cubed**
- 8 **eggs, lightly beaten**
- 1½ **cups half-and-half cream**
- ½ **cup sugar**
- ½ **cup maple syrup**
- 2 **tablespoons vanilla extract**
- 1 **tablespoon ground cinnamon**
- ⅛ **teaspoon ground nutmeg**

1. Place half the bread cubes in a greased 13x9-in. baking dish. Top with the cream cheese and the remaining bread.
2. In a large bowl, whisk remaining ingredients. Pour over top. Cover and refrigerate overnight.
3. Preheat oven to 350°. Remove casserole from refrigerator while oven heats. Cover and bake 30 minutes. Uncover; bake 15-20 minutes longer or until a knife inserted near the center comes out clean.

BREAKFAST PRALINE BREAD PUDDING

Baked French toast inspired this simple make-ahead dish that's perfect for a large holiday meal in the morning. It also travels well.
—**ERIN FURBY** ANCHORAGE, AK

PREP: 20 MIN. + CHILLING • **BAKE:** 40 MIN. • **MAKES:** 12 SERVINGS

- 8 **eggs, lightly beaten**
- 2 **cups half-and-half cream**
- 1 **cup 2% milk**
- 2 **tablespoons brown sugar**
- 3 **teaspoons vanilla extract**
- 1 **teaspoon ground cinnamon**
- ¾ **teaspoon ground nutmeg**
- ½ **teaspoon salt**
- 1 **loaf (1 pound) French bread, cut into 1-inch cubes**
- 1 **cup chopped pecans**
- ½ **cup packed brown sugar**
- ½ **cup butter, melted**

1. In a large bowl, whisk the first eight ingredients until blended. Stir in bread. Transfer to a greased 13x9-in. baking dish. Sprinkle with pecans and brown sugar; drizzle with butter. Refrigerate, covered, several hours or overnight.
2. Preheat oven to 350°. Remove bread pudding from refrigerator; uncover and let stand while oven heats. Bake 40-50 minutes or until puffed, golden and a knife inserted near the center comes out clean. Serve warm.

MICHIGAN FRUIT BAKED OATMEAL

Whole-grain oatmeal is a delicious way to start every day. For a change, swap chunks of Granny Smith apples for the dried fruit. Leftovers warm well in the microwave.
—**JEANETTE KASS** RAVENNA, MI

PREP: 15 MIN. • **BAKE:** 45 MIN. • **MAKES:** 2 SERVINGS

- 1 **cup old-fashioned oats**
- ¼ **cup dried cranberries or cherries**
- 1 **tablespoon brown sugar**
- 2 **cups fat-free milk**
- ½ **cup chunky applesauce**
- ¼ **teaspoon almond extract**
- 2 **tablespoons sliced almonds**
  Optional toppings: vanilla yogurt and additional dried cranberries and sliced almonds

1. Preheat oven to 350°. In a large bowl, combine the first six ingredients. Transfer to a 3-cup baking dish coated with cooking spray; sprinkle with almonds.
2. Bake, uncovered, 45-50 minutes or until set. Serve with toppings if desired.

FAST FIX ▶

PEANUT BUTTER & JELLY WAFFLES

Don't count out the grown-ups when it comes to craving these golden-brown waffles flavored with peanut butter and just a sprinkling of cinnamon. These are guaranteed crowd-pleasers.

—HELENA GEORGETTE MANN SACRAMENTO, CA

START TO FINISH: 25 MIN. • **MAKES:** 10 WAFFLES

- 1¼ cups all-purpose flour
- 3 tablespoons sugar
- 1 tablespoon baking powder
- ¼ teaspoon baking soda
- ¼ teaspoon ground cinnamon
- 2 eggs, separated
- 1¼ cups milk
- ⅓ cup peanut butter
- 3 tablespoons butter, melted
  Jelly of your choice

1. In a large bowl, combine the flour, sugar, baking powder, baking soda and cinnamon. In another bowl, whisk the egg yolks, milk, peanut butter and butter; stir mixture into dry ingredients just until moistened.

2. In a small bowl, beat egg whites until stiff peaks form; fold into batter. Bake in a preheated waffle iron according to manufacturer's directions until waffles are golden brown. Serve with jelly.

FREEZE OPTION *Arrange waffles in a single layer on a baking sheet. Freeze overnight or until frozen. Transfer to a resealable plastic freezer bag. Waffles may be frozen up to 2 months. To use, reheat the frozen waffles in a toaster. Serve with jelly.*

HASH BROWN NESTS WITH PORTOBELLOS AND EGGS

Hash browns make a fabulous crust for individual egg quiches. They look fancy but are actually easy to make. The little nests have been a hit at holiday brunches and other special occasions.

—KATE MEYER BRENTWOOD, TN

PREP: 30 MIN. • **BAKE:** 15 MIN. • **MAKES:** 12 SERVINGS

- 3 cups frozen shredded hash brown potatoes, thawed
- 3 cups chopped fresh portobello mushrooms
- ¼ cup chopped shallots
- 2 tablespoons butter
- 1 garlic clove, minced
- ½ teaspoon salt
- ¼ teaspoon pepper
- 2 tablespoons sour cream
- 1 tablespoon minced fresh basil
  Dash cayenne pepper
- 7 eggs, beaten
- ¼ cup shredded Swiss cheese
- 2 bacon strips, cooked and crumbled
  Additional minced fresh basil, optional

1. Preheat oven to 400°. Press ¼ cup hash browns onto the bottom and up the sides of each of 12 greased muffin cups; set aside.

2. In a large skillet, saute mushrooms and shallots in butter until tender. Add the garlic, salt and pepper; cook 1 minute longer. Remove from the heat; stir in the sour cream, basil and cayenne.

3. Divide eggs among potato-lined muffin cups. Top with mushroom mixture. Sprinkle with cheese and bacon.

4. Bake 15-18 minutes or until eggs are completely set. If desired, garnish with additional basil. Serve warm.

CHOCOLATE CHIP ELVIS PANCAKES

In a family of thirteen children, finding a recipe that everyone likes can be a challenge. This one was a Saturday-morning special that we all loved.

—KEENAN MCDERMOTT SPRINGFIELD, MO

PREP: 15 MIN. • **COOK:** 5 MIN./BATCH • **MAKES:** 16 PANCAKES

- 1¼ cups all-purpose flour
- 2 tablespoons brown sugar
- 3 teaspoons baking powder
- ½ teaspoon salt
- 1 egg
- ¼ cup peanut butter
- 1½ cups 2% milk
- 3 tablespoons butter, melted
- 1 teaspoon vanilla extract
- ½ cup chopped ripe banana
- ½ cup semisweet chocolate chips

1. In a large bowl, whisk flour, brown sugar, baking powder and salt. In another bowl, whisk egg, peanut butter, milk, melted butter and vanilla until blended. Add to flour mixture; stir just until moistened. Fold in banana and chocolate chips.

2. Lightly grease a griddle; heat over medium heat. Pour batter by ¼ cupfuls onto griddle. Cook until bubbles on top begin to pop and bottoms are golden brown. Turn; cook until second side is golden brown.

JACK CHEESE OVEN OMELET

Although it's easy, this omelet looks impressive. Sometimes I toss in mushrooms and cheddar cheese for a different flavor.

—LAUREL ROBERTS VANCOUVER, WA

PREP: 20 MIN. • **BAKE:** 35 MIN. • **MAKES:** 6 SERVINGS

- 8 bacon strips, diced
- 4 green onions, sliced
- 8 eggs
- 1 cup 2% milk
- ½ teaspoon seasoned salt
- 2½ cups (10 ounces) shredded Monterey Jack cheese, divided

1. Preheat oven to 350°. In a large skillet, cook bacon over medium heat until crisp. Drain, reserving 1 tablespoon drippings. Set bacon aside. Saute onions in drippings until tender; set aside.

2. In a large bowl, beat eggs. Add milk, seasoned salt, 2 cups cheese, bacon and sauteed onions. Transfer to a greased shallow 2-qt. baking dish.

3. Bake, uncovered, 35-40 minutes or until set. Sprinkle with remaining cheese.

FREEZE OPTION *Freeze unbaked omelet until firm; cover with foil. To use, remove from freezer 30 minutes before baking (do not thaw). Preheat oven to 350°. Bake as directed, increasing time as necessary for a knife inserted near the center to come out clean. Sprinkle with ½ cup cheese.*

ASPARAGUS PHYLLO BAKE

I'm Greek, and I grew up wrapping most foods in p[...] asparagus is in season, I bring out the phyllo and s[...]

—BONNIE GEAVARAS-BOOTZ SCOTTSDALE, AZ

PREP: 25 MIN. • **BAKE:** 50 MIN. • **MAKES:** 12 SERVINGS

- 2 pounds fresh asparagus, trimmed and cut into 1-inch pieces
- 5 eggs, lightly beaten
- 1 carton (15 ounces) ricotta cheese
- 1 cup (4 ounces) shredded Swiss cheese
- 2 tablespoons grated Parmesan cheese
- 2 garlic cloves, minced
- ½ teaspoon salt
- ½ teaspoon grated lemon peel
- ½ teaspoon pepper
- ½ cup slivered almonds, toasted
- ¾ cup butter, melted
- 16 sheets phyllo dough (14x9 inches)

1. In a large saucepan, bring 8 cups water to a boil. Add asparagus; cook, uncovered, 30 seconds or just until asparagus turns bright green. Remove asparagus and immediately drop it into ice water. Drain and pat dry. In a large bowl, mix the eggs, cheeses and seasonings; stir in almonds and asparagus.

2. Preheat oven to 375°. Brush a 13x9-in. baking dish with some of the butter. Unroll phyllo dough. Layer eight sheets of phyllo in prepared dish, brushing each with butter. (Keep remaining phyllo covered with plastic wrap and a damp towel to prevent it from drying out.)

3. Spread ricotta mixture over phyllo layers. Top with remaining phyllo sheets, brushing each with butter. Cut into 12 rectangles. Bake 50-55 minutes or until golden brown.

NOTE *To toast nuts, spread in a 15x10x1-in. baking pan. Bake at 350° for 5-10 minutes or until lightly browned, stirring occasionally. Or, spread in a dry nonstick skillet and heat over low heat until lightly browned, stirring occasionally.*

MAPLE-GLAZED SAUSAGES

It's so easy to simmer up a sugar-and-spice syrup to cover a skillet full of breakfast sausages. They go well with eggs, French toast, pancakes—just about anything, really.

—**TRUDIE HAGEN** ROGGEN, CO

START TO FINISH: 20 MIN.
MAKES: 10 SERVINGS

- **2 packages (6.4 ounces each) frozen fully cooked breakfast sausage links**
- **1 cup maple syrup**
- **½ cup packed brown sugar**
- **1 teaspoon ground cinnamon**

In a large skillet, brown sausage links. In a small bowl, combine the syrup, brown sugar and cinnamon; pour over sausages. Bring to a boil. Reduce heat; simmer, uncovered, until the sausages are glazed.

> **TOP TIP**
>
> ## Does Your Maple Syrup Make the Grade?
>
> Maple syrup is made in late winter to early spring, when the sap is flowing in maple trees. Water is evaporated from the sap in the syrup-making process. The U.S. grades maple syrup as Fancy (Grade AA), Grade A, Grade B or Grade C. Grade AA is light amber and has a mild maple flavor. Grade C, on the other hand, is dark and has a molasseslike flavor.

BREAKFAST & BRU

BACON & EGG POTATO BAKE

Frozen hash browns make this yummy recipe simple to prepare. Featuring bacon and cheddar cheese, it's tasty as breakfast or brunch fare. You can even make it the night before, keep it in the fridge overnight and bake it in the morning.

—**CHERYL JOHNSON** PLYMOUTH, MN

PREP: 20 MIN. • **BAKE:** 45 MIN. • **MAKES:** 8 SERVINGS

- 1 **package (30 ounces) frozen cubed hash brown potatoes, thawed**
- 1 **pound bacon strips, cooked and crumbled**
- 1 **cup (4 ounces) shredded cheddar cheese, divided**
- ¼ **to ½ teaspoon salt**
- 8 **eggs**
- 2 **cups milk**
  Paprika

1. Preheat oven to 350°. In a large bowl, combine the hash browns, bacon, ½ cup cheese and salt. Spoon into a greased 13x9-in. baking dish. In another large bowl, beat eggs and milk until blended; pour over hash brown mixture. Sprinkle with paprika.

2. Bake, uncovered, 45-50 minutes or until a knife inserted near center comes out clean. Sprinkle with remaining cheese.

NOTE *This dish may be prepared in advance, covered and refrigerated overnight. Remove from refrigerator 30 minutes before baking.*

BLUEBERRY CHEESECAKE FLAPJACKS

This stunning stack of pancakes is just downright pretty. It's tempting to just sit and stare at them, but not for long! Pair them with your favorite breakfast meat and dig in.

—**DONNA CLINE** PENSACOLA, FL

PREP: 30 MIN. • **COOK:** 5 MIN./BATCH
MAKES: 12 PANCAKES (¾ CUP TOPPING)

- 1 **package (3 ounces) cream cheese, softened**
- ¾ **cup whipped topping**
- 1 **cup all-purpose flour**
- ½ **cup graham cracker crumbs**
- 1 **tablespoon sugar**
- 1 **teaspoon baking powder**
- ½ **teaspoon baking soda**
- ¼ **teaspoon salt**
- 2 **eggs, lightly beaten**
- 1¼ **cups buttermilk**
- ¼ **cup butter, melted**
- 1 **cup fresh or frozen blueberries**
- ¾ **cup maple syrup, warmed**
  Additional blueberries, optional

1. For topping, in a small bowl, beat cream cheese and whipped topping until smooth. Chill until serving.

2. In a large bowl, combine the flour, cracker crumbs, sugar, baking powder, baking soda and salt. Combine the eggs, buttermilk and butter; add to dry ingredients just until moistened. Fold in blueberries.

3. Pour batter by ¼ cupfuls onto a greased hot griddle; turn when bubbles form on top. Cook until the second side is golden brown. Spread topping over pancakes. Top with warm syrup; if desired, sprinkle with additional blueberries.

NOTE *If using frozen blueberries, do not thaw them before adding to the pancake batter. Be sure to thaw any berries used in the optional garnish.*

SOUTHWESTERN CHICKEN SOUP, PAGE 46

GRILLED VEGETABLE SANDWICH, 51

PEAR, HAM & CHEESE PASTRY POCKETS, 55

BUFFALO TURKEY BURGERS, 57

Soups & Sandwiches

What goes together better than a hot bowl of soup and a tasty sandwich? Not a thing!
The selection here ranges from classics, such as Easy Beef Barley Soup and Tex-Mex
Sloppy Joes, to new favorites like Tuscan Chicken Soup and Grilled Vegetable Sandwiches.
Use your imagination and create a special soup-and-sandwich combo, or just relish each
recipe on its own.

CLASSIC FRENCH ONION SOUP

Enjoy my signature soup the way my granddaughter Becky does. I make it for her in a French onion soup bowl complete with garlic croutons and a puddle of melted Swiss cheese on top.
—**LOU SANSEVERO** FERRON, UT

PREP: 20 MIN. • **COOK:** 2 HOURS
MAKES: 12 SERVINGS

- 5 **tablespoons olive oil, divided**
- 1 **tablespoon butter**
- 8 **cups thinly sliced onions (about 3 pounds)**
- 3 **garlic cloves, minced**
- ½ **cup port wine**
- 2 **cartons (32 ounces each) beef broth**
- ½ **teaspoon pepper**
- ¼ **teaspoon salt**
- 24 **slices French bread baguette (½ inch thick)**
- 2 **large garlic cloves, peeled and halved**
- ¾ **cup shredded Gruyere or Swiss cheese**

1. In a Dutch oven, heat 2 tablespoons oil and butter over medium heat. Add onions; cook and stir 10-13 minutes or until softened. Reduce heat to medium-low; cook 30-40 minutes or until deep golden brown, stirring occasionally. Add minced garlic; cook 2 minutes longer.

2. Stir in wine. Bring to a boil; cook until liquid is reduced by half. Add the broth, pepper and salt; return to a boil. Reduce heat; simmer 1 hour, stirring occasionally.

3. Meanwhile, place baguette slices on a baking sheet; brush both sides with remaining oil. Bake at 400° for 3-5 minutes on each side or until toasted. Rub toasts with halved garlic.

4. To serve, place twelve 8-oz. broiler-safe bowls or ramekins on baking sheets. Place two toasts in each. Ladle with soup; top with cheese. Broil 4 in. from heat until cheese is melted.

LOADED GRILLED CHICKEN SANDWICH

I threw these ingredients together on a whim, and the sandwich turned out so well, I surprised myself! If you're in a rush, microwave the bacon. Just cover it with a paper towel to keep it from splattering too much.

—**DANA YORK** KENNEWICK, WA

START TO FINISH: 30 MIN.
MAKES: 4 SERVINGS

- 4 **boneless skinless chicken breast halves (4 ounces each)**
- 2 **teaspoons Italian salad dressing mix**
- 4 **slices pepper jack cheese**
- 4 **ciabatta or kaiser rolls, split**
- 2 **tablespoons mayonnaise**
- ¾ **teaspoon Dijon mustard**
- 4 **cooked bacon strips, halved**
- 4 **slices tomato**
- ½ **medium ripe avocado, peeled and thinly sliced**
- ½ **pound deli coleslaw (about 1 cup)**

1. Pound chicken with a meat mallet to flatten slightly; sprinkle both sides with dressing mix. Moisten a paper towel with cooking oil; using long-handled tongs, rub on the grill rack to coat lightly.

2. Grill the chicken, covered, over medium heat or broil 4 in. from heat 4-6 minutes on each side or until a thermometer reads 165°. Place cheese on chicken; grill, covered, 1-2 minutes longer or until the cheese is melted. Meanwhile, grill rolls, cut side down, 1-2 minutes or until toasted.

3. Mix mayonnaise and mustard; spread on roll tops. Layer roll bottoms with chicken, bacon, tomato, avocado and coleslaw. Replace tops.

ITALIAN MUFFULETTA

Our family and friends came over for a deck party where they all pitched in to build our deck. I served this sandwich to keep up their strength. They savored it so much that I have made it several times since. It also makes a quick and impressive entree for casual entertaining!

—**DANA SCHMITT** AMES, IA

START TO FINISH: 25 MIN.
MAKES: 6 SERVINGS

- ⅔ **cup pimiento-stuffed olives, chopped**
- 1 **can (4¼ ounces) chopped ripe olives**
- 6 **tablespoons shredded Parmesan cheese**
- ¼ **cup Italian salad dressing**
- 2 **teaspoons minced garlic**
- 1 **loaf (1 pound) Italian bread**
- ½ **pound sliced deli turkey**
- ¼ **pound sliced Swiss cheese**
- ¼ **pound thinly sliced hard salami**
- ¼ **pound sliced provolone cheese**
- ¼ **pound thinly sliced bologna**

1. In a small bowl, combine the first five ingredients; set aside.

2. Cut bread in half horizontally; carefully hollow out top and bottom, leaving a 1-in. shell (discard removed bread or save for another use).

3. Spoon half of olive mixture over bottom half of bread. Layer with turkey, Swiss cheese, salami, provolone cheese, bologna and remaining olive mixture. Replace bread top. Cut into six wedges.

BAKED POTATO CHEDDAR SOUP

A few simple kitchen staples make for an impressive soup. Use a better-quality yellow cheddar cheese; it adds greater depth of color and flavor to this dish.

—**KRISTIN REYNOLDS** VAN BUREN, AR

START TO FINISH: 30 MIN.
MAKES: 4 SERVINGS

- ⅓ **cup all-purpose flour**
- 3 **cups milk**
- 2 **large potatoes, baked, peeled and coarsely mashed (1½ pounds)**
- ⅓ **cup plus 2 tablespoons shredded cheddar cheese, divided**
- ½ **teaspoon salt**
- ¼ **teaspoon pepper**
- ½ **cup sour cream**
- ½ **cup thinly sliced green onions, divided**
  Crumbled cooked bacon, optional

1. In a large saucepan, whisk flour and milk until smooth. Bring to a boil; cook and stir for 2 minutes or until thickened. Stir in potatoes, ⅓ cup cheese, salt and pepper. Cook over medium heat 2-3 minutes or until cheese is melted. Remove from heat.

2. Stir in the sour cream and ¼ cup onions until blended. Cover; cook over medium heat 10-12 minutes or until heated through (do not boil). Garnish with remaining cheese and onions and, if desired, bacon.

SOUTHWESTERN CHICKEN SOUP

The spices really liven up the flavor in this filling soup. The recipe is easily doubled and freezes well.

—ANNE SMITHSON CARY, NC

PREP: 10 MIN. • **COOK:** 1¼ HOURS • **MAKES:** 8 SERVINGS

- 1 carton (32 ounces) plus 1 can (14½ ounces) reduced-sodium chicken broth
- 1 can (14½ ounces) crushed tomatoes, undrained
- 1 can (14½ ounces) diced tomatoes, undrained
- 1 pound boneless skinless chicken breast, cut into ½-inch cubes
- 1 large onion, chopped
- ⅓ cup minced fresh cilantro
- 1 can (4 ounces) chopped green chilies
- 1 garlic clove, minced
- 1 teaspoon chili powder
- 1 teaspoon ground cumin
- ½ teaspoon dried oregano
- ¼ teaspoon cayenne pepper
- 3 cups frozen corn, thawed
  Tortilla chips
- 1 cup (4 ounces) shredded reduced-fat cheddar or Mexican cheese blend

In a large saucepan, combine the first 12 ingredients. Bring to a boil. Reduce heat; cover and simmer 1 hour. Add corn; cook 10 minutes longer. Top each serving with tortilla chips; sprinkle with cheese.

FAST FIX ▶

BBQ BACON BURGERS

With a slice of bacon inside and a tasty barbecue-mayo sauce on top, these are definitely not ordinary burgers. I think you'll agree.

—JOAN SCHOENHERR EASTPOINTE, MI

START TO FINISH: 30 MIN. • **MAKES:** 4 SERVINGS

- ¼ cup mayonnaise
- ¼ cup barbecue sauce
- 4 bacon strips, cooked and crumbled
- 1½ teaspoons dried minced onion
- 1½ teaspoons steak seasoning
- 1 pound ground beef
- 4 slices Swiss cheese
- 4 hamburger buns, split
  Lettuce leaves and tomato slices

1. In a small bowl, combine mayonnaise and barbecue sauce. In another bowl, combine the bacon, 2 tablespoons mayonnaise mixture, onion and steak seasoning; crumble beef over mixture and mix well. Shape into four patties.
2. Grill burgers, covered, over medium heat for 5-7 minutes on each side or until a thermometer reads 160° and juices run clear. Top with cheese. Cover and cook 1-2 minutes longer or until the cheese is melted. Spread the remaining mayonnaise mixture over cut side of bun bottoms. Layer with lettuce, burger and tomato. Replace tops.

TOP TIP

Crumbling Bacon

Bacon is usually too hot to crumble right after it's been cooked. If your time is short, cut the raw bacon into chunks with scissors. The bacon will cook faster, and will already be in small pieces when it is cooked.

FAST FIX

GRILLED GOAT CHEESE & ARUGULA SANDWICHES

To create a more grown-up grilled cheese sandwich, I threw in tangy goat cheese and peppery arugula. I enjoy a similar combination on pizza, and it works here, too.
—**JESSIE APFE** BERKELEY, CA

START TO FINISH: 30 MIN. • **MAKES:** 4 SERVINGS

- ½ cup sun-dried tomato pesto
- 8 slices sourdough bread
- 1½ cups roasted sweet red peppers, drained and patted dry
- 8 slices part-skim mozzarella cheese
- ½ cup crumbled goat cheese
- 1 cup fresh arugula
- ¼ cup butter, softened

1. Spread pesto over four slices of bread. Layer with peppers, mozzarella cheese, goat cheese and arugula; top with the remaining bread. Spread outsides of sandwiches with butter.
2. In a large skillet, toast the sandwiches over medium heat 3-4 minutes on each side or until bread is golden brown and cheese is melted.

COUSCOUS MEATBALL SOUP

This soup is easy, healthy and tasty. It chases the chill away on a wintery day and is perfect with fresh crusty bread.
—**JONATHAN PACE** SAN FRANCISCO, CA

PREP: 25 MIN. • **COOK:** 40 MIN. • **MAKES:** 10 SERVINGS (2½ QUARTS)

- 1 pound lean ground beef (90% lean)
- 2 teaspoons dried basil
- 2 teaspoons dried oregano
- ½ teaspoon salt
- 1 large onion, finely chopped
- 2 teaspoons canola oil
- 8 cups chopped collard greens
- 8 cups chopped fresh kale
- 2 cartons (32 ounces each) vegetable stock
- 1 tablespoon white wine vinegar
- ½ teaspoon crushed red pepper flakes
- ¼ teaspoon pepper
- 1 package (8.8 ounces) pearl (Israeli) couscous

1. In a small bowl, combine the beef, basil, oregano and salt. Shape into ½-in. balls. In a large nonstick skillet coated with cooking spray, brown meatballs; drain. Remove meatballs and set aside.
2. In the same skillet, brown onion in oil. Add greens and kale; cook 6-7 minutes longer or until wilted.
3. In a Dutch oven, combine the greens mixture, meatballs, stock, vinegar, pepper flakes and pepper. Bring to a boil. Reduce heat; cover and simmer 10 minutes. Return to a boil. Stir in the couscous. Reduce heat; cover and simmer 10-15 minutes or until couscous is tender, stirring once.

NO-BEAN CHILI

I like to combine the ingredients for this zesty chili the night before. In the morning, I load up the slow cooker and let it do the rest of the work for me.
—**MOLLY BUTT** GRANVILLE, OH

PREP: 10 MIN. • **COOK:** 4 HOURS • **MAKES:** 6 SERVINGS

- 1½ pounds lean ground beef (90% lean)
- 1 can (14½ ounces) stewed tomatoes, undrained
- 1 can (8 ounces) tomato sauce
- 1 small onion, chopped
- 1 small green pepper, chopped
- 1 can (4 ounces) chopped green chilies
- ½ cup minced fresh parsley
- 1 tablespoon chili powder
- 1 garlic clove, minced
- 1¼ teaspoons salt
- ½ teaspoon paprika
- ¼ teaspoon pepper
  Hot cooked rice or pasta
  Optional toppings: shredded cheddar cheese, sour cream and sliced green onions

Crumble beef into a 3-qt. slow cooker. Add the next 11 ingredients and mix well. Cover and cook on high 4-6 hours or until meat is no longer pink. Serve with rice or pasta and the toppings of your choice.

GOLDEN CLAM CHOWDER

Enjoy delicious homemade clam chowder any night with this easy recipe. Bits of crispy bacon are more than just traditional—they also make the chowder feel rich and indulgent.
—**AMANDA BOWYER** CALDWELL, ID

PREP: 20 MIN. • **COOK:** 20 MIN. • **MAKES:** 7 SERVINGS

- 2 celery ribs
- 2 medium carrots
- 1 medium onion
- 2 teaspoons olive oil
- 4 garlic cloves, minced
- 4 medium potatoes, peeled and diced

- 2 cans (6½ ounces each) minced clams, undrained
- 1 bottle (8 ounces) clam juice
- 1 cup plus 1 tablespoon water, divided
- 1 teaspoon dried thyme
- ½ teaspoon salt
- ½ teaspoon pepper
- 1 can (12 ounces) evaporated milk
- 2 teaspoons cornstarch
- 2 bacon strips, cooked and crumbled

1. Finely chop the celery, carrots and onion. In a Dutch oven, saute vegetables in oil until tender. Add garlic; cook 1 minute longer. Stir in the potatoes, clams, clam juice, 1 cup water, thyme, salt and pepper. Bring to a boil. Reduce heat; cover and simmer 12-15 minutes or until potatoes are tender.
2. Gradually stir in milk; heat through. Combine cornstarch and remaining water until smooth; stir into chowder. Bring to a boil; cook and stir 2 minutes or until thickened. Stir in the bacon.

FAST FIX
BUFFALO CHICKEN QUESADILLAS

My quesadillas are versatile enough to serve as a meal or to win big points as a snack while the big game is on TV. Feel free to sub in your favorite flavor of tortillas, or kick up the spice factor with pepper jack cheese instead of the Mexican cheese blend.
—**CRYSTAL SCHLUETER** NORTHGLENN, CO

START TO FINISH: 25 MIN. • **MAKES:** 4 SERVINGS

- 2 cups shredded rotisserie chicken
- ½ cup buffalo wing sauce
- 2 teaspoons canola oil
- 1 cup chopped sweet onion
- 2 celery ribs, chopped
- ¼ teaspoon salt
- ⅛ teaspoon pepper
- 4 tomato-flavored flour tortillas (10 inches)
- 2 cups (8 ounces) shredded Mexican cheese blend
- ¼ cup finely chopped pitted green olives
- ⅔ cup sour cream
- ½ cup crumbled blue cheese
- 2 tablespoons chopped celery leaves
  Additional buffalo wing sauce, optional

1. Preheat oven to 350°. In a small bowl, toss chicken with wing sauce. In a large skillet, heat oil over medium-high heat. Add onion, celery, salt and pepper; cook and stir until onion is tender.
2. Place two tortillas on an ungreased baking sheet; top with chicken and onion mixtures. Sprinkle with Mexican cheese and olives. Top with remaining tortillas. Bake 8-10 minutes or until golden brown and cheese is melted.
3. In a small bowl, mix sour cream and blue cheese. Serve quesadilla wedges with celery leaves, blue cheese sauce and, if desired, additional wing sauce.

3. In a small bowl, combine the mayonnaise, sour cream, lemon juice, sugar, ground mustard, Dijon mustard and horseradish. Serve pork on rolls with lettuce and mustard-horseradish sauce.

FAST FIX ▸
CREAM OF WILD RICE SOUP

Tender cubes of chicken, fresh vegetables and wild rice make this soup filling enough for a meal. You can't beat the down-home comfort of a warm bowlful. I like to serve it with whole wheat rolls.
—**J. BEATRICE HINTZ** NEENAH, WI

START TO FINISH: 30 MIN. • **MAKES:** 10 SERVINGS (2½ QUARTS)

- 1 **large onion, chopped**
- 1 **large carrot, shredded**
- 1 **celery rib, chopped**
- ¼ **cup butter**
- ½ **cup all-purpose flour**
- 8 **cups chicken broth**
- 3 **cups cooked wild rice**
- 1 **cup cubed cooked chicken breast**
- ¼ **teaspoon salt**
- ¼ **teaspoon pepper**
- 1 **cup fat-free evaporated milk**
- ¼ **cup minced chives**

In a large saucepan, saute the onion, carrot and celery in butter until tender. Stir in flour until blended. Gradually add broth. Stir in the rice, chicken, salt and pepper. Bring to a boil over medium heat; cook and stir 2 minutes or until thickened. Stir in milk; cook 3-5 minutes longer. Garnish with chives.

GRILLED PORK TENDERLOIN SANDWICHES

A friend from work shared this delectable pork sandwich with me years ago. I'm always asked for the recipe when I serve it to someone for the first time.
—**GERI BIERSCHBACH** WEIDMAN, MI

PREP: 15 MIN. + MARINATING • **GRILL:** 25 MIN. • **MAKES:** 6 SERVINGS

- 2 **tablespoons canola oil**
- 2 **tablespoons reduced-sodium soy sauce**
- 2 **tablespoons steak sauce**
- 2 **garlic cloves, minced**
- 1½ **teaspoons brown sugar**
- ½ **teaspoon ground mustard**
- ½ **teaspoon minced fresh gingerroot**
- 2 **pork tenderloins (1 pound each)**

MUSTARD-HORSERADISH SAUCE
- ¼ **cup fat-free mayonnaise**
- ¼ **cup reduced-fat sour cream**
- 1½ **teaspoons lemon juice**
- 1 **teaspoon sugar**
- ½ **teaspoon ground mustard**
- ½ **teaspoon Dijon mustard**
- ½ **teaspoon prepared horseradish**
- 6 **kaiser rolls, split**
- 6 **lettuce leaves**

1. In a large resealable plastic bag, combine the first seven ingredients. Add pork; seal bag and turn to coat. Refrigerate 8 hours or overnight.
2. Drain pork, discarding marinade. Moisten a paper towel with cooking oil; using long-handled tongs, rub on grill rack to coat lightly. Grill pork, covered, over indirect medium heat for 25-40 minutes or until a thermometer reads 145°. Let stand for 5 minutes before slicing.

GRILLED VEGETABLE SANDWICH

Wow! Meat lovers won't even miss the meat, but they will rave about the simply fabulous flavor of this hearty grilled veggie sandwich. It's wonderful with ciabatta bread's crispy crust and light, airy texture.

—**DIANA TSEPERKAS** HAMDEN, CT

PREP: 20 MIN. + MARINATING • **GRILL:** 10 MIN. • **MAKES:** 4 SERVINGS

- 1 medium zucchini, thinly sliced lengthwise
- 1 medium sweet red pepper, quartered
- 1 small red onion, cut into ½-inch slices
- ¼ cup prepared Italian salad dressing
- 1 loaf ciabatta bread (14 ounces), split
- 2 tablespoons olive oil
- ¼ cup reduced-fat mayonnaise
- 1 tablespoon lemon juice
- 2 teaspoons grated lemon peel
- 1 teaspoon minced garlic
- ½ cup crumbled feta cheese

1. In a large resealable plastic bag, combine the zucchini, pepper, onion and salad dressing. Seal bag and turn to coat; refrigerate for at least 1 hour. Drain and discard marinade.

2. Brush cut sides of bread with oil; set aside. Place the vegetables on grill rack. Grill, covered, over medium heat 4-5 minutes on each side or until crisp-tender. Remove and keep warm. Grill bread, oil side down, over medium heat 30-60 seconds or until toasted.

3. In a small bowl, combine the mayonnaise, lemon juice, peel and garlic. Spread over bread bottom; sprinkle with cheese. Top with vegetables and remaining bread. Cut into four slices.

HEARTY NAVY BEAN SOUP

Beans were a commodity you did not survive without in the '30s. This bean soup was excellent back then and still is now. It's a real family favorite, and I make it often.

—**MILDRED LEWIS** TEMPLE, TX

PREP: 30 MIN. + STANDING • **COOK:** 1¾ HOURS
MAKES: 10 SERVINGS (2½ QUARTS)

- 3 cups (1½ pounds) dried navy beans
- 1 can (14½ ounces) diced tomatoes, undrained
- 1 large onion, chopped
- 1 meaty ham hock or 1 cup diced cooked ham
- 2 cups chicken broth
- 2½ cups water
   Salt and pepper to taste
   Minced fresh parsley

1. Rinse and sort beans. Place beans in a Dutch oven or stockpot; add water to cover by 2 in. Bring to a boil; boil 2 minutes. Remove from heat; cover and let stand 1 to 4 hours or until beans are softened.

2. Drain and rinse beans, discarding liquid. Place in a large Dutch oven or stockpot. Add tomatoes with juice, onion, ham hock, broth, water, salt and pepper. Bring to a boil. Reduce heat; cover and simmer until beans are tender, about 1½ hours.

3. Add more water if necessary. Remove ham hock and let stand until cool enough to handle. Remove meat from bone; discard bone. Cut meat into bite-size pieces; set aside. (For a thicker soup, cool slightly, then puree beans in a food processor or blender and return to pan.) Return ham to soup and heat through. Garnish with parsley.

FAST FIX

TEX-MEX SLOPPY JOES

Sloppy joes are popular with adults and kids. I deviated from the traditional recipe by adding a little Southwestern spiciness.

—**GERALDINE SAUCIER** ALBUQUERQUE, NM

START TO FINISH: 30 MIN. • **MAKES:** 6 SERVINGS

- 1 **pound ground beef**
- 1 **small onion, chopped**
- 2 **garlic cloves, minced**
- 1 **cup ketchup**
- 1 **can (4 ounces) chopped green chilies**
- ½ **cup beef broth**
- ¼ **cup chili sauce**
- 1 **teaspoon chili powder**
- ½ **teaspoon ground cumin**
- ¼ **teaspoon crushed red pepper flakes**
- ¼ **teaspoon salt**
- ¼ **teaspoon coarsely ground pepper**
- 6 **hamburger buns, split**
- 2 **tablespoons butter, softened**

1. In a large skillet, cook beef and onion over medium heat 6-8 minutes or until beef is no longer pink, breaking up beef into crumbles; drain. Add garlic; cook 1-2 minutes longer. Stir in ketchup, chilies, broth, chili sauce and seasonings. Bring to a boil. Reduce heat; simmer, uncovered, 5 minutes, stirring occasionally.

2. Meanwhile, spread cut sides of buns with butter. Place on baking sheets, buttered side up. Broil 4 in. from the heat for 1-2 minutes or until toasted. Serve beef mixture in buns.

SAUSAGE LENTIL SOUP

I found this good-for-you recipe in a men's magazine and lightened it up. I ate a lot of it when I was pregnant because it's so tasty and loaded with fiber, vitamins and iron. It uses low-fat ingredients without sacrificing taste.

—**SUZANNE DABKOWSKI** BLYTHEWOOD, SC

PREP: 25 MIN. • **COOK:** 40 MIN. • **MAKES:** 6 SERVINGS

- 1 **medium onion, chopped**
- 1 **celery rib, chopped**
- ¼ **pound reduced-fat smoked sausage, halved and thinly sliced**
- 1 **medium carrot, halved and thinly sliced**
- 2 **garlic cloves, minced**
- 2 **cans (14½ ounces each) reduced-sodium chicken broth**
- ⅓ **cup water**
- 1 **cup dried lentils, rinsed**
- ½ **teaspoon dried oregano**
- ¼ **teaspoon ground cumin**
- ¼ **teaspoon pepper**
- 1 **can (14½ ounces) stewed tomatoes, cut up**
- 1 **tablespoon Worcestershire sauce**
- 1 **cup chopped fresh spinach**

1. In a large saucepan coated with cooking spray, cook and stir onion and celery over medium-high heat 2 minutes. Add sausage, carrot and garlic; cook 2-3 minutes longer or until onion is tender.

2. Stir in the broth, water, lentils, oregano, cumin and pepper. Bring to a boil. Reduce heat; cover and simmer for 25-30 minutes or until lentils and vegetables are tender.

3. Stir in the tomatoes, Worcestershire sauce and spinach; cook until heated through and spinach is wilted.

❝Unbelievable. This is a staple soup for us. No-fuss preparation.❞

—**KMARQUI** TASTEOFHOME.COM

APRES-SKI SOUP

Apres-ski is French for "after skiing," and this microwave soup is perfect when we get together after hitting the slopes. Full of healthy veggies, it warms you from head to toe.

—NANCY HAMLIN LITTLETON, CO

START TO FINISH: 30 MIN.
MAKES: 6 SERVINGS (1½ QT.)

1 tablespoon butter
1¼ cups cubed acorn squash
1 carrot, thinly sliced
1 medium leek (white portion only), thinly sliced
3 cans (14½ ounces each) reduced-sodium chicken broth
1 small zucchini, halved and sliced
½ cup uncooked elbow macaroni
1 bay leaf
½ teaspoon dried basil
¼ teaspoon dried thyme
⅛ teaspoon salt
⅛ teaspoon pepper

1. Place butter in a 3-qt. microwave-safe bowl; microwave on high for 15-20 seconds or until melted. Add squash, carrot and leek; stir to coat. Cook, covered, on high 6 minutes.
2. Stir in remaining ingredients; cook, covered, on high 12-14 minutes or until vegetables and macaroni are tender, stirring twice. Remove the bay leaf.
NOTE *This recipe was tested in a 1,100-watt microwave.*

TOP TIP

Preparing Leeks

Remove any withered outer leaves. Trim root end. Cut off and discard the green upper leaves at the point where the pale green becomes dark green. Leeks often contain sand between their many layers. If leeks are to be sliced or chopped, cut the leek open lengthwise down one side and rinse under cold running water, If using the leek whole, cut an X about ¼- to ½-in. deep in the root end. Soak for 30 minutes in water containing a splash of vinegar. Rinse under cold running water, gently separating the leaves and opening the slit area while rinsing.

CHICKEN POTPIE SOUP

My grandmother hand-wrote a cookbook. She supplied the best pie crust, and I created the delicious soup for it.
—KAREN LEMAY PEARLAND, TX

PREP: 20 MIN. + CHILLING • **COOK:** 20 MIN.
MAKES: 6 SERVINGS

2 cups all-purpose flour
1¼ teaspoons salt
⅔ cup shortening
5 to 6 tablespoons 2% milk
SOUP
2 tablespoons butter
1 cup cubed peeled potatoes
1 cup chopped sweet onion
2 celery ribs, chopped
2 medium carrots, chopped
½ cup all-purpose flour
½ teaspoon salt
¼ teaspoon pepper
3 cans (14½ ounces each) chicken broth
2 cups shredded cooked chicken
1 cup frozen petite peas
1 cup frozen corn

1. In a large bowl, mix flour and salt; cut in shortening until crumbly. Gradually add the milk, tossing with a fork until dough holds together when pressed. Shape into a disk; wrap in plastic wrap. Refrigerate 30 minutes or overnight.
2. On a lightly floured surface, roll dough to ⅛-in. thickness. Using a floured 2½-in. heart-shaped or round cutter, cut 18 shapes. Place 1 in. apart on ungreased baking sheets. Bake at 425° for 8-11 minutes or until golden brown. Cool on a wire rack.
3. For soup, in a Dutch oven, heat butter over medium-high heat. Add potatoes, onion, celery and carrots; cook and stir 5-7 minutes or until onion is tender.
4. Stir in the flour, salt and pepper until blended; gradually whisk in the broth. Bring to a boil, stirring occasionally. Reduce heat; simmer, uncovered, 8-10 minutes or until potatoes are tender. Stir in remaining ingredients; heat through. Serve with the pastries.

MINI HAWAIIAN BURGERS

These are ideal burgers for a luau or any backyard gathering. I came up with the dish while trying to find something new that my husband would enjoy, and now he asks for them all the time.

—KATHLEEN MANASIAN WHITMORE LAKE, MI

START TO FINISH: 25 MIN. • **MAKES:** 12 SERVINGS

- 1 can (8 ounces) unsweetened crushed pineapple
- 1 green onion, finely chopped
- 1 teaspoon Worcestershire sauce
- ½ teaspoon salt
- ½ teaspoon garlic powder
- ½ teaspoon salt-free seasoning blend
- ½ teaspoon pepper
- 1 pound ground turkey
- ½ pound uncooked chorizo or bulk spicy pork sausage
- ⅔ cup ketchup
- 12 Hawaiian sweet rolls, split
- 6 lettuce leaves, cut in half
- 12 slices tomato

1. Drain pineapple, reserving ½ cup juice. In a large bowl, combine pineapple, green onion, Worcestershire sauce and seasonings. Add turkey and chorizo; mix lightly but thoroughly. Shape into twelve ½-in.-thick patties.

2. Place on a broiler pan. Broil burgers 4 in. from heat 4-5 minutes on each side or until a thermometer reads 165°.

3. In a small bowl, mix ketchup and reserved pineapple juice. Serve burgers on rolls with lettuce, tomato and ketchup mixture.

SIMPLE TACO SOUP

We first sampled this chili-like soup at a church dinner. Since it uses packaged seasonings and several cans of vegetables, it's a snap to prepare.

—GLENDA TAYLOR SAND SPRINGS, OK

START TO FINISH: 25 MIN.
MAKES: 6-8 SERVINGS (ABOUT 2 QUARTS)

- 2 pounds ground beef
- 1 envelope taco seasoning
- 1½ cups water
- 1 can (16 ounces) mild chili beans, undrained
- 1 can (15¼ ounces) whole kernel corn, drained
- 1 can (15 ounces) pinto beans, rinsed and drained
- 1 can (14½ ounces) stewed tomatoes
- 1 can (10 ounces) diced tomato with green chilies
- 1 can (4 ounces) chopped green chilies, optional
- 1 envelope ranch salad dressing mix

In a Dutch oven, cook beef over medium heat until no longer pink; drain. Add taco seasoning and mix well. Stir in the remaining ingredients. Bring to a boil. Reduce heat; simmer, uncovered, 15 minutes or until heated through, stirring occasionally.

CHICKEN CHILI CHOWDER

One chilly April afternoon, I craved a hearty soup but had less than an hour to prepare a meal. I created my chowder with items I had in the pantry, and everyone thought it hit the spot.
—**JENNA REMPE** LINCOLN, NE

PREP: 15 MIN. • **COOK:** 25 MIN. • **MAKES:** 6 SERVINGS (2 QUARTS)

- 1 medium onion, chopped
- 2 teaspoons canola oil
- 5 medium red potatoes, cubed
- 1 can (14½ ounces) chicken broth
- 1 can (10¾ ounces) condensed cream of chicken soup, undiluted
- ½ cup salsa verde
- 1 teaspoon chili powder
- ½ teaspoon garlic powder
- ½ teaspoon ground cumin
- ½ teaspoon pepper
- ¼ teaspoon salt
- 2 cups cubed cooked chicken breast
- 1 can (15½ ounces) great northern beans, rinsed and drained
- 1 can (14¾ ounces) cream-style corn
  Shredded cheddar cheese and sour cream, optional

Saute onion in oil in a large saucepan until tender. Add potatoes, broth, soup, salsa and seasonings. Bring to a boil. Reduce heat; cover and simmer 15-20 minutes or until potatoes are tender. Stir in chicken, beans and corn; heat through. Serve with cheese and sour cream if desired.

FAST FIX ▶
PEAR, HAM & CHEESE PASTRY POCKETS

While looking at what I had in the fridge one night, I came up with this recipe. Add a cup of soup and supper's ready.
—**TERRI CRANDALL** GARDNERVILLE, NV

START TO FINISH: 30 MIN. • **MAKES:** 8 SERVINGS

- 1 package (17.3 ounces) frozen puff pastry, thawed
- ¼ cup honey Dijon mustard
- 1 egg, lightly beaten
- 8 slices deli ham
- 4 slices Muenster cheese, halved diagonally
- 1 medium red pear, very thinly sliced
- 1 small red onion, thinly sliced

1. Preheat oven to 400°. Unfold each sheet of puff pastry. Cut each into four squares. Spread 1½ teaspoons mustard over each square to within ½ in. of edges. Brush egg over edges of pastry.

2. On one corner of each square, layer ham, cheese, pear and onion. Fold opposite corner over filling, forming a triangle; press edges with a fork to seal. Transfer to ungreased baking sheets. Brush tops with remaining egg. Bake 10-14 minutes or until golden brown. Serve warm.

FREEZE OPTION *Freeze cooled pockets in a freezer container, separating with waxed paper. To use, reheat pockets on a baking sheet in a preheated 400° oven until they are crisp and heated through.*

BACON-CHICKEN SANDWICHES

Everyone likes these tasty sandwiches. Flattening the chicken breasts helps them cook faster, and the mango chutney and other toppings make them better than anything you could order in a restaurant.

—AGNES WARD STRATFORD, ON

START TO FINISH: 25 MIN.
MAKES: 4 SERVINGS

- 4 **boneless skinless chicken breast halves (5 ounces each)**
- ½ **teaspoon salt**
- ½ **teaspoon pepper**
- 2 **teaspoons canola oil**
- 4 **tomato slices**
- 4 **slices process Swiss cheese**
- ¼ **cup mango chutney**
- 3 **tablespoons mayonnaise**
- 4 **kaiser rolls, split and toasted**
- 1 **cup fresh baby spinach**
- 8 **slices ready-to-serve fully cooked bacon, warmed**

1. Flatten chicken to ½-in. thickness; sprinkle with salt and pepper. In a large skillet over medium heat, cook chicken in oil 4-5 minutes on each side or until chicken juices run clear. Top each chicken breast half with a tomato slice and cheese slice; cover and cook 2-3 minutes or until cheese is melted.
2. Combine chutney and mayonnaise; spread over the roll bottoms. Layer with the spinach, chicken and bacon; replace tops.

TUSCAN CHICKEN SOUP

Change up your traditional chicken soup by adding a bit of fiber with white kidney beans. Soup is a smart way to use up leftover chicken.

—ROSEMARY GOETZ HUDSON, NY

PREP: 15 MIN. • **COOK:** 20 MIN.
MAKES: 4 SERVINGS

- 1 **small onion, chopped**
- 1 **small carrot, sliced**
- 1 **tablespoon olive oil**
- 2 **cans (14½ ounces each) chicken broth**
- 1 **cup water**
- ¾ **teaspoon salt**
- ¼ **teaspoon pepper**
- 1 **can (15 ounces) white kidney or cannellini beans, rinsed and drained**
- ⅔ **cup uncooked small spiral pasta**
- 3 **cups thinly sliced fresh escarole or spinach**
- 2 **cups shredded cooked chicken**

1. In a large saucepan, saute onion and carrot in oil until onion is tender. Add the broth, water, salt and pepper; bring to a boil. Stir in beans and pasta; return to a boil.
2. Reduce heat; cover and simmer 15 minutes or until the pasta and the vegetables are tender, stirring occasionally. Add escarole and chicken; heat through.

EASY BEEF BARLEY SOUP

It takes only a few minutes before my soup is bubbling away on the stovetop. Any leftovers make a fabulous lunch.

—CAROLE LANTHIER COURTICE, ON

PREP: 15 MIN. • **COOK:** 55 MIN.
MAKES: 4 SERVINGS

- ½ **pound lean ground beef (90% lean)**
- 2 **large fresh mushrooms, sliced**
- 1 **celery rib, chopped**
- 1 **small onion, chopped**
- 2 **teaspoons all-purpose flour**
- 3 **cans (14½ ounces each) reduced-sodium beef broth**
- 2 **medium carrots, sliced**
- 1 **large potato, peeled and cubed**
- ½ **teaspoon pepper**
- ⅛ **teaspoon salt**
- ⅓ **cup medium pearl barley**
- 1 **can (5 ounces) evaporated milk**
- 2 **tablespoons tomato paste**

1. In a Dutch oven over medium heat, cook and stir the beef, mushrooms, celery and onion until meat is no longer pink; drain. Stir in flour until blended; gradually add broth. Stir in the carrots, potato, pepper and salt. Bring to a boil. Stir in barley.
2. Reduce heat; cover and simmer for 45-50 minutes or until barley is tender. Whisk in the milk and tomato paste; heat through.

> 66 Thought these burgers were delicious. My personal preference would be to slightly reduce amount of cumin and increase hot sauce. All in all, most flavorful. 99
> —NORAROBERTS TASTEOFHOME.COM

BUFFALO TURKEY BURGERS

There's nothing bland about these turkey burgers! Celery and blue cheese salad dressing help tame the hot sauce. For an even skinnier version, skip the bun and add sliced onion and chopped tomato.
—**MARY PAX-SHIPLEY** BEND, OR

START TO FINISH: 25 MIN.
MAKES: 4 SERVINGS

- 2 tablespoons Louisiana-style hot sauce, divided
- 2 teaspoons ground cumin
- 2 teaspoons chili powder
- 2 garlic cloves, minced
- ½ teaspoon salt
- ⅛ teaspoon pepper
- 1 pound lean ground turkey
- 4 whole wheat hamburger buns, split
- 1 cup shredded lettuce
- 2 celery ribs, chopped
- 2 tablespoons fat-free blue cheese salad dressing

1. In a large bowl, mix 1 tablespoon hot sauce, cumin, chili powder, garlic, salt and pepper. Add the turkey; mix lightly but thoroughly. Shape into four ½-in.-thick patties.

2. In a large nonstick skillet coated with cooking spray, cook burgers over medium heat 4-6 minutes on each side or until a thermometer reads 165°.

3. Serve burgers on buns with lettuce, celery, salad dressing and remaining hot sauce.

FREEZE OPTION *Place uncooked patties on a plastic wrap-lined baking sheet; wrap and freeze until firm. Remove from pan and transfer to a large resealable plastic bag; return to freezer. To use, grill frozen patties as directed, increasing time as necessary for a thermometer to read 165°.*

CAULIFLOWER SOUP

Cauliflower and carrots share the stage in this cheddary soup that will warm you to your toes. We like it with hot pepper sauce; however, it can be omitted with equally flavorful results.

—DEBBIE OHLHAUSEN CHILLIWACK, BC

START TO FINISH: 30 MIN.
MAKES: 8 SERVINGS (ABOUT 2 QUARTS)

- 1 medium head cauliflower, broken into florets
- 1 medium carrot, shredded
- ¼ cup chopped celery
- 2½ cups water
- 2 teaspoons chicken bouillon or 1 vegetable bouillon cube
- 3 tablespoons butter
- 3 tablespoons all-purpose flour
- ¾ teaspoon salt
- ⅛ teaspoon pepper
- 2 cups 2% milk
- 1 cup (4 ounces) shredded cheddar cheese
- ½ to 1 teaspoon hot pepper sauce, optional

1. In a large bowl, combine cauliflower, carrot, celery, water and bouillon. Bring to a boil. Reduce heat; cover and simmer 12-15 minutes or until vegetables are tender (do not drain).
2. In another large saucepan, melt butter. Stir in flour, salt and pepper until smooth. Gradually add the milk. Bring to a boil over medium heat; cook and stir 2 minutes or until thickened. Reduce heat. Stir in cheese until melted. Add hot pepper sauce if desired. Stir into cauliflower mixture.

⑤ INGREDIENTS FAST FIX ▶

QUICK RAVIOLI & SPINACH SOUP

I love my Italian-American traditions, but I still like to have shortcuts when I'm cooking. For a quick Italian wedding soup, I created this version using refrigerated ravioli.

—CYNTHIA BENT NEWARK, DE

START TO FINISH: 25 MIN. • **MAKES:** 6 SERVINGS

- 2 cartons (32 ounces each) chicken broth
- ¼ teaspoon onion powder
    Dash pepper
- 1 package (9 ounces) refrigerated small cheese ravioli
- 4 cups coarsely chopped fresh spinach (about 4 ounces)
- 3 cups shredded cooked chicken
    Grated Parmesan cheese, optional

In a large saucepan, bring broth, onion powder and pepper to a boil. Add ravioli; cook, uncovered, 7-10 minutes or until tender. Add spinach and chicken during the last 3 minutes of cooking. If desired, serve with cheese.

CHIPOTLE ROAST BEEF SANDWICHES

Rustic ciabatta is an ideal match for tender roast beef, bold blue cheese and chipotle in this easy, tasty recipe.

—ANDRE HOUSEKNECHT FEASTERVILLE, PA

START TO FINISH: 25 MIN. • **MAKES:** 4 SERVINGS

- 1 loaf (14 ounces) ciabatta bread, halved lengthwise
- ⅔ cup mayonnaise
- 1 tablespoon chopped chipotle pepper in adobo sauce
- 1 small garlic clove, minced
- 1 teaspoon lime juice
- ¼ teaspoon pepper
- ⅛ teaspoon salt
- ½ cup crumbled blue cheese
- ¾ pound sliced deli roast beef
- 1 small onion, thinly sliced
- 1 medium tomato, sliced
- 4 lettuce leaves

1. Place bread, cut side up, on a baking sheet. Broil 3-4 in. from heat 2-3 minutes or until toasted.
2. Meanwhile, in a small bowl, combine the mayonnaise, chipotle pepper, garlic, lime juice, pepper and salt; spread over cut sides of bread. Sprinkle bottom half with blue cheese. Layer with roast beef, onion, tomato and lettuce; replace top. Cut into four sandwiches.

TOP TIP

Spinach Math

When a recipe calls for cooked fresh spinach, remember this: A pound of fresh spinach will yield 10-12 cups of torn leaves, which will cook down to about 1 cup.

FAST FIX ▶

BEEF VEGETABLE SOUP

At the end of a long day, you want to put something quick, warm and substantial on the table for your family. This satisfying beef vegetable soup fills the bill and will have you out of the kitchen in no time flat!

—**D. M. HILLOCK** HARTFORD, MI

START TO FINISH: 25 MIN.
MAKES: 4 SERVINGS

- 1 **pound ground beef**
- ½ **cup chopped onion**
- 1 **can (15 ounces) tomato sauce**
- 1½ **cups frozen mixed vegetables, thawed**
- 1¼ **cups frozen corn, thawed**
- 1¼ **cups beef broth**
- 1 **tablespoon soy sauce**
- 1 **tablespoon molasses**

In a large skillet, cook beef and onion over medium heat until meat is no longer pink; drain. Stir in remaining ingredients. Bring to a boil. Reduce heat; cover and simmer 10 minutes or until hot and bubbly.

FAST FIX ▶

COBB SALAD SANDWICHES

Satisfy the whole family with these fun, hearty sandwiches. It's easy to customize them to suit each person's tastes.

—*TASTE OF HOME* TEST KITCHEN

START TO FINISH: 20 MIN.
MAKES: 4 SERVINGS

- ¼ **cup mayonnaise**
- ½ **teaspoon prepared horseradish**
- ¼ **teaspoon dried basil**
- 4 **croissants, split**
- 4 **lettuce leaves**
- 1 **medium tomato, sliced**
- 4 **cooked bacon strips, halved**
- 4 **slices deli ham**
- 3 **hard-cooked eggs, sliced**

In a small bowl, combine the mayonnaise, horseradish and basil; spread over cut side of croissant bottoms. Layer with lettuce, tomato, bacon, ham and eggs; replace tops.

❝This was great. I did add a little bit more beef broth because it just wasn't 'soupy' enough with the recommended amount. It had good flavor and was super easy/quick. Definitely will make again.❞

—**SBHAYES05** TASTEOFHOME.COM

SLOW COOKER PASTA E FAGIOLI

This is my favorite soup to make because it's so flavorful, hearty and healthy. I have served this comforting dish to guests and received many compliments.

—**PENNY NOVY** BUFFALO GROVE, IL

PREP: 30 MIN. • **COOK:** 7½ HOURS
MAKES: 8 SERVINGS (2½ QUARTS)

- 1 **pound ground beef**
- 1 **medium onion, chopped**
- 1 **carton (32 ounces) chicken broth**
- 2 **cans (14½ ounces each) diced tomatoes, undrained**
- 1 **can (15 ounces) white kidney or cannellini beans, rinsed and drained**
- 2 **medium carrots, chopped**
- 1½ **cups finely chopped cabbage**
- 1 **celery rib, chopped**
- 2 **tablespoons minced fresh basil or 2 teaspoons dried basil**
- 2 **garlic cloves, minced**
- ½ **teaspoon salt**
- ½ **teaspoon pepper**
- 1 **cup ditalini or other small pasta Grated Parmesan cheese, optional**

1. In a large skillet, cook beef and onion over medium heat until the beef is no longer pink and the onion is tender; drain.

2. Transfer to a 4- or 5-qt. slow cooker. Stir in the broth, tomatoes, beans, carrots, cabbage, celery, basil, garlic, salt and pepper. Cover and cook on low 7-8 hours or until vegetables are tender.

3. Stir in pasta. Cover and cook on high 30 minutes longer or until pasta is tender. Sprinkle with cheese if desired.

TOP TIP

Why Rinse Canned Beans?

The liquid surrounding canned beans is high in sodium, and it is best not to use it. To remove the excess sodium, empty the can into a colander and rinse the beans with cold water. Let them drain in the colander before using them.

ARTICHOKE TUNA MELT

Artichokes, spinach and a lemony mayonnaise give this melt a tasty advantage over plain tuna sandwiches.
—*TASTE OF HOME* TEST KITCHEN

START TO FINISH: 25 MIN.
MAKES: 6 SERVINGS

- 1 **loaf (1 pound) French bread**
- 1 **tablespoon olive oil**
- 1 **garlic clove, halved**
- ¾ **cup mayonnaise**
- 1 **tablespoon lemon juice**
- 1 **tablespoon Dijon mustard**
- ½ **teaspoon garlic powder**
- ½ **teaspoon pepper**
- 4 **cans (5 ounces each) albacore white tuna in water**
- 1 **can (14 ounces) water-packed artichoke hearts, rinsed, drained and chopped**
- 1 **cup fresh baby spinach**
- 2 **plum tomatoes, sliced**
- 1 **cup (4 ounces) shredded part-skim mozzarella cheese**

1. Cut bread in half lengthwise (save one half for another use). Brush bread with oil. Place cut side up on an ungreased baking sheet. Broil 4-6 in. from heat 2-3 minutes or until golden brown. Rub cut sides of garlic clove over bread; discard garlic.

2. In a large bowl, combine the mayonnaise, lemon juice, mustard, garlic powder and pepper. Stir in tuna and artichokes.

3. Arrange spinach over bread; top with tuna mixture, tomatoes and cheese. Broil 1-2 minutes or until cheese is melted. Cut into six slices.

PORCINI MAC & CHEESE, PAGE 77

BACON POTATO SALAD, 64

MINTY WATERMELON–CUCUMBER SALAD, 74

CREAMY BLUEBERRY GELATIN SALAD, 78

Side Dishes, Salads & More

A meal isn't complete without a few sides to enhance the entree. The sides, salads and condiments here won raves from households just like yours, and they're sure to add flair to your dinners. Whether you're looking for a quick dish on a busy weeknight, a cool salad for an outdoor barbecue or a festive item for a special celebration, you'll find what you need on the following pages.

BACON POTATO SALAD

My family was tired of the same old potato salad at family functions, so I created this with the ingredients I had on hand. Now I'm always asked to bring it to potluck gatherings.

—**TAMI GALLAGHER** EAGAN, MN

PREP: 30 MIN. + CHILLING
MAKES: 8 SERVINGS

- 4 cups cubed red potatoes
- 1 cup chopped onion
- 7 bacon strips, cooked and crumbled
- 2 tablespoons minced fresh parsley
- 1⅓ cups mayonnaise
- 3 tablespoons grated Parmesan cheese
- 3 tablespoons prepared ranch salad dressing
- 2 tablespoons prepared mustard
- 4 teaspoons white vinegar
- ½ teaspoon minced garlic
- ¼ teaspoon salt
- ¼ teaspoon pepper

1. Place potatoes in a large saucepan and cover with water. Bring to a boil. Reduce heat; cover and cook for 10-15 minutes or until tender. Drain.
2. In a large bowl, combine potatoes, onion, bacon and parsley. In a small bowl, combine remaining ingredients. Pour over potato mixture; toss to coat. Refrigerate 1 hour or until chilled.

CRISP & SPICY CUCUMBER SALAD

Sweet-hot Asian flavors using rice vinegar, sesame oil and cayenne will light up your taste buds!

—**ALIVIA DOCKERY** PARKER, CO

PREP: 25 MIN. + MARINATING
MAKES: 6 SERVINGS

- 2 small English cucumbers, thinly sliced
- 2 medium carrots, thinly sliced
- 1 large sweet red pepper, julienned
- ½ medium red onion, thinly sliced
- 2 green onions, sliced
- ½ serrano or jalapeno pepper, seeded and thinly sliced, optional

MARINADE
- ⅓ cup sugar
- ⅓ cup rice vinegar
- ⅓ cup water
- 1 teaspoon each salt, garlic powder and pepper
- 1 teaspoon sesame oil
- 1 teaspoon reduced-sodium soy sauce
- 1 small garlic clove, minced
- ½ teaspoon minced fresh gingerroot
- ¼ teaspoon cayenne pepper, optional
  Optional toppings: minced fresh cilantro, chopped peanuts and additional sliced green onion

1. In a large bowl, combine the first six ingredients. In a small bowl, mix marinade ingredients, stirring to dissolve sugar. Pour over vegetables; toss to combine. Refrigerate, covered, 30 minutes or overnight.
2. Serve with a slotted spoon. If desired, sprinkle with toppings.
NOTE *Wear disposable gloves when cutting hot peppers; the oils can burn skin. Avoid touching your face.*

REFRIGERATOR PICKLES

These pickles are so good and easy to prepare, you'll want to keep them on hand all the time. My in-laws send over produce just so I'll make more!

—**LOY JONES** ANNISTON, AL

PREP: 25 MIN. + CHILLING • **MAKES:** 6 CUPS

- 3 cups sliced peeled cucumbers
- 3 cups sliced peeled yellow summer squash
- 2 cups chopped sweet onions
- 1½ cups white vinegar
- 1 cup sugar
- ½ teaspoon salt
- ½ teaspoon celery seed
- ½ teaspoon mustard seed

1. Place the cucumbers, squash and onions in a large bowl; set aside. In a small saucepan, combine remaining ingredients; bring to a boil. Cook and stir just until the sugar is dissolved. Pour over cucumber mixture; cool.
2. Cover tightly and refrigerate at least 24 hours. Serve with a slotted spoon.

⑤INGREDIENTS
CORN WITH CILANTRO-LIME BUTTER

I grow cilantro in my garden. When I created a lime butter for grilled corn, I made sure to include some fresh cilantro in the recipe.

—**ANDREA REYNOLDS** WESTLAKE, OH

PREP: 15 MIN. + CHILLING • **GRILL:** 15 MIN.
MAKES: 12 SERVINGS

- ½ cup butter, softened
- ¼ cup minced fresh cilantro
- 1 tablespoon lime juice
- 1½ teaspoons grated lime peel
- 12 medium ears sweet corn, husks removed
  Grated cotija cheese, optional

1. In a small bowl, mix the butter, cilantro, lime juice and lime peel. Shape into a log; wrap in plastic wrap. Refrigerate 30 minutes or until firm. Wrap each ear of corn with a piece of heavy-duty foil (about 14 in. square).

2. Grill corn, covered, over medium heat 15-20 minutes or until tender, turning occasionally. Meanwhile, cut lime butter into 12 slices. Remove corn from grill. Carefully open foil, allowing steam to escape. Serve corn with butter and, if desired, cheese.

❝ This butter was a HUGE hit at my last BBQ! The tanginess of the lime and the freshness of the cilantro take this over the top. It is even good served on steaks. ❞

—**RANDCBRUNS**
TASTEOFHOME.COM

SLOW-COOKED BEAN MEDLEY

I often change the variety of beans in this classic recipe, using whatever I have on hand to total five 15- to 16-ounce cans. The sauce makes any combination delicious.
—**PEGGY GWILLIM** STRASBOURG, SK

PREP: 25 MIN. • **COOK:** 5 HOURS
MAKES: 12 SERVINGS (¾ CUP EACH)

- 1½ cups ketchup
- 2 celery ribs, chopped
- 1 medium onion, chopped
- 1 medium green pepper, chopped
- 1 medium sweet red pepper, chopped
- ½ cup packed brown sugar
- ½ cup water
- ½ cup Italian salad dressing
- 2 bay leaves
- 1 tablespoon cider vinegar
- 1 teaspoon ground mustard
- ⅛ teaspoon pepper
- 1 can (16 ounces) kidney beans, rinsed and drained
- 1 can (15½ ounces) black-eyed peas, rinsed and drained
- 1 can (15½ ounces) great northern beans, rinsed and drained
- 1 can (15¼ ounces) whole kernel corn, drained
- 1 can (15¼ ounces) lima beans, rinsed and drained
- 1 can (15 ounces) black beans, rinsed and drained

In a 5-qt. slow cooker, combine the first 12 ingredients. Stir in the remaining ingredients. Cover and cook on low for 5-6 hours or until onion and peppers are tender. Discard the bay leaves.

FAST FIX ASIAN SPAGHETTI

Give a simple entree an Asian twist with a quick side that has a hint of heat. We enjoy the spaghetti with its bright, crisp-tender snow peas and carrots, but you could easily substitute any veggies you have on hand.
—**ANNE SMITHSON** CARY, NC

START TO FINISH: 20 MIN. • **MAKES:** 5 SERVINGS

- 8 ounces uncooked angel hair pasta
- 1 cup sliced fresh mushrooms
- 1 cup fresh snow peas
- ¾ cup shredded carrots
- 4 green onions, cut into 1-inch pieces
- 2 tablespoons canola oil
- 1 garlic clove, minced
- ¼ cup reduced-sodium soy sauce
- 1 teaspoon sugar
- ¼ teaspoon cayenne pepper
- 2 tablespoons sesame seeds, toasted

1. Cook pasta according to package directions.
2. Meanwhile, in a large skillet, saute the mushrooms, snow peas, carrots and onions in oil until crisp-tender. Add garlic; cook 1 minute longer.
3. In a small bowl, combine soy sauce, sugar and cayenne. Drain pasta. Add pasta and soy sauce mixture to skillet and toss to coat. Heat through. Sprinkle with sesame seeds.

CARROT CAKE JAM

For a change of pace from berry jams, try this unique option. Spread on a bagel with cream cheese, it tastes almost as good as real carrot cake!

—**RACHELLE STRATTON** ROCK SPRINGS, WY

PREP: 45 MIN. • **PROCESS:** 5 MIN. • **MAKES:** 8 HALF-PINTS

- 1 **can (20 ounces) unsweetened crushed pineapple, undrained**
- 1½ **cups shredded carrots**
- 1½ **cups chopped peeled ripe pears**
- 3 **tablespoons lemon juice**
- 1 **teaspoon ground cinnamon**
- ¼ **teaspoon ground cloves**
- ¼ **teaspoon ground nutmeg**
- 1 **package (1¾ ounces) powdered fruit pectin**
- 6½ **cups sugar**

1. In a large saucepan, combine the first seven ingredients. Bring the mixture to a boil. Reduce heat; cover and simmer 15-20 minutes or until the pears are tender, stirring occasionally. Stir in pectin. Bring to a full rolling boil over high heat, stirring constantly. Stir in sugar; return to a full rolling boil. Boil and stir 1 minute.

2. Remove from heat; skim off foam. Ladle hot mixture into eight hot sterilized half-pint jars, leaving ¼-in. headspace. Remove air bubbles and adjust headspace, if necessary, by adding hot mixture. Wipe rims. Center lids on jars; screw on bands until fingertip tight.

3. Place jars into canner with simmering water, ensuring that they are completely covered with water. Bring to a boil; process for 5 minutes. Remove jars and cool.

NOTE *The processing time listed is for altitudes of 1,000 feet or less. Add 1 minute to the processing time for each 1,000 feet of additional altitude.*

⑤ INGREDIENTS

BROCCOLI CASSEROLE

Everybody who has tried my side dish absolutely raves about it. People who don't even like broccoli beg me to make it.

—**ELAINE HUBBARD** POCONO LAKE, PA

PREP: 20 MIN. • **BAKE:** 35 MIN. • **MAKES:** 6-8 SERVINGS

- 2 **packages (16 ounces each) frozen broccoli florets**
- 1 **can (10¾ ounces) condensed cream of mushroom soup, undiluted**
- 1 **cup (8 ounces) sour cream**
- 1½ **cups (6 ounces) shredded sharp cheddar cheese, divided**
- 1 **can (6 ounces) french-fried onions, divided**

1. Preheat oven to 325°. Cook broccoli according to package directions; drain well. In a large saucepan, combine soup, sour cream, 1 cup cheese and 1¼ cups onions. Cook over medium heat 4-5 minutes or until heated through. Stir in the broccoli.

2. Pour into a greased 2-qt. baking dish. Bake, uncovered, 25-30 minutes or until bubbly. Sprinkle with the remaining cheese and onions. Bake 10-15 minutes longer or until cheese is melted.

(5)INGREDIENTS

ROASTED CAULIFLOWER & BRUSSELS SPROUTS

This is a surefire way to get my husband to eat Brussels sprouts. Between the roasted flavor of the veggies and the crisp, smoky bacon, the delicious side dish will convert even the pickiest eater.
—**LISA SPEER** PALM BEACH, FL

PREP: 30 MIN. • **BAKE:** 20 MIN.
MAKES: 10 SERVINGS

- 2 **pounds fresh Brussels sprouts, thinly sliced**
- 1 **pound fresh cauliflowerets (about 7 cups), thinly sliced**
- ¼ **cup olive oil**
- 1 **teaspoon freshly ground pepper**
- ½ **teaspoon salt**
- 1 **pound bacon strips, cooked and crumbled**
- ⅓ **to ½ cup balsamic vinaigrette**

1. Preheat oven to 375°. In a very large bowl, toss Brussels sprouts and cauliflower with oil, pepper and salt. Transfer to two greased 15x10x1-in. baking pans.
2. Roast 20-25 minutes or until vegetables are tender. Transfer to a serving bowl. Just before serving, add bacon and drizzle with vinaigrette; toss to coat.

FAST FIX

GLAZED CARROT COINS

These glossy carrots, flavored with orange juice, cinnamon and ginger, are pretty enough for a special meal.
—**HELEN BETHEL** MAYSVILLE, NC

START TO FINISH: 25 MIN.
MAKES: 4 SERVINGS

- 2 **tablespoons butter**
- 2 **tablespoons brown sugar**
- 2 **tablespoons orange juice**
- ¼ **teaspoon salt**
- ¼ **teaspoon ground ginger**
- ⅛ **teaspoon ground cinnamon**
- 6 **medium carrots, cut into ½-inch slices**

In a small saucepan, melt butter over medium heat. Stir in sugar, juice, salt, ginger and cinnamon. Add carrots; cover and cook 20-25 minutes or until tender, stirring occasionally.

TRIPLE CRANBERRY SAUCE

Cranberry fans will ask for this sauce again and again. It's loaded with their favorite fruit—in fresh, dried and juice form. Orange and allspice make it awesome.
—**ARLENE SMULSKI** LYONS, IL

PREP: 10 MIN. • **COOK:** 15 MIN. + CHILLING • **MAKES:** 3 CUPS

- 1 **package (12 ounces) fresh or frozen cranberries**
- 1 **cup thawed cranberry juice concentrate**
- ½ **cup dried cranberries**
- ⅓ **cup sugar**
- 3 **tablespoons orange juice**
- 3 **tablespoons orange marmalade**
- 2 **teaspoons grated orange peel**
- ¼ **teaspoon ground allspice**

1. In a small saucepan, combine the cranberries, cranberry juice concentrate, dried cranberries and sugar. Cook over medium heat until the berries pop, about 15 minutes.
2. Remove from heat; stir in the orange juice, marmalade, orange peel and allspice. Transfer to a small bowl; refrigerate until chilled.

TOP TIP

Buying Fresh Cranberries

Fresh cranberries are in season from early fall through December. When buying, look for packages with shiny, bright red (light or dark) berries. Avoid berries that are bruised or shriveled or have brown spots. Refrigerate fresh unwashed cranberries for about 1 month or freeze up to 1 year.

NEVER-FAIL SCALLOPED POTATOES

Take the chill off any blustery day and make something special to accompany meaty entrees. This creamy, stick-to-the-ribs potato-and-onion side dish is one you'll turn to often.
—**AGNES WARD** STRATFORD, ON

PREP: 30 MIN. • **BAKE:** 1 HOUR • **MAKES:** 6 SERVINGS

- 2 **tablespoons butter**
- 3 **tablespoons all-purpose flour**
- 1 **teaspoon salt**
- ¼ **teaspoon pepper**
- 1½ **cups fat-free milk**
- ½ **cup shredded reduced-fat cheddar cheese**
- 1¾ **pounds potatoes, peeled and thinly sliced (about 5 medium)**
- 1 **medium onion, halved and thinly sliced**

1. Preheat oven to 350°. In a small nonstick skillet, melt butter. Stir in flour, salt and pepper until smooth; gradually add milk. Bring to a boil. Cook and stir 2 minutes or until thickened. Remove from heat; stir in cheese until blended.
2. Place half of the potatoes in a 1½-qt. baking dish coated with cooking spray; layer with half of the onion and cheese sauce. Repeat layers.
3. Cover and bake 50 minutes. Uncover; bake 10-15 minutes longer or until bubbly and potatoes are tender.

❝ Loved this recipe! So simple but so delicious! Loved the addition of the sliced onion in this dish and the subtleness of the cheese. ❞
—**CHRISTYCINCY** TASTEOFHOME.COM

ROASTED BUTTERNUT SQUASH & RICE SALAD

We have end-of-season picnics for my son's flag football team. My salad makes enough to serve the hungry boys and their families.

—**DOLORES DEIFEL** MUNDELEIN, IL

PREP: 25 MIN. + CHILLING • **COOK:** 25 MIN. + COOLING
MAKES: 12 SERVINGS (¾ CUP EACH)

3 **tablespoons brown sugar**
3 **tablespoons balsamic vinegar**
2 **tablespoons olive oil**
1 **teaspoon kosher salt**
1 **medium butternut squash (2½ to 3 pounds), peeled and cut into ¾-inch cubes**
2 **cups uncooked jasmine rice**
2 **large sweet red peppers, cut into ½-inch pieces**
1 **cup pine nuts, toasted**
6 **green onions, thinly sliced**
3 **tablespoons snipped fresh dill**
3 **tablespoons coarsely chopped fresh parsley**
DRESSING
½ **cup olive oil**
3 **tablespoons red wine vinegar**
½ **teaspoon kosher salt**
¼ **teaspoon pepper**

1. Preheat oven to 425°. In a large bowl, combine the brown sugar, balsamic vinegar, oil and salt. Add the squash; toss to coat. Transfer to a greased, foil-lined 15x10x1-in. baking pan. Bake 25-30 minutes or until tender, stirring occasionally. Cool completely.
2. Meanwhile, cook rice according to package directions. Remove from heat; cool completely.
3. In a large bowl, combine red peppers, pine nuts, green onions, dill, parsley, squash and rice. In a small bowl, whisk dressing ingredients. Pour over salad; toss to coat. Serve at room temperature. Cover and refrigerate leftovers.
NOTE *To toast nuts, spread in a 15x10x1-in. baking pan. Bake at 350° for 5-10 minutes or until lightly browned, stirring occasionally. Or, spread in a dry nonstick skillet and heat over low heat until lightly browned, stirring occasionally.*

CAMPERS' COLESLAW

Crispy and crunchy, this traditional, no-fuss slaw makes a refreshing side dish for summer picnics and parties.

—**KIMBERLY WALLACE** DENNISON, OH

PREP: 20 MIN. + CHILLING • **MAKES:** 12 SERVINGS (¾ CUP EACH)

1½ **cups sugar**
¾ **cup white vinegar**
¾ **cup olive oil**
3 **teaspoons salt**
1 **teaspoon celery seed**
1 **medium head cabbage, shredded**
1 **large onion, chopped**
1 **medium green pepper, chopped**

1. In a small saucepan, combine the first five ingredients. Bring to a boil; boil for 1-2 minutes or until sugar is dissolved. Remove from the heat; cool to room temperature.
2. In a large bowl, combine the cabbage, onion and pepper; add dressing and toss to coat. Refrigerate until chilled. Serve with a slotted spoon.

APPLE PIE JAM

My husband and I love this jam so much because it tastes just like apple pie without the crust.

—**AUDREY GODELL** STANTON, MI

PREP: 30 MIN. • **PROCESS:** 10 MIN. • **MAKES:** 7 HALF-PINTS

4 **to 5 large Golden Delicious apples, peeled and sliced (about 2 pounds)**
1 **cup water**
5 **cups sugar**
½ **teaspoon butter**
1 **pouch (3 ounces) liquid fruit pectin**
1½ **teaspoons ground cinnamon**
1 **teaspoon ground nutmeg**
¼ **teaspoon ground mace, optional**

1. In a Dutch oven, combine apples and water. Cover and cook slowly until tender. Measure 4½ cups apples; return to the pan. (Save remaining apple mixture for another use or discard.)
2. Stir in sugar and butter. Bring to a full rolling boil over high heat, stirring constantly. Stir in pectin. Continue to boil 1 minute, stirring constantly.
3. Remove from heat; skim off foam. Stir in spices. Carefully ladle hot mixture into seven hot half-pint jars, leaving ¼-in. headspace. Remove air bubbles and adjust headspace, if necessary, by adding hot mixture. Wipe rims. Center lids on jars; screw on bands until fingertip tight.
4. Place jars into canner with simmering water, ensuring that they are completely covered with water. Bring to a boil; process for 10 minutes. Remove jars and cool.
NOTE *The processing time listed is for altitudes of 1,000 feet or less. Add 1 minute to the processing time for each 1,000 feet of additional altitude.*

GRILLED THREE-CHEESE POTATOES

While this is delicious grilled, I've also cooked it in the oven at 350° for an hour. Add cubed ham to it and you can serve it as a full-meal main dish.

—MARGARET RILEY TALLAHASSEE, FL

PREP: 15 MIN. • **GRILL:** 35 MIN. • **MAKES:** 6-8 SERVINGS

- 6 **large potatoes, sliced ¼ inch thick**
- 2 **medium onions, chopped**
- ⅓ **cup grated Parmesan cheese**
- 1 **cup (4 ounces) shredded sharp cheddar cheese, divided**
- 1 **cup (4 ounces) shredded part-skim mozzarella cheese, divided**
- 1 **pound sliced bacon, cooked and crumbled**
- ¼ **cup butter, cubed**
- 1 **tablespoon minced chives**
- 1 **to 2 teaspoons seasoned salt**
- ½ **teaspoon pepper**

1. Divide the potatoes and onions equally between two pieces of heavy-duty foil (about 18 in. square) that have been coated with cooking spray.

2. Combine Parmesan cheese and ¾ cup each cheddar and mozzarella; sprinkle over potatoes and onions. Top with the bacon, butter, chives, seasoned salt and pepper. Bring opposite ends of foil together over the filling and fold down several times. Fold the unsealed ends toward filling and crimp tightly.

3. Grill, covered, over medium heat 35-40 minutes or until potatoes are tender. Remove from grill. Open foil carefully and sprinkle with remaining cheeses.

FAST FIX
DIJON GREEN BEANS

I relish this recipe because it combines the freshness of garden green beans with a warm and tangy dressing.

—JANNINE FISK MALDEN, MA

START TO FINISH: 20 MIN. • **MAKES:** 10 SERVINGS

- 1½ **pounds fresh green beans, trimmed**
- 2 **tablespoons red wine vinegar**
- 2 **tablespoons olive oil**
- 2 **teaspoons Dijon mustard**
- ½ **teaspoon salt**
- ¼ **teaspoon pepper**
- 1 **cup grape tomatoes, halved**
- ½ **small red onion, sliced**
- 2 **tablespoons grated Parmesan cheese**

1. Place beans in a large saucepan and cover with water. Bring to a boil. Cook, covered, 10-15 minutes or until crisp-tender.

2. Meanwhile, whisk the vinegar, oil, mustard, salt and pepper in a small bowl. Drain beans; place in a large bowl. Add tomatoes and onion. Drizzle with dressing and toss to coat. Sprinkle with cheese.

FAST FIX ▶

RICE ON THE GRILL

When it's hot outside, we do entire meals on the grill. Since our kids like rice, we often include this tangy side as part of the menu.
—**SHIRLEY HOPKINS** OLDS, AB

START TO FINISH: 30 MIN. • **MAKES:** 4 SERVINGS

- 1⅓ cups uncooked instant rice
- ⅓ cup sliced fresh mushrooms
- ¼ cup chopped green pepper
- ¼ cup chopped onion
- ½ cup water
- ½ cup chicken broth
- ⅓ cup ketchup
- 1 tablespoon butter

1. In a 9-in. round disposable foil pan, combine the first seven ingredients. Dot with butter. Cover with heavy-duty foil; seal edges tightly.

2. Grill, covered, over medium heat 12-15 minutes or until liquid is absorbed. Remove foil carefully to allow steam to escape. Fluff with a fork.

❝Perfect for a summer BBQ. I was looking for something to cook along with the outdoor meal; this worked great in a pan on the side burner. It was moist, and I had mushrooms, celery and spices in there. Wasn't any left over.❞
—**MAPETE8** TASTEOFHOME.COM

FAST FIX ▶

SALAMI PASTA SALAD

The first time I tasted this fantastic salad was at my wedding, and I recall, even in the blur of that day, that the recipe was in high demand. I made a point to get a copy. That was years ago and I'm still asked to bring it to cookouts and parties.
—**SARAH RYAN** GENEVA, OH

START TO FINISH: 20 MIN. • **MAKES:** 9 SERVINGS

- 2 cups uncooked small pasta shells
- ¾ cup chopped green pepper
- ¾ cup chopped fresh tomatoes
- ½ cup chopped pepperoni
- ½ cup cubed hard salami
- ½ cup whole ripe olives, quartered
- 2 ounces provolone cheese, cubed
- ⅓ cup chopped onion

DRESSING
- ⅓ cup canola oil
- ¼ cup red wine vinegar
- 2 tablespoons sugar
- 1½ teaspoons salt
- 1½ teaspoons dried oregano
- ½ teaspoon pepper

1. Cook pasta according to package directions; drain and rinse in cold water. Place in a large bowl; add the green pepper, tomatoes, pepperoni, salami, olives, cheese and onion.

2. In a small bowl, whisk the dressing ingredients. Pour over the pasta mixture; toss to coat. Cover and refrigerate until serving.

⑤ INGREDIENTS FAST FIX

MINTY WATERMELON-CUCUMBER SALAD

Capturing the delightful flavors of summer, this beautiful salad will be the talk of any picnic or potluck.

—ROBLYNN HUNNISETT GUELPH, ON

START TO FINISH: 20 MIN.
MAKES: 16 SERVINGS (¾ CUP EACH)

- 8 **cups cubed seedless watermelon**
- 2 **medium English cucumbers, halved lengthwise and sliced**
- 6 **green onions, chopped**
- ¼ **cup minced fresh mint**
- ¼ **cup balsamic vinegar**
- ¼ **cup olive oil**
- ½ **teaspoon salt**
- ½ **teaspoon pepper**

In a large bowl, toss the first four ingredients. In a small bowl, whisk remaining ingredients. Pour over salad; toss to coat. Serve immediately or refrigerate, covered, up to 2 hours before serving.

⑤ INGREDIENTS FAST FIX

SPAETZLE DUMPLINGS

These tender homemade noodles take only minutes to make. You can enjoy them with chicken gravy or simply buttered and sprinkled with parsley.

—PAMELA EATON MONCLOVA, OH

START TO FINISH: 15 MIN.
MAKES: 6 SERVINGS

- 2 **cups all-purpose flour**
- 4 **eggs, lightly beaten**
- ⅓ **cup 2% milk**
- 2 **teaspoons salt**
- 8 **cups water**
- 1 **tablespoon butter**

1. In a large bowl, stir flour, eggs, milk and salt until smooth (dough will be sticky). In a large saucepan, bring the water to a boil.

2. Pour dough into a colander or spaetzle maker coated with cooking spray; place over boiling water. With a wooden spoon, press the dough until small pieces drop into boiling water. Cook 2 minutes or until dumplings are tender and float. Remove with a slotted spoon; toss with butter.

SLOW COOKER TZIMMES

Tzimmes is a Jewish dish with a variety of fruits and vegetables that may or may not include meat. Traditionally (as it is here), it's tossed with honey and cinnamon and slowly cooked to meld the flavors.

—LISA RENSHAW KANSAS CITY, MO

PREP: 20 MIN. • **COOK:** 5 HOURS
MAKES: 12 SERVINGS (⅔ CUP EACH)

- ½ **medium butternut squash, peeled and cubed**
- 2 **medium sweet potatoes, peeled and cubed**
- 6 **medium carrots, sliced**
- 2 **medium tart apples, peeled and sliced**
- 1 **cup chopped sweet onion**
- 1 **cup chopped dried apricots**
- 1 **cup golden raisins**
- ½ **cup orange juice**
- ¼ **cup honey**
- 2 **tablespoons finely chopped crystallized ginger**
- 3 **teaspoons ground cinnamon**
- 3 **teaspoons pumpkin pie spice**
- 2 **teaspoons grated orange peel**
- 1 **teaspoon salt**
  Vanilla yogurt, optional

1. Place the first seven ingredients in a 5- or 6-qt. slow cooker. Combine the orange juice, honey, ginger, cinnamon, pie spice, orange peel and salt; pour over top and mix well.

2. Cover and cook on low 5-6 hours or until vegetables are tender. Dollop servings with yogurt if desired.

FAST FIX
SUNNY STRAWBERRY & CANTALOUPE SALAD

My little ones absolutely love this salad and ask me to make it all the time. Fruit and cheese taste great together and the kids like the crunch of the sunflower seeds.

—AYSHA SCHURMAN AMMON, ID

START TO FINISH: 15 MIN.
MAKES: 4 SERVINGS

- 1 **cup sliced fresh strawberries**
- 1 **cup cubed cantaloupe**
- ½ **cup (about 2 ounces) cubed part-skim mozzarella cheese**
- 2 **tablespoons raspberry vinaigrette**
- ½ **cup fresh raspberries**
- 1 **tablespoon sunflower kernels**
  Thinly sliced fresh mint leaves, optional

In a large bowl, combine strawberries, cantaloupe and cheese. Drizzle with vinaigrette and toss to coat. Just before serving, gently stir in raspberries; top with sunflower kernels. If desired, sprinkle with mint.

ORZO CHEESECAKE FRUIT SALAD

This features my favorite fruits, complemented by the creamy pudding mix. It even works as a dessert.

—PRISCILLA GILBERT
INDIAN HARBOUR BEACH, FL

PREP: 30 MIN. + CHILLING
MAKES: 16 SERVINGS

- 1 **cup uncooked orzo pasta**
- 1 **package (3.4 ounces) instant cheesecake or vanilla pudding mix**
- ⅓ **cup sour cream**
- 1 **can (20 ounces) crushed pineapple, undrained**
- 1 **large banana, sliced**
- 2 **teaspoons lemon juice**
- 2 **cans (11 ounces each) mandarin oranges, drained**
- 2 **cups miniature marshmallows**
- 1 **cup chopped pecans, toasted**
- 1 **cup canned sliced peaches, drained and chopped**
- ½ **cup maraschino cherries, drained and quartered**
- 1 **carton (8 ounces) frozen whipped topping, thawed**
- ½ **cup flaked coconut, toasted**

1. Cook orzo according to package directions. Drain and rinse in cold water; set aside.

2. In a large bowl, combine pudding mix, sour cream and pineapple. Toss banana with lemon juice; stir into pudding mixture. Stir in the oranges, marshmallows, pecans, peaches, cherries and orzo. Fold in the whipped topping. Sprinkle with the coconut. Cover and refrigerate for 2 hours or until chilled.

PORCINI MAC & CHEESE

I had a mushroom mac and cheese at a local restaurant and thought I could make it at home. I incorporated the fall flavor of a pumpkin ale, and it turned out better than the original.
—**LAURA DAVIS** CHINCOTEAGUE ISLAND, VA

PREP: 30 MIN. + STANDING • **BAKE:** 35 MIN. • **MAKES:** 6 SERVINGS

- 1 package (1 ounce) dried porcini mushrooms
- 1 cup boiling water
- 1 package (16 ounces) small pasta shells
- 6 tablespoons butter, cubed
- 1 cup chopped baby portobello mushrooms
- 1 shallot, finely chopped
- 1 garlic clove, minced
- 3 tablespoons all-purpose flour
- 2½ cups 2% milk
- ½ cup pumpkin or amber ale
- 2 cups (8 ounces) shredded sharp white cheddar cheese
- 1 cup (4 ounces) shredded fontina cheese
- 1 teaspoon salt
- 1 cup soft bread crumbs

1. Preheat oven to 350°. In a small bowl, combine dried mushrooms and boiling water; let stand 15-20 minutes or until mushrooms are softened. Remove with a slotted spoon; rinse and finely chop. Discard liquid. Cook pasta according to package directions for al dente.
2. Meanwhile, in a Dutch oven, heat butter over medium-high heat. Add portobello mushrooms and shallot; cook and stir 2-3 minutes or until tender. Add garlic; cook 1 minute longer. Stir in flour until blended; gradually stir in milk and beer. Bring to a boil, stirring constantly; cook and stir for 3-4 minutes or until slightly thickened. Stir in cheeses, salt and reserved mushrooms.
3. Drain pasta; add to mushroom mixture and toss to combine. Transfer to a greased 13x9-in. baking dish. Top with bread crumbs. Bake, uncovered, for 35-40 minutes or until golden brown.

NOTE *To make soft bread crumbs, tear bread into pieces and place in a food processor or blender. Cover and pulse until crumbs form. One slice of bread yields ½ to ¾ cup crumbs.*

FAST FIX

SPRING GREENS WITH BEETS AND GOAT CHEESE

Here's one of my signature salads. I sometimes vary the ingredients slightly, depending on what I have on hand, but this version is my absolute favorite. I adore the flavor combination.
—**KRISTIN KOSSAK** BOZEMAN, MT

START TO FINISH: 20 MIN. • **MAKES:** 8 SERVINGS

- ⅔ cup pecan halves
- 3 tablespoons balsamic vinegar, divided
- 1 tablespoon water
- 1 tablespoon sugar
- ¼ cup olive oil
- 2 tablespoons maple syrup
- 1 teaspoon stone-ground mustard
- ⅛ teaspoon salt
- 1 package (5 ounces) spring mix salad greens
- 1 can (14½ ounces) sliced beets, drained
- 1 cup crumbled goat cheese

1. In a large heavy skillet, cook the pecans, 1 tablespoon vinegar and water over medium heat until nuts are toasted, about 4 minutes. Sprinkle with the sugar. Cook and stir 2-4 minutes or until sugar is melted. Spread on foil to cool.
2. In a small bowl, whisk the oil, syrup, mustard, salt and remaining vinegar. Refrigerate until serving.
3. In a large bowl, combine salad greens and dressing; toss to coat. Divide among eight salad plates. Top with beets, goat cheese and glazed pecans.

TOP TIP

About Goat Cheese

This soft, easily spread cheese with a distinctively tangy flavor is made from the milk of goats. Goat cheese is often found in Middle Eastern or Mediterranean cuisines. Chevre is a variety that may be made with goat and cow milk; if the label says *pur chevre* then the cheese is made from 100 percent goat's milk. Tightly wrap goat cheese and store in the refrigerator up to 2 weeks. If goat cheese has a sour taste rather than a tangy, tart taste, it is old and should be discarded.

TUSCAN-STYLE ROASTED ASPARAGUS

I turn to this recipe when locally grown asparagus is in season. It is so easy for parties because the dish can be served hot or cold.
—**JANNINE FISK** MALDEN, MA

PREP: 20 MIN. • **BAKE:** 15 MIN. • **MAKES:** 8 SERVINGS

- 1½ **pounds fresh asparagus, trimmed**
- 1½ **cups grape tomatoes, halved**
- 3 **tablespoons pine nuts**
- 3 **tablespoons olive oil, divided**
- 2 **garlic cloves, minced**
- 1 **teaspoon kosher salt**
- ½ **teaspoon pepper**
- 1 **tablespoon lemon juice**
- ⅓ **cup grated Parmesan cheese**
- 1 **teaspoon grated lemon peel**

1. Preheat oven to 400°. Place the asparagus, tomatoes and pine nuts on a foil-lined 15x10x1-in. baking pan. Mix 2 tablespoons oil, garlic, salt and pepper; add to asparagus and toss to coat.

2. Bake 15-20 minutes or just until asparagus is tender. Drizzle with remaining oil and lemon juice; sprinkle with cheese and lemon peel. Toss to combine.

> ❝ I made this a few weeks ago for a family gathering and it was a hit, even with those who aren't big veggie eaters. Great recipe! ❞
> —**KRISTINECHAYES** TASTEOFHOME.COM

CREAMY BLUEBERRY GELATIN SALAD

Plump blueberries and a fluffy topping star in my mom's pretty, refreshing salad. Her blueberry creation was served at every holiday and celebration. Now, Mom's grandchildren request it for all the holiday menus.
—**SHARON HOEFERT** GREENDALE, WI

PREP: 30 MIN. + CHILLING • **MAKES:** 12-15 SERVINGS

- 2 **packages (3 ounces each) grape gelatin**
- 2 **cups boiling water**
- 1 **can (21 ounces) blueberry pie filling**
- 1 **can (20 ounces) unsweetened crushed pineapple, undrained**

TOPPING
- 1 **package (8 ounces) cream cheese, softened**
- 1 **cup (8 ounces) sour cream**
- ½ **cup sugar**
- 1 **teaspoon vanilla extract**
- ½ **cup chopped walnuts**

1. In a large bowl, dissolve gelatin in boiling water. Cool 10 minutes. Stir in pie filling and pineapple until blended. Transfer to a 13x9-in. dish. Cover and refrigerate until partially set, about 1 hour.

2. For topping, in a small bowl, combine the cream cheese, sour cream, sugar and vanilla. Carefully spread over gelatin; sprinkle with walnuts. Cover and refrigerate until firm.

GARDEN SALSA

My mouthwatering salsa is made from ripe garden ingredients and subtle seasonings. It's one of my go-to dishes for parties.
—**MICHELLE BERAN** CLAFLIN, KS

START TO FINISH: 15 MIN.
MAKES: 5 CUPS

- 6 medium tomatoes, finely chopped
- ¾ cup finely chopped green pepper
- ½ cup finely chopped onion
- ½ cup thinly sliced green onions
- 6 garlic cloves, minced
- 2 teaspoons cider vinegar
- 2 teaspoons lemon juice
- 2 teaspoons olive oil
- 1 to 2 teaspoons minced jalapeno pepper
- 1 to 2 teaspoons ground cumin
- ½ teaspoon salt
- ¼ to ½ teaspoon cayenne pepper
  Tortilla chips

In a large bowl, combine tomatoes, green pepper, onions, garlic, vinegar, lemon juice, oil, jalapeno and the seasonings. Cover and refrigerate until serving. Serve with chips.
NOTE *Wear disposable gloves when cutting hot peppers; the oils can burn skin. Avoid touching your face.*

TOP TIP

Seeding Jalapeno Peppers

To reduce the heat of jalapenos and other hot peppers, remove and discard the seeds. To do so quickly, cut off the tops of the peppers, then cut them lengthwise in half. Use the tip of a spoon to scrap out the seeds and membranes. If you like very spicy foods, add the seeds to the dish you're making instead of discarding them.

FAST FIX ▶

ZUCCHINI ONION PIE

Zucchini always seems to grow in abundance in our garden. This is a good and different way to use the excess.

—LUCIA JOHNSON MASSENA, NY

START TO FINISH: 30 MIN. • **MAKES:** 6 SERVINGS

- 3 eggs
- 1 cup grated Parmesan cheese
- ½ cup canola oil
- 1 tablespoon minced fresh parsley
- 1 garlic clove, minced
- ¼ teaspoon salt
- ⅛ teaspoon pepper
- 3 cups sliced zucchini
- 1 cup biscuit/baking mix
- 1 small onion, chopped

Preheat oven to 350°. In a large bowl, whisk the first seven ingredients. Stir in the zucchini, baking mix and onion. Pour into a greased 9-in. deep-dish pie plate. Bake 25-35 minutes or until lightly browned.

FAST FIX ▶

SUPER ITALIAN CHOPPED SALAD

Antipasto ingredients are sliced and diced to make this substantial salad. I like to buy sliced meat from the deli and chop it all up so you can get a bit of everything in each bite.

—KIM MOLINA DUARTE, CA

START TO FINISH: 25 MIN. • **MAKES:** 10 SERVINGS

- 3 cups torn romaine
- 1 can (15 ounces) garbanzo beans or chickpeas, rinsed and drained
- 1 jar (6½ ounces) marinated artichoke hearts, drained and chopped
- 1 medium green pepper, chopped
- 2 medium tomatoes, chopped
- 1 can (2¼ ounces) sliced ripe olives, drained
- 5 slices deli ham, chopped
- 5 thin slices hard salami, chopped
- 5 slices pepperoni, chopped
- 3 slices provolone cheese, chopped
- 2 green onions, chopped
- ¼ cup olive oil
- 2 tablespoons red wine vinegar
- ¼ teaspoon salt
- ⅛ teaspoon pepper
- 2 tablespoons grated Parmesan cheese
   Pepperoncini, optional

In a large bowl, combine the first 11 ingredients. For dressing, in a small bowl, whisk the oil, vinegar, salt and pepper. Pour over salad; toss to coat. Sprinkle with cheese. If desired, top with pepperoncini.

TEXAS JALAPENO JELLY

A jar of this jelly is always warmly received. I like to add a Southwestern accent by trimming the lid with a bandanna.

—**LORI MCMULLEN** VICTORIA, TX

PREP: 20 MIN. • **PROCESS:** 10 MIN. • **MAKES:** 7 HALF-PINTS

- 2 jalapeno peppers, seeded and chopped
- 3 medium green peppers, cut into 1-inch pieces, divided
- 1½ cups white vinegar, divided
- 6½ cups sugar
- ½ to 1 teaspoon cayenne pepper
- 2 pouches (3 ounces each) liquid fruit pectin
  About 6 drops green food coloring, optional
  Cream cheese and crackers, optional

1. In a blender or food processor, place jalapenos, half of the green peppers and ½ cup vinegar; cover and process until pureed. Pour into a large Dutch oven. Repeat with remaining green peppers and another ½ cup vinegar. Add the sugar, cayenne and remaining vinegar to pan. Bring to a rolling boil over high heat, stirring constantly. Quickly stir in pectin. Return to a rolling boil; boil 1 minute, stirring constantly.
2. Remove from heat; skim off foam. If desired, add food coloring. Ladle hot mixture into seven hot half-pint jars, leaving ¼-in. headspace. Wipe rims. Center lids on jars; screw on bands until fingertip tight.
3. Place jars into canner with simmering water, ensuring that they are completely covered with water. Bring to a boil; process for 10 minutes. Remove jars and cool. If desired, serve over cream cheese with crackers.

NOTE *When cutting hot peppers, disposable gloves are recommended. Avoid touching your face. The processing time listed is for altitudes of 1,000 feet or less. Add 1 minute to the processing time for each 1,000 feet of additional altitude.*

BRAVO BROCCOLI

Here's a fast, delicious way to dress up crisp-tender broccoli. Just toss with a simple sweet-sour mixture that gets a slight kick from crushed red pepper flakes.

—*TASTE OF HOME* TEST KITCHEN

START TO FINISH: 20 MIN. • **MAKES:** 4 SERVINGS

- 1 bunch broccoli, cut into florets
- 1 tablespoon butter, melted
- 1 tablespoon rice vinegar
- 1½ teaspoons brown sugar
- ¼ teaspoon salt
- ¼ teaspoon crushed red pepper flakes
- ⅛ teaspoon garlic powder

1. Place broccoli in a steamer basket; place in a large saucepan over 1 in. of water. Bring to a boil; cover and steam 3-4 minutes or until tender. Transfer to a large bowl.
2. Combine the remaining ingredients; drizzle over broccoli and gently toss to coat.

❝ Something new for my broccoli! Everyone loved it, even the toddler! ❞

—**KRISTIEKS** TASTEOFHOME.COM

HOMEMADE PIZZA SAUCE

For years, I had trouble finding a pizza my family liked, so I started making my own. The evening I served it to company and they asked for my recipe, I thought, *I finally got it right!* Feel free to spice up the sauce to suit your own family's tastes.
—**CHERYL KRAVIK** SPANAWAY, WA

PREP: 10 MIN. • **COOK:** 70 MIN.
MAKES: ABOUT 4 CUPS

- 2 **cans (15 ounces each) tomato sauce**
- 1 **can (12 ounces) tomato paste**
- 1 **tablespoon Italian seasoning**
- 1 **tablespoon dried oregano**
- 1 **to 2 teaspoons fennel seed, crushed**
- 1 **teaspoon onion powder**
- 1 **teaspoon garlic powder**
- ½ **teaspoon salt**

1. Rinse four 1-cup plastic containers and lids with boiling water. Dry the containers and lids thoroughly.
2. In a large saucepan over medium heat, mix tomato sauce and paste. Add remaining ingredients; mix well. Bring to a boil, stirring constantly. Reduce heat; cover and simmer 1 hour, stirring occasionally. Cool.
3. Fill all the containers to within ½ in. of tops. Wipe off the top edges of containers. Freeze up to 12 months. Thaw frozen sauce in refrigerator before serving.
NOTE *Use the sauce with crust and toppings of your choice to make a pizza; 1⅓ cups of sauce will cover a crust in a 15x10x1-in. pan.*

" Absolutely loved this pizza sauce! So easy to make and it tastes amazing! Will never have pizza any other way now!! "
—GUENSLERM
TASTEOFHOME.COM

YELLOW SUMMER SQUASH RELISH

My friends can barely wait for the growing season to arrive so I can make this incredible relish. The color really dresses up a hot dog.
—**RUTH HAWKINS** JACKSON, MS

PREP: 1 HOUR + MARINATING
PROCESS: 15 MIN. • **MAKES:** 6 PINTS

- **10 cups shredded yellow summer squash (about 4 pounds)**
- **2 large onions, chopped**
- **1 large green pepper, chopped**
- **6 tablespoons canning salt**
- **4 cups sugar**
- **3 cups cider vinegar**
- **1 tablespoon each celery seed, ground mustard and ground turmeric**
- **½ teaspoon ground nutmeg**
- **½ teaspoon pepper**

1. In a large container, combine the squash, onions, green pepper and salt. Cover and refrigerate overnight. Drain; rinse and drain again.
2. In a Dutch oven, combine sugar, vinegar and seasonings; bring to a boil. Add squash mixture; return to a boil. Reduce heat; simmer 15 minutes. Remove from heat.
3. Carefully ladle hot mixture into six hot pint jars, leaving ½-in. headspace. Remove the air bubbles and adjust headspace, if necessary, by adding hot mixture. Wipe the rims. Center the lids on jars; screw on bands until fingertip tight.
4. Place the jars into canner with simmering water, ensuring that they are completely covered with water. Bring to a boil; process for 15 minutes. Remove jars and cool. Refrigerate remaining relish up to 1 week.
NOTE *The processing time listed is for altitudes of 1,000 feet or less. For altitudes up to 3,000 feet, add 5 minutes; 6,000 feet, add 10 minutes; 8,000 feet, add 15 minutes; 10,000 feet, add 20 minutes.*

SWEET POTATO & CHICKPEA SALAD

Take this colorful dish to the buffet at a family gathering, or enjoy it as a satisfying meal all by itself.
—**BRENDA GLEASON** HARTLAND, WI

PREP: 15 MIN. • **BAKE:** 20 MIN.
MAKES: 8 SERVINGS

- **2 medium sweet potatoes (about 1 pound), peeled and cubed**
- **1 tablespoon olive oil**
- **½ teaspoon salt**
- **¼ teaspoon pepper**
- **1 can (15 ounces) garbanzo beans or chickpeas, rinsed and drained**

DRESSING
- **2 tablespoons seasoned rice vinegar**
- **4 teaspoons olive oil**
- **1 tablespoon minced fresh gingerroot**
- **1 garlic clove, minced**
- **¼ teaspoon salt**
- **¼ teaspoon pepper**

SALAD
- **4 cups spring mix salad greens**
- **¼ cup crumbled feta cheese**

1. Preheat oven to 425°. In a large bowl, combine sweet potatoes, oil, salt and pepper; toss to coat. Transfer to a 15x10x1-in. baking pan coated with cooking spray. Roast 20-25 minutes or until tender, stirring once.
2. In a large bowl, combine garbanzo beans and sweet potatoes. In a small bowl, whisk the dressing ingredients. Add to sweet potato mixture; toss to coat. Serve over salad greens; top with feta cheese.

TOP TIP

Summer Squash Facts

Summer squash have edible thin skins and soft seeds. Zucchini, pattypan and yellow are the most common varieties. Choose firm summer squash with brightly colored skin that's free from spots and bruises. Generally, the smaller the squash, the more tender it will be. Refrigerate summer squash in a plastic bag for up to 5 days.

BREADED PORK CHOPS, PAGE 95

BARBECUE CHICKEN PIZZA, 99

PLUM-GLAZED COUNTRY RIBS, 90

UNSTUFFED CABBAGE, 113

Hearty Main Dishes

The centerpiece of any meal is the entree, but it can also be the hardest dish to choose. From easy weeknight dinners to impressive special-occasion suppers, the dishes that follow will have your mind bubbling with exciting options, such as Barbecue Chicken Pizza, Thai Red Curry Chicken, Cordon Bleu Pork Chops or Molasses-Glazed Baby Back Ribs.

BLUE-CHEESE FLAT IRON STEAK

If you haven't already enjoyed the rich, creamy pairing of blue cheese with your favorite steak, stop reading and get cooking! I take it a step further by folding in a little butter to make the dish even more indulgent!

—**AMANDA MARTIN** MONSON, MA

PREP: 15 MIN. + MARINATING • **GRILL:** 10 MIN. • **MAKES:** 4 SERVINGS

- ¼ cup olive oil
- 2 tablespoons red wine vinegar
- 2 garlic cloves, minced
- 1 teaspoon dried oregano
- 1 teaspoon dried rosemary, crushed
- 1 teaspoon pepper
- ¼ teaspoon salt
- 1¼ pounds beef flat iron steak or top sirloin steak (1 inch thick)

BLUE CHEESE BUTTER
- ¼ cup crumbled blue cheese
- 3 tablespoons butter, softened
- 1 tablespoon minced fresh chives
- ⅛ teaspoon pepper

1. In a large resealable plastic bag, combine the first seven ingredients. Add beef; seal bag and turn to coat. Refrigerate 30 minutes.
2. In a small bowl, mix blue cheese, butter, chives and pepper; set aside. Drain beef, discarding marinade.
3. Grill the steaks, covered, over medium heat or broil 4 in. from heat 5-7 minutes on each side or until meat reaches desired doneness (for medium-rare, a thermometer should read 145°; medium, 160°; well-done, 170°). Serve with blue cheese butter.

FAST FIX

BACON & TOMATO SPAGHETTI

Here's a summer-perfect pasta that features baby spinach, cherry tomatoes and crisp bacon. It's all tossed with a tangy balsamic vinaigrette.

—*TASTE OF HOME* TEST KITCHEN

START TO FINISH: 25 MIN. • **MAKES:** 4 SERVINGS

- 8 ounces uncooked spaghetti
- ½ pound thick-sliced bacon strips, chopped
- 2 cups cherry tomatoes, halved
- 3 cups fresh baby spinach
- ¼ cup balsamic vinaigrette
- ½ teaspoon salt
- ¼ teaspoon pepper
  Grated Parmesan cheese

1. Cook spaghetti according to package directions.
2. Meanwhile, in a large skillet, cook bacon over medium heat until crisp. Remove to paper towels with a slotted spoon; drain, reserving 2 tablespoons drippings.
3. Saute the tomatoes in drippings until tender. Drain spaghetti; stir into skillet. Add spinach, bacon, vinaigrette, salt and pepper; heat through. Sprinkle with cheese.

GOLDEN CHICKEN CORDON BLEU

Elegance and good taste shine in this tender chicken classic that's an easy entree for a special dinner for two.

—*TASTE OF HOME* TEST KITCHEN

PREP: 20 MIN. • **BAKE:** 20 MIN. • **MAKES:** 2 SERVINGS

- 2 boneless skinless chicken breast halves (6 ounces each)
- 2 slices deli ham (¾ ounce each)
- 2 slices Swiss cheese (¾ ounce each)
- ½ cup all-purpose flour
- ¼ teaspoon salt
- ⅛ teaspoon paprika
- ⅛ teaspoon pepper
- 1 egg
- 2 tablespoons 2% milk
- ½ cup seasoned bread crumbs
- 1 tablespoon canola oil
- 1 tablespoon butter, melted

1. Preheat oven to 350°. Flatten chicken to ¼-in. thickness; top each with a slice of ham and a slice of cheese. Roll up and tuck in ends; secure with toothpicks.
2. In a shallow bowl, combine the flour, salt, paprika and pepper. In another bowl, whisk egg and milk. Place bread crumbs in a third bowl. Dip chicken in flour mixture, then egg mixture; roll in crumbs.
3. In a small skillet, brown the chicken in oil on all sides. Transfer chicken to an 8-in.-square baking dish coated with cooking spray.
4. Bake, uncovered, 20-25 minutes or until a thermometer reads 165°. Discard toothpicks; drizzle with butter.

FAST FIX ▶

PORK CHOPS WITH HONEY-BALSAMIC GLAZE

My husband is something of an expert when it comes to eating pork chops, and he says this recipe is restaurant quality.
—**NICOLE CLAYTON** PRESCOTT, AZ

START TO FINISH: 30 MIN. • **MAKES:** 4 SERVINGS

- 4 **bone-in pork loin chops (1 inch thick and 10 ounces each)**
- ½ **teaspoon crushed red pepper flakes**
- ½ **teaspoon salt**
- ½ **teaspoon pepper**
- 2 **tablespoons olive oil**

GLAZE
- ½ **cup balsamic vinegar**
- ½ **cup honey**
- 3 **green onions, chopped**
- 2 **garlic cloves, minced**
- 1 **teaspoon minced fresh rosemary or ¼ teaspoon dried rosemary, crushed**
- ⅛ **teaspoon salt**
- ⅛ **teaspoon pepper**
- ¼ **cup butter, cubed**

1. Sprinkle pork chops with pepper flakes, salt and pepper. In a large skillet, heat oil over medium heat. Add pork; cook 5-7 minutes on each side or until meat reaches desired doneness (for medium-rare, a thermometer should read 145°; medium, 160°). Remove and keep warm.

2. In the same skillet, whisk the vinegar, honey, green onions, garlic, rosemary, salt and pepper; bring to a boil.

Reduce heat; simmer, uncovered, 6-8 minutes or until slightly thickened, stirring occasionally. Remove from heat; whisk in butter until melted. Serve with pork chops.

FAST FIX ▶

SEASONED TILAPIA FILLETS

If you need a healthy, keep-it-simple solution to dinner tonight, you just found it. This dish relies on everyday spices to deliver big flavor.
—**DANA ALEXANDER** LEBANON, MO

START TO FINISH: 30 MIN. • **MAKES:** 2 SERVINGS

- 2 **tilapia fillets (6 ounces each)**
- 1 **tablespoon butter, melted**
- 1 **teaspoon steak seasoning**
- ½ **teaspoon dried parsley flakes**
- ¼ **teaspoon dried thyme**
- ¼ **teaspoon paprika**
- ⅛ **teaspoon onion powder**
- ⅛ **teaspoon salt**
- ⅛ **teaspoon pepper**
  Dash garlic powder

1. Preheat oven to 425°. Place fillets in a greased 11x7-in. baking dish. Drizzle with butter. In a small bowl, combine the remaining ingredients; sprinkle over fillets.

2. Cover and bake for 15 minutes. Uncover and bake for 5-8 minutes longer or until fish flakes easily with a fork.

NOTE *This recipe was tested with McCormick's Montreal Steak Seasoning. Look for it in the spice aisle.*

MEATBALL STEW

Many years ago, the *Farm Journal* published a recipe that became the jumping-off point for my version. It's as colorful as it is delicious. I often serve it over wide egg noodles or atop steamed rice—but it's also good just as it is.

—**SAVILLA ZOOK** SEABROOK, MD

PREP: 15 MIN. • **COOK:** 45 MIN.
MAKES: 8-10 SERVINGS

- 1 egg, lightly beaten
- 1 cup soft bread crumbs
- ¼ cup finely chopped onion
- 1 teaspoon salt
- ½ teaspoon dried marjoram
- ¼ teaspoon dried thyme
- 1½ pounds lean ground beef (90% lean)
- 2 tablespoons canola oil
- 2 cans (10¾ ounces each) condensed tomato soup, undiluted
- 2 cans (10½ ounces each) condensed beef broth, undiluted
- 4 medium potatoes, peeled and diced
- 4 medium carrots, diced
- 1 jar (16 ounces) whole onions, drained
- ¼ cup minced fresh parsley

1. In a large bowl, combine the egg, bread crumbs, chopped onion, salt, marjoram and thyme. Crumble beef over the top and mix well. Shape into 24 meatballs. Heat oil in a Dutch oven. Brown meatballs in batches; drain.
2. Add the soup, broth, potatoes, carrots and whole onions. Bring to a boil; reduce heat and simmer for 30 minutes or until meat is no longer pink. Garnish with parsley.

BAKED CHICKEN CHIMICHANGAS

I developed this quick and easy recipe through trial and error. I used to garnish the chimis with sour cream, but I eliminated it to lighten the recipe. My friends all love when I cook these chimichangas, which are much more healthful than deep-fried versions.

—RICKEY MADDEN CLINTON, SC

PREP: 20 MIN. • **BAKE:** 20 MIN.
MAKES: 6 SERVINGS

- 1½ cups cubed cooked chicken breast
- 1½ cups picante sauce, divided
- ½ cup shredded reduced-fat cheddar cheese
- ⅔ cup chopped green onions, divided
- 1 teaspoon ground cumin
- 1 teaspoon dried oregano
- 6 flour tortillas (8 inches), warmed
- 1 tablespoon butter, melted

1. Preheat oven to 375°. In a small bowl, combine chicken, ¾ cup picante sauce, cheese, ¼ cup onions, cumin and oregano. Spoon ½ cup mixture down the center of each tortilla. Fold sides and ends over filling and roll up. Place seam side down in a 15x10x1-in. baking pan coated with cooking spray. Brush with butter.
2. Bake, uncovered, 20-25 minutes or until heated through. Top with remaining picante sauce and onion

❝Very easy and they do crisp up as if they are fried. I know the recipe is meant to be light, but I did go heavier with the cheese in the recipe.❞

—DANERLEA
TASTEOFHOME.COM

BACON & CHEESE MEAT LOAF

We created this recipe to persuade my son to try meat loaf. After I added blue cheese and bacon, he did try it—and he liked it.

—LILA ALLEN FALLON, NV

PREP: 30 MIN. • **BAKE:** 1¼ HOURS
MAKES: 1 LOAF (8 SERVINGS)

- 1 teaspoon canola oil
- ½ cup shredded carrot
- ½ cup finely chopped onion
- 1 cup soft bread crumbs
- ½ pound bacon strips, cooked and crumbled
- 2 eggs, lightly beaten
- 4 teaspoons Worcestershire sauce
- 2 teaspoons garlic powder
- 2 teaspoons pepper
- 1 teaspoon salt
- 2 pounds ground beef
TOPPING
- ¾ cup crumbled blue cheese
- 2 tablespoons minced fresh sage
- 2 tablespoons minced fresh chives

1. In a small skillet, heat oil over medium-high heat. Add carrot and onion; cook and stir until tender. Cool slightly.
2. In a large bowl, combine bread crumbs, crumbled bacon, eggs, Worcestershire sauce, seasonings and carrot mixture. Add beef; mix lightly but thoroughly.
3. Shape into an 8x4-in. loaf in an ungreased 13x9-in. baking dish. Bake, uncovered, at 350° for 1¼ to1½ hours or until a thermometer reads 160°.
4. In a small bowl, combine the topping ingredients; mix well. Pat onto meat loaf; let stand for 10 minutes before serving. Remove to a platter.

BAKED CREOLE TILAPIA

We think the champagne dressing in this recipe is yummy on almost anything, but it's excellent with this lovely fish. The tilapia is terrific in tacos, too!

—**BERNADETTE BENNETT** WACO, TX

PREP: 10 MIN. + MARINATING • **BAKE:** 20 MIN. • **MAKES:** 6 SERVINGS

- 1 cup champagne salad dressing
- 2 tablespoons lemon juice
- 1 tablespoon Creole seasoning
- 1 teaspoon dried parsley flakes
- 1 teaspoon dill weed
- 6 tilapia fillets (6 ounces each)

1. Combine the first five ingredients in a small bowl. Pour marinade into a large resealable plastic bag. Add tilapia; seal bag and turn to coat. Refrigerate 15 minutes.
2. Meanwhile, preheat oven to 375°.
3. Drain fish, discarding marinade. Place fillets in a greased 15x10x1-in. baking pan. Bake, uncovered, 20-25 minutes or until fish flakes easily with a fork.
NOTE *The following spices may be substituted for 1 teaspoon Creole seasoning: ¼ teaspoon each salt, garlic powder and paprika; and a pinch each of dried thyme, ground cumin and cayenne pepper.*

TOP TIP

Popular Tilapia

A mild, sweet flavor makes tilapia a much-in-demand fish for the dinner table. Its firm, lean texture makes it ideal for a variety of cooking methods: baking, broiling, grilling, pan frying, sauteing and steaming.

BARBECUE PORK AND PENNE SKILLET

I'm the proud mother of wonderful and active children. Simple, delicious and quick meals like this are perfect for us to enjoy together following our after-school activities, errands and sports.
—**JUDY ARMSTRONG** PRAIRIEVILLE, LA

START TO FINISH: 25 MIN. • **MAKES:** 8 SERVINGS

- 1 package (16 ounces) penne pasta
- 1 cup chopped sweet red pepper
- ¾ cup chopped onion
- 1 tablespoon butter
- 1 tablespoon olive oil
- 3 garlic cloves, minced
- 1 carton (16 ounces) refrigerated fully cooked barbecued shredded pork
- 1 can (14½ ounces) diced tomatoes with mild green chilies, undrained
- ½ cup beef broth
- 1 teaspoon ground cumin
- 1 teaspoon pepper
- ¼ teaspoon salt
- 1¼ cups shredded cheddar cheese
- ¼ cup chopped green onions

1. Cook pasta according to package directions.
2. Meanwhile, in a large skillet, saute red pepper and onion in butter and oil until tender. Add garlic; saute 1 minute longer. Stir in the pork, tomatoes, broth, cumin, pepper and salt; heat through.
3. Drain pasta. Add pasta and cheese to pork mixture; stir until blended. Sprinkle with green onions.

---

5 INGREDIENTS

PLUM-GLAZED COUNTRY RIBS

When preparing to make ribs one day, I remembered that a friend had given me homemade plum jelly. I mixed some into the sauce for a pleasant fruity accent.
—**ILA MAE ALDERMAN** GALAX, VA

PREP: 5 MIN. • **BAKE:** 1¼ HOURS • **MAKES:** 8 SERVINGS

- 4 to 4½ pounds bone-in country-style pork ribs
- 1 bottle (12 ounces) chili sauce
- 1 jar (12 to 13 ounces) plum preserves or preserves of your choice
- ¼ cup soy sauce
- ¼ teaspoon hot pepper sauce

1. Preheat oven to 350°. Place ribs in two ungreased 13x9-in. baking dishes. Bake, uncovered, 45 minutes; drain.
2. In a small saucepan, combine the remaining ingredients. Bring to a boil, stirring occasionally. Remove from heat. Set aside ¾ cup sauce for serving.
3. Brush ribs with some of the remaining sauce. Bake, uncovered, 30-45 minutes or until ribs are tender, turning and basting frequently with remaining sauce. Serve with reserved sauce.

" Very good recipe.
My family loved it. "
—PALOPINTOMOM
tasteofhome.com

FAST FIX ▶

SIMPLE SHRIMP PAD THAI

Stir in soy sauce and brown sugar, then add a sprinkle of cilantro and roasted peanuts, and no one will guess the secret ingredient in this dish is marinara sauce.

—**ERIN CHILCOAT** CENTRAL ISLIP, NY

START TO FINISH: 30 MIN. • **MAKES:** 4 SERVINGS

- 8 **ounces uncooked thick rice noodles**
- 1 **pound uncooked medium shrimp, peeled and deveined**
- 3 **garlic cloves, minced**
- 2 **tablespoons canola oil**
- 2 **eggs, beaten**
- 1 **cup marinara sauce**
- ¼ **cup reduced-sodium soy sauce**
- 2 **tablespoons brown sugar**
- ¼ **cup chopped dry roasted peanuts**
   Fresh cilantro leaves
- 1 **medium lime, cut into wedges**
   Sriracha Asian hot chili sauce or hot pepper sauce, optional

1. Cook noodles according to package directions.

2. Meanwhile, stir-fry shrimp and garlic in oil in a large nonstick skillet or wok until shrimp turn pink; remove and keep warm. Add eggs to skillet; cook and stir until set.

3. Add the marinara, soy sauce and brown sugar; heat through. Return shrimp to pan. Drain noodles; toss with shrimp mixture.

4. Sprinkle with peanuts and cilantro. Serve with lime and, if desired, Sriracha.

FAST FIX ▶

STEAK TORTILLAS

When I fix steak, I always grill one extra so I have leftovers to make these delicious filled tortillas. The steak strips are seasoned with salsa, chili powder and cumin, then tucked inside soft flour tortillas with tasty toppings.

—**KRIS WELLS** HEREFORD, AZ

START TO FINISH: 15 MIN. • **MAKES:** 6 SERVINGS

- 2 **cups thinly sliced cooked beef ribeye or sirloin steak (about ¾ pound)**
- 1 **small onion, chopped**
- ¼ **cup salsa**
- ½ **teaspoon ground cumin**
- ½ **teaspoon chili powder**
- ¼ **teaspoon garlic powder**
- 1½ **teaspoons all-purpose flour**
- ½ **cup cold water**
- 6 **flour tortillas (8 inches), warmed**
   Shredded cheese, chopped lettuce and tomatoes and additional salsa, optional

1. In a large nonstick skillet, saute the steak and onion for 1 minute. Stir in the salsa and seasonings.

2. In a small bowl, combine flour and water until smooth; gradually add to the skillet. Bring to a boil; cook and stir for 1-2 minutes or until thickened. Place beef mixture on tortillas; top as desired with cheese, lettuce, tomatoes and additional salsa. Fold in sides.

PIZZA MARGHERITA

This classic pie starts with a chewy homemade crust topped with tomatoes, mozzarella, oregano and fresh basil. It's so delicious that you'll be glad the recipe makes two 13-inch pizzas!

—LORETTA LAWRENCE MYRTLE BEACH, SC

PREP: 30 MIN. + RISING • **BAKE:** 15 MIN.
MAKES: 2 PIZZAS (8 SLICES EACH)

3	teaspoons active dry yeast
1	cup warm water (110° to 115°)
2	tablespoons olive oil
1	teaspoon sugar
1	teaspoon salt
3	cups bread flour

TOPPINGS

2	cans (14½ ounces each) diced tomatoes, drained
20	fresh basil leaves, thinly sliced
2	tablespoons minced fresh oregano or 2 teaspoons dried oregano
8	cups (2 pounds) shredded part-skim mozzarella cheese
½	teaspoon crushed red pepper flakes
⅛	teaspoon salt
⅛	teaspoon pepper
2	tablespoons olive oil

1. In a small bowl, dissolve yeast in warm water. In a large bowl, combine the oil, sugar, salt and 1 cup flour; beat until smooth. Stir in enough remaining flour to form a soft dough.

2. Turn onto a floured surface; knead until smooth and elastic, about 6-8 minutes. Place in a greased bowl, turning once to grease the top. Cover with plastic wrap and let rise in a warm place until doubled, about 1 hour.

3. Punch dough down; divide in half. Roll each portion into a 13-in. circle. Transfer to two greased 14-in. pizza pans; build up edges slightly. Cover with a clean kitchen towel; let rest for 10 minutes. Preheat oven to 450°.

4. Spoon tomatoes over dough. Top with basil, oregano, cheese, pepper flakes, salt and pepper. Drizzle with oil. Bake 15-20 minutes or until crust is golden brown.

SPICY CHICKEN BREASTS WITH PEPPER PEACH RELISH

Here's a summery entree that's packed with the good-for-your-eyes vitamins found in both the fresh peaches and peppers.

—ROXANNE CHAN ALBANY, CA

PREP: 20 MIN. • **GRILL:** 15 MIN. • **MAKES:** 4 SERVINGS

½	teaspoon salt
¼	teaspoon each ground cinnamon, cloves and nutmeg
4	boneless skinless chicken breast halves (6 ounces each)

GLAZE

¼	cup peach preserves
2	tablespoons lemon juice
¼	teaspoon crushed red pepper flakes

RELISH

2	medium peaches, peeled and finely chopped
⅓	cup finely chopped sweet red pepper
⅓	cup finely chopped green pepper
1	green onion, finely chopped
2	tablespoons minced fresh mint

1. Combine the salt, cinnamon, cloves and nutmeg; rub over chicken. In a small bowl, combine the glaze ingredients; set aside. In another bowl, combine the peaches, peppers, onion, mint and 2 tablespoons glaze; set aside.

2. Moisten a paper towel with cooking oil; using long-handled tongs, rub on grill rack to coat lightly. Grill the chicken, covered, over medium heat or broil 4 in. from heat 6-8 minutes on each side or until a thermometer reads 170°, basting frequently with reserved glaze. Serve with the reserved relish.

OKTOBERFEST STRUDELS

My husband was born and raised in Wisconsin, and he loves bratwurst. I tweaked this strudel filling to include some of his favorite hometown ingredients. Serve the strudel with extra mustard for dipping.

—CLEO GONSKE REDDING, CA

PREP: 30 MIN. • **BAKE:** 25 MIN. + STANDING
MAKES: 2 STRUDELS (3 SERVINGS EACH)

- 1 tablespoon butter
- 5 fully cooked bratwurst links, chopped
- 1 medium onion, chopped
- 1 can (14 ounces) sauerkraut, rinsed and well drained
- ½ cup sour cream
- 3 tablespoons Dijon mustard
- 2½ teaspoons caraway seeds, divided
- 1 package (17.3 ounces) frozen puff pastry, thawed
- 1 cup (4 ounces) shredded Muenster cheese
- 1 cup (4 ounces) shredded sharp cheddar cheese

1. Preheat oven to 400°. In a large skillet, heat butter over medium heat. Add bratwurst and onion; cook and stir 8-10 minutes or until onion is tender. Stir in the sauerkraut and cool slightly.

2. In a small bowl, mix the sour cream, mustard and ½ teaspoon caraway seeds. Unfold one sheet of puff pastry. Spread with ⅓ cup sour cream mixture to within ½ in. of edges. Spoon 2½ cups sausage mixture down center of the pastry; sprinkle with ½ cup each Muenster and cheddar cheeses.

3. Lightly brush edges of pastry with water; bring edges together, pinching to seal. Transfer to an ungreased baking sheet, seam side down; pinch ends and fold under. Repeat with remaining ingredients.

4. Brush tops with water; sprinkle with remaining caraway seeds. Cut slits in pastry. Bake 25-30 minutes or until golden brown. Let stand 10 minutes before slicing.

FAST FIX ▶

GRILLED HALIBUT STEAKS

No one would guess you use pantry ingredients like brown sugar, soy sauce and lemon juice in this simple recipe. I always receive compliments.

—MARY ANN DELL PHOENIXVILLE, PA

START TO FINISH: 25 MIN. • **MAKES:** 4 SERVINGS

- 2 tablespoons brown sugar
- 2 tablespoons butter
- 1 tablespoon lemon juice
- 2 teaspoons soy sauce
- 1 teaspoon minced garlic
- ½ teaspoon pepper
- 4 halibut steaks (5 ounces each)

1. In a small saucepan, combine the first six ingredients. Cook and stir until butter is melted. Remove from heat; set aside.

2. Using long-handled tongs, moisten a paper towel with cooking oil and lightly coat the grill rack. Grill halibut, covered, over medium heat or broil 4 in. from heat 4-5 minutes on each side or until fish flakes easily with a fork, basting frequently with butter mixture.

❝ Had a nice glaze with the sauce that added a little sweetness. It was very good and I will make it again. ❞

—JANADELE TASTEOFHOME.COM

TACO BUBBLE PIZZA

Your entire family's going to be requesting this meal! Luckily for you, it's a cinch with tomato soup, taco seasoning and refrigerated biscuits. Set up a taco bar and let everyone add his or her favorite toppings.

—**DAWN SCHUTTER** TITONKA, IA

PREP: 20 MIN. • **BAKE:** 30 MIN. • **MAKES:** 8 SERVINGS

- 1½ pounds lean ground beef (90% lean)
- 1 can (10¾ ounces) condensed tomato soup, undiluted
- ¾ cup water
- 1 envelope taco seasoning
- 1 can (12 ounces) refrigerated buttermilk biscuits
- 2 cups (8 ounces) shredded cheddar cheese

TOPPINGS
- 2 cups torn leaf lettuce
- 2 medium tomatoes, seeded and chopped
- 1 cup salsa
- 1 cup (8 ounces) sour cream
- 1 can (2¼ ounces) sliced ripe olives, drained
  Green onions, optional

1. Preheat oven to 375°. Cook beef in a large skillet over medium heat until no longer pink; drain. Stir in soup, water and taco seasoning; bring to a boil. Reduce heat; simmer, uncovered, for 3 minutes.

2. Meanwhile, cut each biscuit into 8 pieces. Remove beef mixture from heat and gently stir in biscuits. Transfer to an ungreased 13x9-in. baking dish.

3. Bake, uncovered, 20-25 minutes or until biscuits are golden brown. Sprinkle with cheese; bake 8-10 minutes longer or until cheese is melted. Serve with toppings.

BREADED PORK CHOPS

Need a perky update for pork chops? These chops with ranch dressing and a light breading will bring a delightful zing to your dinner table.

—**ANN INGALLS** GLADSTONE, MO

START TO FINISH: 25 MIN. • **MAKES:** 6 SERVINGS

- ⅓ cup prepared ranch salad dressing
- 1 cup seasoned bread crumbs
- 2 tablespoons grated Parmesan cheese
- 6 bone-in pork loin chops (½ inch thick and 8 ounces each)

1. Preheat oven to 425°. Place salad dressing in a shallow bowl. In a separate shallow bowl, mix bread crumbs and cheese. Dip pork chops in dressing, then in crumb mixture, patting to help coating adhere.

2. Place on a rack in an ungreased 15x10x1-in. baking pan. Bake 15-20 minutes or until a thermometer reads 145°. Let stand 5 minutes before serving.

TOP TIP

Know Your Pork Chops

A pork loin chop has a T-bone-shaped bone, with meat on both sides of the bone. The rib chop has meat nestled between the rib and backbone. Center cut chops are boneless. A blade chop may have bones from the shoulder blade, rib and back.

TACO SALAD FOR A LARGE CROWD

When I took this salad to a party, people were scrambling to figure out who made it. Needless to say, I took home an empty bowl and each guest went home with a satisfied stomach.

—LISA HOMER AVON, NY

PREP: 25 MIN. • **COOK:** 10 MIN.
MAKES: 26 SERVINGS (1⅓ CUPS EACH)

- 1½ pounds ground beef
- 2 envelopes taco seasoning, divided
- 1 medium head iceberg lettuce
- 1 package (12½ ounces) nacho tortilla chips, coarsely crushed
- 2 pints grape tomatoes, halved
- 2 cans (16 ounces each) kidney beans, rinsed and drained
- 3 cans (2¼ ounces each) sliced ripe olives, drained
- 1½ cups (6 ounces) shredded cheddar cheese
- 1 large sweet onion, chopped
- 2 cans (4 ounces each) chopped green chilies
- 1½ cups Thousand Island salad dressing
- 1⅓ cups salsa
- ⅓ cup sugar

1. In a Dutch oven over medium heat, cook the beef with 1 envelope plus 2 tablespoons taco seasoning until no longer pink; drain.
2. In a very large serving bowl, combine the lettuce, chips, tomatoes, kidney beans, olives, cheese, onion, chilies and beef mixture.
3. In a small bowl, combine the salad dressing, salsa, sugar and remaining taco seasoning; pour over the salad and toss to coat.

---

⑤ INGREDIENTS FAST FIX

BAKED SALMON

I often make this very moist and flavorful salmon for company because I can have it ready in less than half an hour. I like to serve it with rice or with a green vegetable and a tossed salad.

—EMILY CHANEY BLUE HILL, ME

START TO FINISH: 30 MIN. • **MAKES:** 8 SERVINGS

- 1 salmon fillet (2 pounds)
- 2 tablespoons butter, softened
- ¼ cup white wine or chicken broth
- 2 tablespoons lemon juice
- ½ teaspoon pepper
- ½ teaspoon dried tarragon

1. Preheat oven to 425°. Pat salmon dry. Place in a greased 13x9-in. baking dish. Brush with butter. Combine remaining ingredients; pour over salmon.
2. Bake, uncovered, 20-25 minutes or until fish flakes easily with a fork.

TOP TIP

Removing Salmon Skin

Peeling the skin from fresh salmon can be difficult, but not with my method. I bring ½ inch of water to a slow boil in a frying pan. I put the salmon, skin side down, in the water for a minute. I carefully remove the salmon from the water, and the skin peels right off. I gently rinse the fish and proceed with the recipe. **—FREDA COHEN** LOS ANGELES, CA

GLAZED BBQ RIBS

After trying a fruit salad at a backyard barbecue, I wanted to make a rib sauce that tasted as sweet. Everyone loves the raspberry-red wine sauce combo.
—STEVE MARINO NUTLEY, NJ

PREP: 2 HOURS • **BROIL:** 10 MIN. • **MAKES:** 4 SERVINGS

    4 pounds pork baby back ribs
    ½ cup olive oil
    2 teaspoons salt
    2 teaspoons pepper
    1 bottle (18 ounces) barbecue sauce
    1 cup seedless raspberry preserves
    ¼ cup dry red wine
    ½ teaspoon onion powder
    ½ teaspoon cayenne pepper

1. Preheat oven to 325°. Place ribs in a shallow roasting pan, bone side down. In a small bowl, mix oil, salt and pepper; rub over ribs. Bake, covered, 1½ to 2 hours or until tender; drain.
2. In another bowl, mix remaining ingredients; reserve ¾ cup for serving with ribs. Brush some of the remaining sauce over ribs. Bake, uncovered, 25-30 minutes or until ribs are glazed, basting occasionally with additional sauce.
3. Preheat broiler. Transfer ribs to a broiler pan, bone side down. Broil 4-5 in. from heat 8-10 minutes or until browned. Serve with reserved sauce.

BACON-CHICKEN CRESCENT RING

This ring is really very easy to put together. It's simple and so good that people always ask for the recipe.
—MICHELE MCWHORTER JACKSONVILLE, NC

PREP: 25 MIN. • **BAKE:** 20 MIN. • **MAKES:** 8 SERVINGS

    2 tubes (8 ounces each) refrigerated crescent rolls
    1 can (10 ounces) chunk white chicken, drained and flaked
 1½ cups (6 ounces) shredded Swiss cheese
    ¾ cup mayonnaise
    ½ cup finely chopped sweet red pepper
    ¼ cup finely chopped onion
    6 bacon strips, cooked and crumbled
    2 tablespoons Dijon mustard
    1 tablespoon Italian salad dressing mix

1. Preheat oven to 375°. Grease a 14-in. pizza pan. Unroll crescent roll dough; separate into 16 triangles. Place wide end of one triangle 3 in. from edge of prepared pan with point overhanging edge of pan. Repeat with remaining triangles along outer edge of pan, overlapping the wide ends (dough will look like a sun when complete). Lightly press the wide ends together.
2. In a small bowl, combine the remaining ingredients. Spoon over wide ends of dough. Fold points of triangles over filling and tuck the points under the wide ends (filling will be visible). Bake 20-25 minutes or until golden brown.

“ This was made for a family party and vanished so fast, I had to make another one. ”
—TKARINAS TASTEOFHOME.COM

<FAST FIX>
BAKED SALMON CAKES

Baked in muffin pans and served with sauce on the side, these cute cakes make a fantastic light meal. You can also bake a double batch and freeze some for a quick, healthful supper later in the month.

—**NIKKI HADDAD** GERMANTOWN, MD

START TO FINISH: 30 MIN.
MAKES: 4 SERVINGS

- 1 **can (14¾ ounces) salmon, drained, bones and skin removed**
- 1½ **cups soft whole wheat bread crumbs**
- ½ **cup finely chopped sweet red pepper**
- ½ **cup egg substitute**
- 3 **green onions, thinly sliced**
- ¼ **cup finely chopped celery**
- ¼ **cup minced fresh cilantro**
- 3 **tablespoons fat-free mayonnaise**
- 1 **tablespoon lemon juice**
- 1 **garlic clove, minced**
- ⅛ **to ¼ teaspoon hot pepper sauce**

SAUCE
- 2 **tablespoons fat-free mayonnaise**
- ¼ **teaspoon capers, drained**
- ¼ **teaspoon dill weed**
  Dash lemon juice

1. Preheat oven to 425°. In a large bowl, combine the first 11 ingredients. Place ⅓ cup salmon mixture into each of eight muffin cups coated with cooking spray. Bake 10-15 minutes or until a thermometer reads 160°.
2. Meanwhile, combine the sauce ingredients. Serve with salmon.

SAVORY SPAGHETTI SAUCE

This fresh-tasting spaghetti sauce is a real crowd-pleaser. With a husband and 12 kids to feed every day, I rely on this flavorful recipe often. It tastes especially good in the summer made with fresh herbs.

—**ANNE HEINONEN** HOWELL, MI

PREP: 5 MIN. • **COOK:** 70 MIN.
MAKES: 4-6 SERVINGS (ABOUT 1 QUART)

- 1 **pound ground beef**
- 1 **large onion, chopped**
- 2 **cans (15 ounces each) tomato sauce**
- 1 **garlic clove, minced**
- 1 **bay leaf**
- 1 **tablespoon minced fresh basil or 1 teaspoon dried basil**
- 2 **teaspoons minced fresh oregano or ¾ teaspoon dried oregano**
- 2 **teaspoon sugar**
- ½ **to 1 teaspoon salt**
- ½ **teaspoon pepper**
  Hot cooked spaghetti
  Fresh oregano, optional

1. In a Dutch oven, cook ground beef and onion until meat is no longer pink and onion is tender; drain. Add the next eight ingredients; bring to a boil.
2. Reduce heat; cover and simmer for 1 hour, stirring occasionally. Remove and discard bay leaf. Serve sauce with spaghetti. If desired, garnish with fresh oregano.

POTLUCK SPARERIBS

When I want to bring an empty pan home from a potluck, I turn to this recipe. The ribs disappear in minutes!

—**SHERI KIRKMAN** LANCASTER, NY

PREP: 10 MIN. • **BAKE:** 1 HOUR 50 MIN.
MAKES: 12 SERVINGS

- 6 **pounds pork spareribs**
- 1½ **cups ketchup**
- ¾ **cup packed brown sugar**
- ½ **cup white vinegar**
- ½ **cup honey**
- ⅓ **cup soy sauce**
- 1½ **teaspoons ground ginger**
- 1 **teaspoon salt**
- ¾ **teaspoon ground mustard**
- ½ **teaspoon garlic powder**
- ¼ **teaspoon pepper**

1. Preheat oven to 350°. Cut ribs into serving-size pieces; place with the meaty side up on racks in two greased 13x9-in. baking pans. Cover tightly with foil. Bake 1¼ hours or until meat is tender.
2. Remove racks; drain and return ribs to pans. Combine the remaining ingredients; pour over ribs. Bake, uncovered, for 35 minutes or until the sauce coats the ribs, basting occasionally. Ribs can also be grilled over medium-hot heat for the last 35 minutes instead of being baked.

BARBECUE CHICKEN PIZZA

My husband and I love barbecue chicken pizza, but I decided to take it up a notch by adding other toppings that we love, including smoky bacon and creamy Gorgonzola. My mouth starts to water just thinking about it!

—**MEGAN CROW** LINCOLN, NE

PREP: 40 MIN. • **BAKE:** 20 MIN.
MAKES: 8 SERVINGS

- 2 **tablespoons olive oil**
- 1 **medium red onion, sliced**
- 1 **tube (13.8 ounces) refrigerated pizza crust**
- ¾ **cup barbecue sauce**
- 2 **cups shredded cooked chicken breast**
- 6 **bacon strips, cooked and crumbled**
- ¼ **cup crumbled Gorgonzola cheese**
- 2 **jalapeno peppers, seeded and minced**
- 1 **teaspoon paprika**
- 1 **teaspoon garlic powder**
- 2 **cups (8 ounces) shredded part-skim mozzarella cheese**

1. Preheat oven to 425°. In a large skillet, heat the oil over medium heat. Add onion; cook and stir 4-6 minutes or until softened. Reduce heat to medium-low; cook 20-25 minutes or until the onion is deep golden brown, stirring occasionally.

2. Unroll and press the dough onto bottom and ½ in. up sides of a greased 15x10x1-in. baking pan. Bake for 8 minutes.

3. Spread the barbecue sauce over dough; top with the chicken, cooked onion, bacon, Gorgonzola cheese and jalapenos. Sprinkle with paprika and garlic powder; top with mozzarella cheese. Bake 8-10 minutes longer or until the crust is golden and cheese is melted.

FREEZE OPTION *Bake pizza crust as directed; cool. Top with all the ingredients as directed; wrap securely and freeze unbaked pizza. To use, unwrap pizza; bake as directed, increasing time as necessary.*

NOTE *Wear disposable gloves when cutting hot peppers; the oils can burn skin. Avoid touching your face.*

"My husband could not quit eating these! I made them with panko but followed the rest of the recipe. I think he would have me make them every night! LOL!"
—DEBMANSUR
TASTEOFHOME.COM

FAST FIX ▶

FRIED CHICKEN STRIPS

I recently made this recipe of Mom's for my in-laws and they said it was the "best fried chicken ever." Slicing the chicken breasts into strips cuts down on cooking time and ensures that every piece is crunchy and evenly coated.

—GENNY MONCHAMP REDDING, CA

START TO FINISH: 20 MIN. • **MAKES:** 6 SERVINGS

2⅔ cups crushed saltines (about 80 crackers)
 1 teaspoon garlic salt
 ½ teaspoon dried basil
 ½ teaspoon paprika
 ⅛ teaspoon pepper
 1 egg
 1 cup milk
1½ pounds boneless skinless chicken breasts, cut into ½-inch strips
    Oil for frying

1. In a shallow bowl, combine the first five ingredients. In another shallow bowl, beat egg and milk. Dip chicken into egg mixture, then cracker mixture.
2. In an electric skillet or deep-fat fryer, heat oil to 375°. Fry chicken, a few strips at a time, 2-3 minutes on each side or until golden brown. Drain on paper towels.

HERBED LONDON BROIL

My stepfather passed this recipe along to me. It's good whether you grill or broil the meat, and I've never met a person who didn't enjoy the well-seasoned asparagus or tender beef as much as we do.

—SHARON PATNOE ELKINS, AR

PREP: 10 MIN. + MARINATING • **GRILL:** 15 MIN. • **MAKES:** 2 SERVINGS

¼ cup chopped onion
¼ cup lemon juice
 2 tablespoons canola oil
 1 garlic clove, minced
¼ teaspoon each celery seed, salt, dried thyme and oregano
¼ teaspoon dried rosemary, crushed
    Dash pepper
½ pound beef flank steak

1. In a large resealable bag, combine onion, lemon juice, oil, garlic and seasonings; add steak. Seal bag and turn to coat; refrigerate several hours or overnight, turning once.
2. Drain steak, discarding marinade. Grill steak, covered, over medium heat 6-7 minutes on each side or until meat reaches desired doneness (for medium-rare, a thermometer should read 145°; medium, 160°; well-done, 170°). Slice thinly across the grain.

FAST FIX ▶

CURRY CHICKEN

This is a big hit in our house. My young son and daughter gobble it up. With its irresistible blend of curry and sweet coconut milk, your family will, too.

—TRACY SIMIELE CHARDON, OH

START TO FINISH: 30 MIN. • **MAKES:** 4 SERVINGS

1½ cups uncooked instant rice
 1 pound boneless skinless chicken breasts, cut into 1-inch pieces
 2 teaspoons curry powder
¾ teaspoon salt
¼ teaspoon pepper
½ cup chopped onion
 1 tablespoon canola oil
 1 can (13.66 ounces) coconut milk
 2 tablespoons tomato paste
 3 cups fresh baby spinach
 1 cup chopped tomato

1. Cook rice according to package directions. Meanwhile, sprinkle the chicken with curry, salt and pepper. In a large skillet, saute chicken and onion in oil until chicken is no longer pink.
2. Stir in the coconut milk and tomato paste. Bring to a boil. Reduce heat; simmer, uncovered, 5 minutes or until thickened. Add spinach and tomato; cook 2-3 minutes longer or until spinach is wilted. Serve with rice.

CORDON BLEU PORK CHOPS

I found an interesting pork recipe in a church cookbook and tweaked it to my tastes. Now I prepare these cheesy chops year-round.

—MARCIA OBENHAUS PRINCETON, IL

PREP: 15 MIN. + MARINATING • **GRILL:** 10 MIN. • **MAKES:** 4 SERVINGS

- 4 **bone-in pork loin chops (1 inch thick)**
- ½ **cup ketchup**
- ½ **cup water**
- ¼ **cup white vinegar**
- 2 **tablespoons Worcestershire sauce**
- 2 **tablespoons brown sugar**
- 2 **tablespoons dried minced onion**
- 1 **tablespoon soy sauce**
- 1 **tablespoon lemon juice**
- 1 **teaspoon garlic powder**
- 1 **teaspoon ground mustard**
- 4 **thin slices part-skim mozzarella cheese**
- 4 **thin slices fully cooked ham**

1. Cut a pocket in each chop. Mix the next 10 ingredients. Reserve ½ cup for basting and refrigerate. Pour remaining marinade into a large resealable plastic bag or shallow glass container. Add pork and turn to coat. Seal bag or cover container; refrigerate overnight, turning meat occasionally.
2. Place a cheese slice on each slice of ham; roll up jelly-roll style. Drain pork and discard marinade in bag. Insert a ham-cheese roll in each pocket; secure with soaked toothpicks.
3. Grill, covered, over medium heat, 4-5 minutes on each side or until a thermometer reads 145°, basting occasionally with reserved marinade. Let meat stand 5 minutes before serving. Discard toothpicks.

SWEET AND SOUR MEAT LOAF

My husband, Bob, and I like basic hearty meat-and-potatoes meals. The sweet-and-sour flavor adds a deliciously different twist to this longtime standby. I hardly ever make plain meat loaf anymore—and you may not, either, once you've tasted this one.

—DEBBIE HANEKE STAFFORD, KS

PREP: 15 MIN. • **BAKE:** 1 HOUR • **MAKES:** 6 SERVINGS

- 1 **cup dry bread crumbs**
- 1 **teaspoon salt**
- ¼ **teaspoon pepper**
- 2 **eggs**
- 1½ **pounds ground beef**
- 1 **teaspoon dried minced onion**
- 1 **can (15 ounces) tomato sauce, divided**
- ½ **cup sugar**
- 2 **tablespoons brown sugar**
- 2 **tablespoons cider vinegar**
- 2 **teaspoons prepared mustard**

1. Preheat oven to 350°. In a large bowl, combine the bread crumbs, salt, pepper and eggs; crumble beef over top and mix well. Add onion and half of the tomato sauce. Press into a 9x5-in. loaf pan.
2. Bake 50 minutes. In a saucepan, combine sugars, vinegar, mustard and remaining tomato sauce; bring to a boil. Pour over meat loaf; bake 10 minutes longer.

MOLASSES-GLAZED BABY BACK RIBS

My husband sizzles up his luscious ribs recipe for our family of five at least once a month in the summer. The sweet-and-sour barbecue sauce is the perfect condiment for the tender meat. Serve it with other finger-licking foods such as corn on the cob.

—**KIM BRALEY** DUNEDIN, FL

PREP: 20 MIN. + MARINATING • **GRILL:** 70 MIN. • **MAKES:** 4 SERVINGS

- 4½ **pounds pork baby back ribs**
- 1 **bottle (2 liters) cola**
- ½ **teaspoon salt**
- ½ **teaspoon pepper**
- ¼ **teaspoon garlic salt**
- ¼ **teaspoon dried oregano**
- ¼ **teaspoon onion powder**
- ⅛ **teaspoon cayenne pepper**

BARBECUE SAUCE
- ¼ **cup ketchup**
- ¼ **cup honey**
- ¼ **cup molasses**
- 1 **tablespoon prepared mustard**
- ½ **teaspoon cayenne pepper**
- ½ **teaspoon salt**

1. Place the ribs in large resealable plastic bags; add the cola. Seal bags and turn to coat; refrigerate for 8 hours or overnight.

2. Drain and discard cola. Pat ribs dry with paper towels. Combine the seasonings; rub over ribs.

3. Prepare grill for indirect heat, using a drip pan. Place ribs over pan; grill, covered, over indirect medium heat 1 hour or until tender, turning occasionally.

4. In a small bowl, combine barbecue sauce ingredients. Brush sauce over ribs; grill, covered, over medium heat 10-20 minutes longer or until browned, turning and basting occasionally.

PAPRIKA CHICKEN THIGHS

My family is so happy when I serve this dish. It's one of their favorite meals, and the gravy is perfect over rice, grits or mashed potatoes.

—**JUDY ARMSTRONG** PRAIRIEVILLE, LA

PREP: 15 MIN. • **BAKE:** 50 MIN. • **MAKES:** 8 SERVINGS

- ¼ **cup butter**
- 3 **tablespoons all-purpose flour**
- 2 **tablespoons paprika**
- 1 **teaspoon poultry seasoning**
- 8 **bone-in chicken thighs, skin removed**
- ½ **teaspoon salt**
- ½ **teaspoon pepper**
- 1 **can (10¾ ounces) condensed cream of mushroom soup, undiluted**
- 1 **cup 2% milk**
- 8 **ounces sliced fresh mushrooms**
- 2 **tablespoons minced fresh parsley**
  Hot cooked rice, optional

1. Preheat oven to 350°. In a small saucepan, melt butter over medium heat. Remove from the heat; stir in the flour, paprika and poultry seasoning. Sprinkle chicken with salt and pepper; place in an ungreased 13x9-in. baking dish. Spread butter mixture over chicken.

2. In a bowl, whisk soup and milk; stir in mushrooms. Pour over chicken. Bake, covered, 35 minutes. Uncover; bake 15-20 minutes longer or until a thermometer inserted in chicken reads 170° to 175°. Sprinkle with parsley. If desired, serve with rice.

CREAMY CHICKEN ENCHILADAS

My daughter brought 10 pans of these yummy enchiladas to my wedding reception and it was the biggest hit of all the food. So many people wanted the recipe that we sent it out with our Christmas cards.

—PAT COFFEE KINGSTON, WA

PREP: 30 MIN. • **BAKE:** 35 MIN. • **MAKES:** 10 SERVINGS

- 1 package (8 ounces) cream cheese, softened
- 2 tablespoons water
- 2 teaspoons onion powder
- 2 teaspoons ground cumin
- ½ teaspoon salt
- ¼ teaspoon pepper
- 5 cups diced cooked chicken
- 20 flour tortillas (6 inches), room temperature
- 2 cans (10¾ ounces each) condensed cream of chicken soup, undiluted
- 2 cups (16 ounces) sour cream
- 1 cup 2% milk
- 2 cans (4 ounces each) chopped green chilies
- 2 cups (8 ounces) shredded cheddar cheese

1. Preheat oven to 350°. In a large bowl, beat cream cheese, water, onion powder, cumin, salt and pepper until smooth. Stir in chicken.

2. Place ¼ cup chicken mixture down the center of each tortilla. Roll up and place seam side down in two greased 13x9-in. baking dishes. In a large bowl, combine soup, sour cream, milk and chilies; pour over enchiladas.

3. Bake, uncovered, 30-40 minutes or until heated through. Sprinkle with cheese; bake 5 minutes longer or until cheese is melted.

BRUSCHETTA PIZZA

Loaded with Italian flavor and plenty of fresh tomatoes, this is bound to become a family favorite. It's even better with a homemade whole wheat crust.

—DEBRA KEIL OWASSO, OK

PREP: 25 MIN. • **BAKE:** 10 MIN. • **MAKES:** 8 SLICES

- ½ pound reduced-fat bulk pork sausage
- 1 prebaked 12-inch pizza crust
- 1 package (6 ounces) sliced turkey pepperoni
- 2 cups (8 ounces) shredded part-skim mozzarella cheese
- 1½ cups chopped plum tomatoes
- ½ cup fresh basil leaves, thinly sliced
- 1 tablespoon olive oil
- 2 garlic cloves, minced
- ½ teaspoon minced fresh thyme or ⅛ teaspoon dried thyme
- ½ teaspoon balsamic vinegar
- ¼ teaspoon salt
- ⅛ teaspoon pepper
  Additional fresh basil leaves, optional

1. Preheat oven to 450°. In a small skillet, cook sausage over medium heat until no longer pink; drain. Place crust on an ungreased baking sheet. Top with pepperoni, sausage and cheese. Bake for 10-12 minutes or until cheese is melted.

2. In a small bowl, combine the tomatoes, sliced basil, oil, garlic, thyme, vinegar, salt and pepper. Spoon over pizza. Garnish with additional basil if desired.

FAST FIX >

THAI RED CURRY CHICKEN

I re-created a delicious dish from a restaurant, and now I cook it almost weekly for my family. On a busy night, frozen stir-fry veggies really speed things up.

—**MARY SHENK** DEKALB, IL

START TO FINISH: 25 MIN. • **MAKES:** 4 SERVINGS

- 1 **can (13.66 ounces) coconut milk**
- ⅓ **cup chicken broth**
- 2 **tablespoons brown sugar**
- 2 **tablespoons fish sauce**
- 1 **tablespoon red curry paste**
- 2 **cups frozen stir-fry vegetable blend**
- 3 **cups cubed cooked chicken breast**
  Cooked jasmine rice
  Minced fresh cilantro, optional

1. Combine the first five ingredients in a large skillet. Bring to a boil; reduce heat and simmer 5 minutes.
2. Stir in vegetables; return to a boil. Reduce heat and simmer, uncovered, for 9-11 minutes or until vegetables are tender and sauce thickens slightly.
3. Add chicken; heat through. Serve with rice. If desired, sprinkle with cilantro.

FAST FIX >

PROSCIUTTO-PEPPER PORK CHOPS

Here's an entree that's easy, fast and, most important, delicious. It's easy to make for two, six, or even eight. Serve these chops with pasta salad for a light and satisfying meal.

—**DONNA PRISCO** RANDOLPH, NJ

START TO FINISH: 20 MIN. • **MAKES:** 4 SERVINGS

- 4 **boneless pork loin chops (4 ounces each)**
- ⅛ **teaspoon garlic powder**
- ⅛ **teaspoon pepper**
- 2 **teaspoons canola oil**
- 4 **thin slices prosciutto or deli ham**
- ½ **cup julienned roasted sweet red peppers**
- 2 **slices reduced-fat provolone cheese, cut in half**

1. Sprinkle pork chops with garlic powder and pepper. In a large nonstick skillet, cook chops in oil over medium heat for 4-5 minutes on each side or until a thermometer reads 145°.
2. Top each pork chop with prosciutto, red peppers and cheese. Cover and cook 1-2 minutes or until cheese is melted. Let stand 5 minutes before serving.

EGGS BENEDICT BURGERS

To feed my daughter's hungry cowboy friends after a rodeo, I created these with leftover burgers, hollandaise and bacon. This is one recipe I'll definitely make again and again!

—BONNIE GEAVARAS-BOOTZ
SCOTTSDALE, AZ

PREP: 25 MIN. • **GRILL:** 10 MIN.
MAKES: 4 SERVINGS

- 1½ **pounds ground beef**
- ½ **teaspoon salt**
- ¼ **teaspoon pepper**
- 4 **hamburger buns, split**
- 1 **envelope hollandaise sauce mix**
- 1½ **teaspoons stone-ground mustard**
- 4 **eggs**
- 4 **lettuce leaves**
- 4 **slices tomato**
- 6 **bacon strips, halved and cooked**

1. In a large bowl, combine the beef, salt and pepper, mixing lightly but thoroughly. Shape mixture into four ½-in.-thick patties.

2. Grill the burgers, covered, over medium heat 4-6 minutes on each side or until a thermometer reads 160°. Grill the buns, cut side down, until toasted.

3. Meanwhile, prepare sauce mix according to package directions using milk; stir in mustard. Keep warm.

4. Heat a large nonstick skillet coated with cooking spray over medium-high heat. Break eggs, one at a time, into pan; reduce heat to low. Cook until desired doneness; if desired, turn after whites are set.

5. Place lettuce, tomato and burgers on bottoms of buns; top with bacon, eggs and sauce. Replace tops.

> I made these for guests last night. Big hit. Only change I made was to add a little of the sauce to the ground beef before forming the patties.
> —REBELWITHOUTACLUE TASTEOFHOME.COM

CHICKEN SALAD-STUFFED PEPPERS

We love this recipe because it combines chicken salad with the fresh flavor of summer bell peppers.

—MARY MARLOWE LEVERETTE
COLUMBIA, SC

PREP: 30 MIN. • **BAKE:** 15 MIN.
MAKES: 4 SERVINGS

- 4 **green onions, finely chopped**
- ½ **cup mayonnaise**
- 2 **tablespoons lemon juice**
- ½ **teaspoon dried tarragon**
- ½ **teaspoon pepper**
- ¼ **teaspoon salt**
- 2 **cups finely chopped rotisserie chicken**
- ½ **cup shredded Monterey Jack cheese**
- 1 **celery rib, finely chopped**
- 4 **medium sweet red peppers**
  Crushed potato chips, optional

1. Preheat oven to 350°. In a small bowl, mix the first six ingredients. Add the chicken, cheese and celery; toss to coat.

2. Cut peppers lengthwise in half; remove seeds. In a Dutch oven, cook peppers in boiling water 3-4 minutes or until crisp-tender; drain.

3. Place in a greased 13x9-in. baking dish. Fill with chicken mixture. If desired, sprinkle with chips. Bake, uncovered, 15-20 minutes or until filling is heated through.

MOM'S SWEDISH MEATBALLS

Mom fixed these meatballs for all sorts of family dinners, potluck suppers and PTA meetings. The scent of browning meat is intoxicating. Add to that the sweet perfume of onions caramelizing, and people's mouths start watering.

—MARYBETH MANK MESQUITE, TX

PREP: 30 MIN. • **COOK:** 40 MIN.
MAKES: 6 SERVINGS

- ¾ **cup seasoned bread crumbs**
- 1 **medium onion, chopped**
- 2 **eggs, lightly beaten**
- ⅓ **cup minced fresh parsley**
- 1 **teaspoon coarsely ground pepper**
- ¾ **teaspoon salt**
- 2 **pounds ground beef**

GRAVY

- ½ **cup all-purpose flour**
- 2¾ **cups 2% milk**
- 2 **cans (10½ ounces each) condensed beef consomme, undiluted**
- 1 **tablespoon Worcestershire sauce**
- 1 **teaspoon coarsely ground pepper**
- ¾ **teaspoon salt**

NOODLES

- 1 **package (16 ounces) egg noodles**
- ¼ **cup butter, cubed**
- ¼ **cup minced fresh parsley**

1. In a large bowl, combine the first six ingredients. Crumble beef over mixture; mix lightly but thoroughly. Shape into 1½-in. meatballs (about 36). In a large skillet, brown meatballs in batches. Using a slotted spoon, remove to paper towels to drain, reserving drippings in pan.

2. For gravy, stir flour into drippings; cook and stir until light brown (do not burn). Gradually whisk in milk until smooth. Stir in the consomme, Worcestershire sauce, pepper and salt. Bring to a boil; cook and stir 2 minutes or until thickened.

3. Return meatballs to pan. Cook, uncovered, 15-20 minutes longer or until meatballs are cooked through, stirring occasionally.

4. Meanwhile, cook noodles according to package directions. Drain; toss with butter. Serve with meatball mixture; sprinkle with parsley.

TOP TIP

How to Make Uniform-Sized Meatballs

Lightly pat meat mixture into a 1-in.-thick rectangle. Cut the rectangle into the same number of squares as meatballs in the recipe. Gently roll each square into a ball.

FAST FIX ▶

CHIPOTLE-SPARKED MUSTARD SALMON

My scrumptious salmon entree packs huge flavors. Chipotle pepper, stone-ground mustard and horseradish come together in a fantastic blend that's anything but boring.

—**HELEN CONWELL** PORTLAND, OR

START TO FINISH: 25 MIN. • **MAKES:** 6 SERVINGS

- 6 **salmon fillets (4 ounces each)**
- ¼ **cup reduced-fat mayonnaise**
- ¼ **cup prepared horseradish**
- ¼ **cup stone-ground mustard**
- ¼ **teaspoon lemon-pepper seasoning**
- 1 **teaspoon minced chipotle pepper in adobo sauce**
- 1 **teaspoon snipped fresh dill**

1. Preheat oven to 350°. Place salmon in a foil-lined 15x10x1-in. baking pan. In a small bowl, mix mayonnaise, horseradish, mustard, lemon pepper and chipotle pepper; spread over fillets.

2. Bake 15-20 minutes or until fish just begins to flake easily with a fork. Sprinkle with dill.

(5) INGREDIENTS

BASIC CHICKEN BARBECUE

As far as I'm concerned, there's no better way to spend a summer night than sitting outdoors with the family and enjoying hot-off-the-grill chicken like this.

—**SHERRY SCHMIDT** FRANKLIN, VA

PREP: 10 MIN. + MARINATING • **GRILL:** 35 MIN. • **MAKES:** 4 SERVINGS

- 1 **cup white vinegar**
- 3 **tablespoons sugar**
- 2 **tablespoons salt**
- 1 **cup water**
- ½ **cup canola oil**
- 1 **tablespoon poultry seasoning**
- 1 **tablespoon pepper**
- 1 **broiler/fryer chicken (3 to 3½ pounds), cut up**

1. In a small bowl, whisk the vinegar, sugar and salt. Whisk in the water, oil, poultry seasoning and pepper. Reserve ½ cup for basting; cover and refrigerate. Pour remaining marinade into a large resealable plastic bag; add the chicken. Seal bag and turn to coat. Refrigerate 2-4 hours.

2. Drain chicken, discarding marinade in bag. Grill, covered, over medium heat 35-45 minutes or until juices run clear, turning and basting occasionally with the reserved marinade.

"Very light, flavorful. It was a change of how I usually prepare salmon. Family loved it. Served it with cheesy pasta & broccoli."

—**SINEY** TASTEOFHOME.COM

ROASTED KIELBASA & VEGETABLES

The number one reason that I like kielbasa with veggies? It's a healthy approach. Number two, it's a one-pan meal.

—**MARIETTA SLATER** JUSTIN, TX

PREP: 20 MIN. • **BAKE:** 40 MIN. • **MAKES:** 6 SERVINGS

- 3 **medium sweet potatoes, peeled and cut into 1-inch pieces**
- 1 **large sweet onion, cut into 1-inch pieces**
- 4 **medium carrots, cut into 1-inch pieces**
- 2 **tablespoons olive oil**
- 1 **pound smoked kielbasa or Polish sausage, halved and cut into 1-inch pieces**
- 1 **medium yellow summer squash, cut into 1-inch pieces**
- 1 **medium zucchini, cut into 1-inch pieces**
- ¼ **teaspoon salt**
- ¼ **teaspoon pepper**
  Dijon mustard, optional

1. Preheat oven to 400°. Divide sweet potatoes, onion and carrots between two greased 15x10x1-in. baking pans. Drizzle with oil; toss to coat. Roast 25 minutes, stirring occasionally.

2. Add kielbasa, squash and zucchini to pans; sprinkle with salt and pepper. Roast 15-20 minutes longer or until vegetables are tender. Transfer to a serving bowl; toss to combine. If desired, serve with mustard.

(5) INGREDIENTS FAST FIX
BAKED TILAPIA

My baked tilapia brings the health benefits of fish into my diet in a delicious way. Just add a side of vegetables for a nutritious, delicious lunch or dinnerl.

—**BRANDI CASTILLO** SANTA MARIA, CA

START TO FINISH: 20 MIN. • **MAKES:** 4 SERVINGS

- ¾ **cup soft bread crumbs**
- ⅓ **cup grated Parmesan cheese**
- 1 **teaspoon garlic salt**
- 1 **teaspoon dried oregano**
- 4 **tilapia fillets (5 ounces each)**

1. Preheat oven to 425°. In a shallow bowl, combine bread crumbs, cheese, garlic salt and oregano. Coat fillets in crumb mixture. Place on a baking sheet coated with cooking spray.

2. Bake 8-12 minutes or until fish flakes easily with a fork.

CHICKEN TACO PIE

This family fave comes to the rescue on busy nights when we've been rushing to soccer, swimming lessons or Scouts. I make it in the morning and just pop it into the oven when we get home.
—**KAREN LATIMER** WINNIPEG, MB

PREP: 20 MIN. • **BAKE:** 30 MIN. • **MAKES:** 6 SERVINGS

- 1 tube (8 ounces) refrigerated crescent rolls
- 1 pound ground chicken
- 1 envelope taco seasoning
- 1 can (4 ounces) chopped green chilies
- ½ cup water
- ½ cup salsa
- ½ cup shredded Mexican cheese blend
- 1 cup shredded lettuce
- 1 small sweet red pepper, chopped
- 1 small green pepper, chopped
- 1 medium tomato, seeded and chopped
- 1 green onion, thinly sliced
- 2 tablespoons pickled jalapeno slices
  Sour cream and additional salsa

1. Preheat oven to 350°. Unroll crescent dough and separate into triangles. Press onto bottom of a greased 9-in. pie plate to form a crust, sealing seams well. Bake 18-20 minutes or until golden brown.
2. Meanwhile, in a large skillet, cook chicken over medium heat 6-8 minutes or until no longer pink, breaking into crumbles; drain. Stir in taco seasoning, green chilies, water and salsa; bring to a boil.
3. Spoon into crust; sprinkle with cheese. Bake 8-10 minutes or until cheese is melted.
4. Top with lettuce, peppers, tomato, green onion and pickled jalapeno. Serve with sour cream and additional salsa.

ASPARAGUS, BACON & HERBED CHEESE PIZZA

My zesty pizza is especially nice with spring asparagus but lovely all year round when you add mozzarella and bacon.
—**DAHLIA ABRAMS** DETROIT, MI

START TO FINISH: 30 MIN. • **MAKES:** 6 SERVINGS

- 1 prebaked 12-inch pizza crust
- 6 teaspoons olive oil, divided
- 1 cup (4 ounces) shredded part-skim mozzarella cheese
- 2¼ cups cut fresh asparagus (1-inch pieces)
- 8 bacon strips, cooked and crumbled
- ½ cup garlic-herb spreadable cheese (about 3 ounces)
- ¼ teaspoon crushed red pepper flakes

1. Preheat oven to 450°. Place crust on an ungreased 12-in. pizza pan or baking sheet; brush top with 4 teaspoons oil. Top with mozzarella cheese, asparagus and bacon. Drop spreadable cheese by teaspoonfuls over pizza. Sprinkle with pepper flakes; drizzle with remaining oil.
2. Bake 12-15 minutes or until cheese is lightly browned.

FRESH CORN & TOMATO FETTUCCINE

Whole wheat pasta tossed with tomatoes, corn, red peppers, green onions and a little feta is a sure-fire winner.
—**ANGELA SPENGLER** MECHANICSBURG, PA

START TO FINISH: 30 MIN. • **MAKES:** 4 SERVINGS

- 8 ounces uncooked whole wheat fettuccine
- 2 medium ears sweet corn, husks removed
- 2 teaspoons plus 2 tablespoons olive oil, divided
- ½ cup chopped sweet red pepper
- 4 green onions, chopped
- 2 medium tomatoes, chopped
- ½ teaspoon salt
- ½ teaspoon pepper
- 1 cup crumbled feta cheese
- 2 tablespoons minced fresh parsley

1. In a Dutch oven, cook fettuccine according to package directions, adding corn during the last 8 minutes of cooking.
2. Meanwhile, in a small skillet, heat 2 teaspoons oil over medium-high heat. Add red pepper and green onions; cook and stir until tender.
3. Drain pasta and corn; transfer pasta to a large bowl. Cool corn slightly; cut corn from cob and add to pasta. Add tomatoes, salt, pepper, remaining oil and pepper mixture; toss to combine. Sprinkle with cheese and parsley.

“ Love it! So good. Added chicken to make it a one-dish meal. Second time, shrimp. This is a phenomenal dish! Even took the recipe to my farmer's market corn provider so she and he could enjoy it. ”

—CINDIHERRES TASTEOFHOME.COM

CHILI-RUBBED STEAK & BREAD SALAD

We love skirt steak. To make it a meal, I created a ranch-inspired bread salad with the best flavor combinations: creamy, tangy, sweet and fresh. While we use skirt steak, you may also use sirloin steak.
—DEVON DELANEY WESTPORT, CT

PREP: 35 MIN. + STANDING • **GRILL:** 15 MIN. • **MAKES:** 6 SERVINGS

- 2 **teaspoons chili powder**
- 2 **teaspoons brown sugar**
- ½ **teaspoon salt**
- ½ **teaspoon pepper**
- 1 **beef top sirloin steak (1 inch thick and 1¼ pounds)**
- 2 **cups cubed multigrain bread**
- 2 **tablespoons olive oil**
- 1 **cup ranch salad dressing**
- 2 **tablespoons finely grated horseradish**
- 1 **tablespoon prepared mustard**
- 3 **large tomatoes, cut into 1-inch pieces**
- 1 **medium cucumber, cut into 1-inch pieces**
- 1 **small red onion, halved and thinly sliced**

1. Mix chili powder, brown sugar, salt and pepper; rub over steak. Let stand 15 minutes.

2. Meanwhile, toss bread cubes with oil. In a large skillet, toast bread over medium heat 8-10 minutes or until crisp and lightly browned, stirring frequently. In a small bowl, whisk salad dressing, horseradish and mustard.

3. Grill steak, covered, over medium heat or broil 4 in. from heat 6-8 minutes on each side or until meat reaches desired doneness (for medium-rare, a thermometer should read 145°; medium, 160°; well-done, 170°). Let stand 5 minutes.

4. In a large bowl, combine tomatoes, cucumber, onion and toasted bread. Add ½ cup dressing mixture; toss to coat. Slice steak; serve with salad and remaining dressing.

TOP TIP
Grilling Meat

Before grilling meats, trim excess fat to avoid flare-ups. Bring meat to a cool room temperature before grilling, because cold foods may burn on the outside before the interior is cooked. Use tongs to turn meat instead of a meat fork to avoid piercing and losing juices. Brush on thick or sweet sauces during the last 10 to 15 minutes of cooking. Baste and turn every few minutes to prevent burning. Use a meat or instant-read thermometer to check the internal temperature of meat and poultry before the recommended cooking time is up.

FAMILY-FAVORITE FRIED CHICKEN

I was never impressed with the fried chicken recipes I'd tried, but then I started to experiment and came up with one that my whole family loves. Once you taste it, you'll know why.

—SAMANTHA PAZDERNIK BRECKENRIDGE, MN

PREP: 20 MIN. • **COOK:** 10 MIN./BATCH • **MAKES:** 4 SERVINGS

- 1 cup all-purpose flour
- ½ cup dry bread crumbs
- 2 tablespoons poultry seasoning
- 1 tablespoon paprika
- ½ teaspoon dried parsley flakes
- ¼ teaspoon salt
- ¼ teaspoon onion powder
- ¼ teaspoon garlic powder
- ¼ teaspoon pepper
- 3 eggs
- 1 broiler/fryer chicken (3 to 4 pounds), cut up
  Oil for deep-fat frying

1. In a shallow bowl, mix the first nine ingredients. In a separate shallow bowl, whisk eggs. Dip chicken pieces, one at a time, in eggs; coat with flour mixture.

2. Heat oil to 375° in an electric skillet or deep-fat fryer. Fry chicken, a few pieces at a time, 4-5 minutes on each side or until golden brown and juices run clear. Drain the chicken on paper towels.

UNSTUFFED CABBAGE

Here is one of my favorite ways to cook and enjoy cabbage. It has all the good flavor of regular cabbage rolls, but it's a lot less bother to make.

—MRS. BERNARD SNOW LEWISTON, MI

PREP: 15 MIN. • **COOK:** 1 HOUR 20 MIN. • **MAKES:** 6-8 SERVINGS

TOMATO SAUCE
- 1 large onion, chopped
- 1 medium head cabbage, coarsely chopped (about 8 cups)
- 1 can (28 ounces) diced tomatoes, undrained
- 1 can (8 ounces) tomato sauce
- 1 cup water
- ¼ cup lemon juice
- ⅓ cup raisins

MEATBALLS
- ½ cup uncooked long grain rice
- 1 teaspoon Worcestershire sauce
- ½ teaspoon salt
- ¼ teaspoon pepper
- 1 pound lean ground beef (90% lean)

1. In a large skillet, combine sauce ingredients. Bring to a boil; reduce heat and simmer.

2. Meanwhile, in a large bowl, combine rice, Worcestershire sauce, salt and pepper. Crumble beef over rice mixture; mix well. Shape into 36 balls, about 1¼ in. in diameter. Add to simmering sauce.

3. Cover and simmer about 45 minutes or until the cabbage is tender. Uncover and cook 15 minutes longer or until sauce is thickened.

PARMESAN CHICKEN WITH MUSHROOM WILD RICE

We call this dish "OMG Chicken"! Frozen veggies and rice make this hearty meal both quick and delicious, and we love the easy prep and cleanup.

—**WENDY GORTON** OAK HARBOR, OH

PREP: 15 MIN. • **BAKE:** 45 MIN. • **MAKES:** 6 SERVINGS

- ½ **pound sliced fresh mushrooms**
- 1 **tablespoon canola oil**
- ½ **cup grated Parmesan cheese**
- ½ **cup mayonnaise**
- ½ **teaspoon Italian seasoning**
- 2 **packages (10 ounces each) frozen brown and wild rice with broccoli and carrots**
- ¼ **teaspoon salt**
- ⅛ **teaspoon pepper**
- 6 **boneless skinless chicken thighs**

1. Preheat oven to 325°. Saute mushrooms in oil in a large skillet until tender.
2. Meanwhile, combine the cheese, mayonnaise and Italian seasoning in small bowl; set aside.
3. Place frozen rice mixture in a greased 13x9-in. baking dish; sprinkle with salt and pepper. Top with mushrooms and chicken. Spread cheese mixture over chicken.
4. Bake, uncovered, 45-50 minutes or until a thermometer reads 170°.

⑤ INGREDIENTS

TERIYAKI BEEF TENDERLOIN

A beautiful glaze coats this fantastic tenderloin that's as easy as it is delicious. The marinade and the oven do all the work.

—**LILY JULOW** LAWRENCEVILLE, GA

PREP: 10 MIN. + MARINATING • **BAKE:** 45 MIN. + STANDING **MAKES:** 8 SERVINGS

- 1 **cup sherry or reduced-sodium beef broth**
- ½ **cup reduced-sodium soy sauce**
- 1 **envelope onion soup mix**
- ¼ **cup packed brown sugar**
- 1 **beef tenderloin roast (2 pounds)**
- 2 **tablespoons water**

1. In a bowl, mix sherry, soy sauce, soup mix and brown sugar. Pour 1 cup into a large resealable plastic bag; add tenderloin. Seal bag and turn to coat; refrigerate for 5 hours or overnight. Cover and refrigerate remaining marinade.
2. Preheat oven to 425°. Drain beef, discarding marinade in bag. Place tenderloin on a rack in a shallow roasting pan. Bake, uncovered, 45-50 minutes or until meat reaches desired doneness (for medium-rare, a thermometer should read 145°; medium, 160°; well-done, 170°), basting often with ⅓ cup reserved marinade. Let stand 10-15 minutes.
3. Meanwhile, in a small saucepan, bring water and remaining marinade to a rolling boil; boil 1 minute or until sauce is slightly reduced. Slice beef; serve with sauce.

❝ Delicious! My husband & son say thumbs-up! We're going to have the leftovers on yeast rolls for dinner tomorrow. We just ate & they're already looking forward to dinner tomorrow night! ❞

—**CHINADOLL2008** TASTEOFHOME.COM

HERO PASTA SALAD

Hide this salad until serving time, or you might be surprised to find it gone! For variety, be creative: Add kalamata olives, peppers or yellow tomatoes.

—ANGELA LEINENBACH MECHANICSVILLE, VA

PREP: 35 MIN. • **MAKES:** 4 SERVINGS

- 3 tablespoons olive oil
- 3 tablespoons balsamic vinegar
- 2 small garlic cloves, minced
- ⅛ teaspoon salt
- ⅛ teaspoon pepper

SALAD

- 2 cups uncooked spiral pasta
- 1 small red onion, halved and thinly sliced
- ¾ cup sliced pepperoncini
- 4 ounces cubed provolone cheese
- 2 ounces thinly sliced deli ham, cut into strips (⅔ cup)
- 2 ounces thinly sliced hard salami, cut into strips (⅔ cup)
- 5 cups shredded lettuce
- 1 large tomato, coarsely chopped
- ¾ cup cherry tomatoes, halved

1. In a small bowl, whisk the first five ingredients until blended. Cook pasta according to package directions. Drain pasta; rinse with cold water.

2. In a large bowl, combine onion, pepperoncini, cheese, meats and pasta. Just before serving, add lettuce and tomatoes. Drizzle with dressing; toss to coat.

CHICKPEA POTPIES

My family enjoys potpies, and with this recipe, no one—not even my carnivores—misses the meat. Hungry teens and adults gobble them up!

—ANNETTE WOOFENDEN MIDDLEBORO, MA

PREP: 15 MIN. • **BAKE:** 25 MIN. • **MAKES:** 4 SERVINGS

- 1 small onion, chopped
- 6 tablespoons butter
- 2 garlic cloves, minced
- 6 tablespoons all-purpose flour
- ½ teaspoon salt
- ¼ teaspoon pepper
- 3 cups vegetable broth
- 2 cups frozen mixed vegetables, thawed
- 1 can (15 ounces) garbanzo beans or chickpeas, rinsed and drained
- 1¼ cups frozen cubed hash brown potatoes
- ¼ cup heavy whipping cream
- ¾ teaspoon Italian seasoning
- 1 sheet refrigerated pie pastry

1. Preheat oven to 400°. Saute onion in butter in a large saucepan until tender. Add garlic; cook 1 minute longer. Stir in flour, salt and pepper until blended. Gradually add broth; bring to a boil. Cook and stir 2 minutes or until thickened.

2. Stir in vegetables, garbanzo beans, potatoes, cream and Italian seasoning. Divide mixture among four ungreased 10-oz. ramekins.

3. Unroll pastry; divide into four portions. Roll out each portion to fit ramekins; place pastry over filling. Trim, seal and flute edges. Cut slits in pastry. Place ramekins on a baking sheet.

4. Bake 25-30 minutes or until pastry is golden brown.

CREAMY TUNA-NOODLE CASSEROLE, PAGE 127

SHORT RIB COBBLER, 119

BUFFALO CHICKEN LASAGNA, 126

TACO CORN BREAD CASSEROLE, 118

Casserole Entrees

Casseroles are fantastic! With a single dish you can serve a meal-in-one favorite—and still have time to tend to other things. After dinner, cleanup is simple with just one dish. Even better, leftovers are easy to reheat in the microwave.

TACO CORN BREAD CASSEROLE

A whole can of chilies adds fire to this corn bread casserole. For less heat, you can use just enough of the can for your taste.

—**LISA PAUL** TERRE HAUTE, IN

PREP: 15 MIN. • **BAKE:** 1 HOUR • **MAKES:** 8 SERVINGS

- 2 **pounds ground beef**
- 2 **envelopes taco seasoning**
- 2 **cans (14½ ounces each) diced tomatoes, drained**
- 1 **cup water**
- 1 **cup cooked rice**
- 1 **can (4 ounces) chopped green chilies**
- 2 **packages (8½ ounces each) corn bread/muffin mix**
- 1 **can (8¾ ounces) whole kernel corn, drained**
- 1 **cup (8 ounces) sour cream**
- 2 **cups corn chips**
- 2 **cups (8 ounces) shredded Mexican or cheddar cheese, divided**
- 1 **can (2¼ ounces) sliced ripe olives, drained**
  Shredded lettuce and chopped tomatoes, optional

1. Preheat oven to 400°. In a Dutch oven, cook beef over medium heat 8-10 minutes or until no longer pink, breaking into crumbles; drain. Stir in the taco seasoning. Add the tomatoes, water, rice and green chilies; heat through, stirring occasionally.

2. Meanwhile, prepare corn bread mix according to package directions; stir in corn. Pour half of the batter into a greased 13x9-in. baking dish. Layer with half of the meat mixture, all the sour cream, half of the corn chips and 1 cup cheese. Top with remaining batter, remaining meat mixture, olives and remaining corn chips.

3. Bake, uncovered, 55-60 minutes or until corn bread is cooked through. Sprinkle with remaining cheese; bake 3-5 minutes longer or until the cheese is melted. If desired, serve with lettuce and chopped tomatoes.

NIKKI'S PERFECT PASTITSIO

My mother used to work so hard in the kitchen to make this classic Greek dish, and the results were always well worth her effort. My recipe for pastitsio is easier, a bit lighter and every bit as great as Mom's.

—**NIKKI TSANGARIS** WESTFIELD, IN

PREP: 45 MIN. • **BAKE:** 50 MIN. • **MAKES:** 12 SERVINGS

- 2½ **cups uncooked penne pasta**
- 2 **tablespoons butter, melted**
- 1 **cup grated Parmesan cheese**
- 1½ **pounds ground sirloin**
- 1 **medium onion, chopped**
- 2 **garlic cloves, minced**
- 1 **can (15 ounces) tomato sauce**
- ½ **teaspoon salt**
- ½ **teaspoon ground cinnamon**
- 1 **cup shredded Parmesan cheese, divided**

BECHAMEL SAUCE
- ½ **cup butter, cubed**
- ⅔ **cup all-purpose flour**
- ½ **teaspoon salt**
- ¼ **teaspoon pepper**
- 4 **cups 2% milk**
- 2 **eggs**

1. Cook pasta according to package directions; drain. Toss with butter; add grated Parmesan cheese. Transfer to a greased 13x9-in. baking dish.

2. Preheat oven to 350°. In a skillet, cook and stir beef and onion over medium heat 8-10 minutes or until beef is no longer pink; drain. Add garlic; cook 2 minutes longer. Stir in tomato sauce, salt and cinnamon; heat through. Spoon over pasta. Sprinkle with ½ cup shredded Parmesan cheese.

3. In a large saucepan, melt butter. Stir in flour, salt and pepper until smooth; gradually add milk. Bring to a boil; cook and stir 1-2 minutes or until thickened.

4. In a small bowl, whisk a small amount of hot mixture into eggs; return all to pan, whisking constantly. Bring to a gentle boil; cook and stir 2 minutes. Pour over the beef mixture. Sprinkle with remaining cheese.

5. Bake, covered, 20 minutes. Uncover and bake casserole 30-40 minutes longer or until golden brown.

SHORT RIB COBBLER

This recipe was inspired by my family's love of two things—beef stew and biscuits. After years of making the two separately, I put the biscuits on top of the stew like a cobbler. This supper is as down-home as it gets.

—**JANINE TALLEY** ORLANDO, FL

PREP: 45 MIN. • **BAKE:** 3 HOURS • **MAKES:** 8 SERVINGS

½ cup plus 3 tablespoons all-purpose flour, divided
1¼ teaspoons salt, divided
½ teaspoon pepper
2 pounds well-trimmed boneless beef short ribs, cut into 1½-inch pieces
5 tablespoons olive oil, divided
1 large onion, chopped
1 medium carrot, chopped
1 celery rib, chopped
1 garlic clove, minced
2 tablespoons tomato paste
5 cups beef stock
1 cup dry red wine or additional beef stock
1 teaspoon poultry seasoning
1 bay leaf
1 package (14 ounces) frozen pearl onions, thawed
4 medium carrots, cut into 2-inch pieces

COBBLER TOPPING
2 cups biscuit/baking mix
⅔ cup 2% milk
Fresh thyme leaves

1. Preheat oven to 350°. In a shallow bowl, mix ½ cup flour, ¾ teaspoon salt and pepper. Dip short ribs in flour mixture to coat all sides; shake off excess.
2. In an ovenproof Dutch oven, heat 3 tablespoons oil over medium heat. Brown beef in batches. Remove from pan.
3. In same pan, heat remaining oil over medium heat. Add onion, chopped carrot and celery; cook and stir 2-3 minutes or until tender. Add garlic; cook 1 minute longer. Stir in the tomato paste and remaining flour until blended. Gradually stir in stock and wine until smooth. Return beef to pan; stir in poultry seasoning, bay leaf and remaining salt. Bring to a boil.
4. Bake, covered, 1¾ hours. Stir in pearl onions and carrot pieces. Bake, covered, 30-45 minutes longer or until beef and onions are tender. Skim fat and remove bay leaf.
5. In a small bowl, mix biscuit mix and milk just until a soft dough forms. Drop by scant ¼ cupfuls over beef mixture. Bake, uncovered, 40-45 minutes longer or until topping is golden brown. Sprinkle with thyme.

CHICKEN & CHEESE NOODLE BAKE

With its creamy spaghetti filling and melted cheese topping, this casserole cuts easily and is comforting.

—FANCHEON RESLER ALBION, IN

PREP: 20 MIN. • **BAKE:** 25 MIN.
MAKES: 2 CASSEROLES (6 SERVINGS EACH)

- 1 package (16 ounces) spaghetti, broken
- 2 medium onions, chopped
- 1 each medium green and sweet red pepper, chopped
- ½ cup butter, cubed
- 6 tablespoons all-purpose flour
- 2 cups 2% milk
- 4 cups cubed cooked chicken
- 1 can (10¾ ounces) condensed cream of chicken and mushroom soup, undiluted
- 1 can (10¾ ounces) condensed cream of mushroom soup, undiluted
- 1 cup (8 ounces) sour cream
- ½ teaspoon celery salt
- ½ teaspoon pepper
- 2 cups (8 ounces) shredded part-skim mozzarella cheese
- 1 cup (4 ounces) shredded cheddar cheese

1. Preheat oven to 350°. Cook pasta according to package directions.
2. Meanwhile, in a Dutch oven, saute onions and peppers in butter until tender. Stir in flour until blended; gradually add milk. Bring to a boil; cook and stir 2 minutes or until thickened. Stir in chicken, soups, sour cream, celery salt and pepper.
3. Drain spaghetti; add to the sauce mixture and toss to coat. Transfer to two greased 11x7-in. baking dishes. Sprinkle with cheeses. Cover and bake 20 minutes. Uncover and bake 5-10 minutes longer or until bubbly.
FREEZE OPTION *Cover and freeze unbaked casseroles up to 3 months. To use, partially thaw in the refrigerator overnight. Remove from refrigerator 30 minutes before baking. Preheat oven to 350°. Cover casserole with foil; bake as directed, increasing covered time to 40 minutes or until heated through and a thermometer inserted in center reads 165°. Uncover; bake 5-10 minutes longer or until bubbly.*

66 This recipe has a delicious flavor and is creamy and comforting. I used mini rotini pasta instead of spaghetti and I used 8x8 pans instead of 11x7 pans. Using the smaller pans resulted in 3 casseroles. My husband loved it! This one will be a regular. 99
—EPHELAN80 TASTEOFHOME.COM

PIZZA-STYLE MANICOTTI

Ham, pepperoni, string cheese and manicotti shells combine in a dish that's so easy to prepare that even small children can help.

—JUDY ARMSTRONG PRAIRIEVILLE, LA

PREP: 20 MIN. • **BAKE:** 25 MIN.
MAKES: 4 SERVINGS

- 8 uncooked manicotti shells
- 1 jar (24 ounces) spaghetti sauce
- 8 slices deli ham (about 6 ounces)
- 8 fresh basil leaves
- 8 pieces string cheese
- 24 slices pepperoni
- 1 can (2¼ ounces) sliced ripe olives, drained
- 1 cup shredded Parmesan cheese

1. Cook the manicotti according to package directions for al dente; drain. Preheat oven to 350°.
2. Pour 1 cup sauce into a 13x9-in. baking dish. On a short side of each ham slice, layer one basil leaf, one piece string cheese and three slices pepperoni; roll up. Insert in manicotti shells; arrange in a single layer in baking dish.
3. Pour remaining sauce over top. Sprinkle with olives and Parmesan cheese. Bake, uncovered, 25-30 minutes or until heated through.
FREEZE OPTION *Cover unbaked casserole and freeze up to 3 months. Thaw in the refrigerator overnight. Remove 30 minutes before baking. Preheat oven to 375°. Cover and bake 25-30 minutes or until pasta is tender. Let stand 10 minutes before serving.*

TORTELLINI SPINACH CASSEROLE

This casserole's fresh taste will delight even those who say they don't like spinach. In fact, people are often surprised at just how good it is! Whenever I bring it to a gathering, it doesn't last long.

—BARBARA KELLEN ANTIOCH, IL

PREP: 20 MIN. • **BAKE:** 20 MIN.
MAKES: 12 SERVINGS

- 1 package (19 ounces) frozen cheese tortellini
- 1 pound sliced fresh mushrooms
- 1 teaspoon garlic powder
- ¼ teaspoon onion powder
- ¼ teaspoon pepper
- ½ cup butter, divided
- 1 can (12 ounces) evaporated milk
- ½ pound brick cheese, cubed
- 3 packages (10 ounces each) frozen chopped spinach, thawed and squeezed dry
- 2 cups (8 ounces) shredded part-skim mozzarella cheese

1. Preheat oven to 350°. Cook the tortellini according to the package directions.
2. Meanwhile, in a large skillet, saute mushrooms, garlic powder, onion powder and pepper in ¼ cup butter until mushrooms are tender. Remove and keep warm.
3. In same skillet, combine milk and remaining butter. Bring to a gentle boil; stir in brick cheese until smooth. Drain tortellini; place in a large bowl. Stir in mushroom mixture and spinach. Add cheese sauce and toss to coat.
4. Transfer to a greased 13x9-in. baking dish; sprinkle with mozzarella cheese. Cover and bake 15 minutes. Uncover and bake 5-10 minutes longer or until casserole is heated through and cheese is melted.

SPAGHETTI PIE CASSEROLE

My family adores this casserole. It's old-time comfort food.
—**PATTI LAVELL** ISLAMORADA, FL

PREP: 30 MIN. • **BAKE:** 25 MIN. • **MAKES:** 8 SERVINGS

- 1 **package (8 ounces) spaghetti**
- 1 **pound ground beef**
- 1 **small onion, chopped**
- 2 **garlic cloves, minced**
- 1 **jar (14 ounces) spaghetti sauce**
- ½ **teaspoon salt**
- ¼ **teaspoon pepper**
- 3 **ounces reduced-fat cream cheese**
- 1 **cup (8 ounces) reduced-fat sour cream**
- 3 **green onions, chopped**
- 1½ **cups (6 ounces each) shredded cheddar-Monterey Jack cheese**

1. Cook spaghetti according to package directions; drain.
2. Preheat oven to 350°. In a large skillet, cook the beef, onion and garlic over medium heat 6-8 minutes or until beef is no longer pink, breaking up beef into crumbles; drain. Stir in the spaghetti sauce, salt and pepper; bring to a boil. Reduce heat; simmer, uncovered, for 20 minutes, stirring occasionally.
3. In a small bowl, mix cream cheese and sour cream until blended; stir in green onions. In a greased 11x7-in. baking dish, layer spaghetti, cream cheese mixture and meat mixture. Top with shredded cheese.
4. Bake, covered, 25 minutes. Uncover; bake 5-10 minutes longer or until cheese is bubbly.

SIMPLE CREAMY CHICKEN ENCHILADAS

Here is one of the first recipes that I created and cooked for my husband right after we got married. He was so impressed! We fix these creamy enchiladas for friends regularly.
—**MELISSA ROGERS** TUSCALOOSA, AL

PREP: 30 MIN. • **BAKE:** 30 MIN.
MAKES: 2 CASSEROLES (5 SERVINGS EACH)

- 1 **rotisserie chicken**
- 2 **cans (14½ ounces each) diced tomatoes with mild green chilies, undrained**
- 2 **cans (10¾ ounces each) condensed cream of chicken soup, undiluted**
- 1 **can (10¾ ounces) condensed cheddar cheese soup, undiluted**
- ¼ **cup 2% milk**
- 1 **tablespoon ground cumin**
- 1 **tablespoon chili powder**
- 2 **teaspoons garlic powder**
- 2 **teaspoons dried oregano**
- 1 **package (8 ounces) cream cheese, cubed**
- 20 **flour tortillas (8 inches), warmed**
- 4 **cups shredded Mexican cheese blend**

1. Preheat oven to 350°. Remove meat from bones; discard bones. Shred chicken with two forks and set aside. In a large bowl, combine the tomatoes, soups, milk and seasonings. Transfer 3½ cups to another bowl; add the chicken and cream cheese.
2. Spread ¼ cup soup mixture into each of two greased 13x9-in. baking dishes. Place ⅓ cup chicken mixture down the center of each tortilla. Roll up and place seam side down in baking dishes. Pour remaining soup mixture over tops; sprinkle with Mexican cheese.
3. Bake, uncovered, 30-35 minutes or until heated through and cheese is melted.
FREEZE OPTION *Cover and freeze unbaked casseroles up to 3 months. To use, partially thaw in refrigerator overnight. Remove from refrigerator 30 minutes before baking. Preheat oven to 350°. Cover casserole with foil; bake as directed, increasing covered time to 45 minutes or until heated through and a thermometer inserted in center reads 165°. Uncover; bake 5-10 minutes longer or until the cheese is melted.*

TOP TIP

Transporting Casseroles Without Spills

If you don't have a casserole carrier, here's an easy way to take a casserole to a potluck. Set the dish inside a clear plastic oven bag and close with a twist tie. The bag won't melt, but it will trap any spills—and the potluck organizers can see what's inside. Wrap the dish in a thick beach towel to keep the food warm if you're traveling a short distance. For long distances, place the cooled dish on ice.

"I've made this dish several times and it's SO yummy. The only thing I do differently is I use a packet of taco seasoning in place of all the spices. It's easier and we like it. Other than that, thumbs up!"

—TIMBERGURL1 TASTEOFHOME.COM

MEXI-MAC CASSEROLE

I typically have all the items in my pantry for this favorite all-in-one meal. Green chilies give it just a little bite, but it's easy to swap in a spicier can of tomatoes if you want to turn up the heat.

—JAN CONKLIN STEVENSVILLE, MT

PREP: 25 MIN. • **BAKE:** 30 MIN. • **MAKES:** 8 SERVINGS

- 1 **package (7¼ ounces) macaroni and cheese dinner mix**
- 1½ **pounds lean ground beef (90% lean)**
- 1 **medium onion, finely chopped**
- 2 **garlic cloves, minced**
- 1 **can (14½ ounces) diced tomatoes with mild green chilies**
- 1 **can (4 ounces) chopped green chilies**
- 1 **envelope reduced-sodium taco seasoning**
- 2½ **cups (10 ounces) shredded Mexican cheese blend, divided**
- 1 **can (16 ounces) kidney beans, rinsed and drained**
- 1 **can (15¼ ounces) whole kernel corn, drained**
- 1 **can (7¾ ounces) Mexican-style hot tomato sauce**
- ½ **cup crushed tortilla chips**

1. Prepare macaroni and cheese mix according to the package directions.

2. Meanwhile, preheat oven to 350°. Cook beef, onion and garlic in a Dutch oven over medium heat until meat is no longer pink; drain.

3. Add diced tomatoes, green chilies and taco seasoning. Stir in 2 cups cheese, beans, corn, tomato sauce and prepared macaroni and cheese dinner.

4. Transfer to a greased 13 x9-in. baking dish; sprinkle with chips and remaining cheese.

5. Bake, uncovered, 30-35 minutes or until bubbly.

FREEZE OPTION *Cool unbaked casserole; cover and freeze. To use, partially thaw in refrigerator overnight. Remove from the refrigerator 30 minutes before baking. Preheat oven to 350°. Bake casserole as directed, increasing time as necessary to heat through and for a thermometer inserted in center to read 165°.*

GOLDEN CHICKEN POTPIES

The golden crust and creamy sauce make this veggie-packed pie a sure hit. Frozen vegetables work extremely well in this mild and comforting family-pleasing dinner.

—TASTE OF HOME TEST KITCHEN

PREP: 20 MIN. • **BAKE:** 35 MIN.
MAKES: 2 POTPIES (6 SERVINGS EACH)

- 4 **cups cubed cooked chicken**
- 4 **cups frozen cubed hash brown potatoes, thawed**
- 1 **package (16 ounces) frozen mixed vegetables, thawed and drained**
- 1 **can (10¾ ounces) condensed cream of chicken soup, undiluted**
- 1 **can (10¾ ounces) condensed cream of onion soup, undiluted**
- 1 **cup milk**
- 1 **cup (8 ounces) sour cream**
- 2 **tablespoons all-purpose flour**
- ½ **teaspoon salt**
- ½ **teaspoon pepper**
- ¼ **teaspoon garlic powder**
- 1 **package (15 ounces) refrigerated pie pastry**

1. Preheat oven to 400°. In a large bowl, combine the first 11 ingredients. Divide between two 9-in. deep-dish pie plates. Roll out pastry to fit the top of each pie. Place over filling; trim, seal and flute edges. Cut slits in top or make decorative cutouts in pastry.

2. Bake 35-40 minutes or until golden brown.

FREEZE OPTION *Cover and freeze unbaked pies for up to 3 months. To use, remove from freezer 30 minutes before baking (do not thaw). Preheat oven to 425°. Place pie on a baking sheet; cover edges loosely with foil. Bake 30 minutes. Reduce heat to 350°; remove foil and bake 50-55 minutes longer or until golden brown, or until heated through and a thermometer inserted in center reads 165°.*

SUMMER VEGETABLE COBBLER

Here's a comforting vegetarian main dish that uses a lot of garden produce. Try different squashes like pattypan and crookneck for the zucchini—whatever you have available.

—**ELISABETH LARSEN** PLEASANT GROVE, UT

PREP: 40 MIN. • **BAKE:** 25 MIN. • **MAKES:** 4 SERVINGS

- 2 tablespoons butter
- 3 small zucchini, sliced
- 1 small sweet red pepper, finely chopped
- 1 small onion, finely chopped
- 2 garlic cloves, minced
- 2 tablespoons all-purpose flour
- 1 cup 2% milk
- ½ teaspoon salt
- ¼ teaspoon pepper

BISCUIT TOPPING
- 1 cup all-purpose flour
- 1 teaspoon baking powder
- ½ teaspoon salt
- 3 tablespoons cold butter
- ¼ cup shredded Parmesan cheese
- 3 tablespoons minced fresh basil
- ⅔ cup 2% milk

1. Preheat oven to 400°. In a large skillet, heat butter over medium-high heat. Add zucchini, red pepper and onion; cook and stir 10-12 minutes or until zucchini is crisp-tender. Add garlic; cook 1 minute longer.

2. In a small bowl, whisk flour, milk, salt and pepper until smooth; stir into vegetables. Bring to a boil, stirring constantly; cook and stir 2-3 minutes or until sauce is thickened. Spoon into a greased 8-in.-square baking dish.

3. For topping, in a small bowl, whisk flour, baking powder and salt. Cut in butter until mixture resembles coarse crumbs. Stir in cheese and basil. Add milk; stir just until moistened. Drop by rounded tablespoonfuls over filling. Bake 25-30 minutes or until filling is bubbly and the biscuits are golden brown.

ALFREDO-PANCETTA STUFFED SHELLS

I thought up this recipe while I was driving home from work. The local paper started a new reader recipe feature, so I sent this in, and I was published! Warm up some bread, pour the chardonnay, and enjoy.

—**TAMI VOLTZ** RUDOLPH, OH

PREP: 30 MIN. • **BAKE:** 35 MIN. • **MAKES:** 6 SERVINGS

- 12 uncooked jumbo pasta shells
- 4 ounces pancetta, finely chopped
- 1 teaspoon olive oil
- 1 package (6 ounces) fresh baby spinach
- 2 garlic cloves, minced
- ½ teaspoon crushed red pepper flakes
- 1 carton (15 ounces) part-skim ricotta cheese
- 2 tablespoons grated Parmesan cheese
- 1 egg yolk, beaten
- ¼ teaspoon pepper
- 1 jar (15 ounces) roasted garlic Alfredo sauce
- ½ cup shredded mozzarella cheese

1. Cook pasta shells according to package directions; drain and rinse with cold water.

2. Meanwhile, preheat oven to 375°. Cook pancetta in oil in a large skillet over medium heat until crisp. Remove to paper towels, reserving drippings. Saute the spinach, garlic and pepper flakes in drippings until spinach is wilted.

3. Transfer spinach mixture to a small bowl. Add ricotta, Parmesan cheese, egg yolk and pepper; mix well.

4. Spread ½ cup Alfredo sauce in a greased 11x7-in. baking dish. Spoon ricotta mixture into pasta shells; place in baking dish. Pour remaining sauce over shells.

5. Cover and bake 25 minutes. Sprinkle with the mozzarella cheese. Bake 10-15 minutes longer or until cheese is melted. Top with pancetta.

BUFFALO CHICKEN LASAGNA

This recipe was inspired by my daughter's favorite food—Buffalo wings! It tastes just like it came from a restaurant.

—MELISSA MILLWOOD LYMAN, SC

PREP: 1 HOUR 40 MIN.
BAKE: 40 MIN. + STANDING
MAKES: 12 SERVINGS

- 1 tablespoon canola oil
- 1½ pounds ground chicken
- 1 small onion, chopped
- 1 celery rib, finely chopped
- 1 large carrot, grated
- 2 garlic cloves, minced
- 1 can (14½ ounces) diced tomatoes, drained
- 1 bottle (12 ounces) Buffalo wing sauce
- ½ cup water
- 1½ teaspoons Italian seasoning
- ½ teaspoon salt
- ¼ teaspoon pepper
- 9 lasagna noodles
- 1 carton (15 ounces) ricotta cheese
- 1¾ cups (7 ounces) crumbled blue cheese, divided
- ½ cup minced Italian flat leaf parsley
- 1 egg, lightly beaten
- 3 cups (12 ounces) shredded part-skim mozzarella cheese
- 2 cups (8 ounces) shredded white cheddar cheese

1. In a Dutch oven, heat oil over medium heat. Add chicken, onion, celery and carrot; cook and stir until meat is no longer pink and vegetables are tender. Add garlic; cook 2 minutes longer. Stir in tomatoes, wing sauce, water and seasonings; bring to a boil. Reduce heat; cover and simmer 1 hour.

2. Meanwhile, cook the noodles according to package directions; drain. In a small bowl, mix the ricotta cheese, ¾ cup blue cheese, parsley and egg. Preheat oven to 350°.

3. Spread 1½ cups sauce into a greased 13x9-in. baking dish. Layer with three noodles, 1½ cups sauce, ⅔ cup ricotta mixture, 1 cup of the mozzarella cheese, ⅔ cup cheddar cheese and ⅓ cup blue cheese. Repeat layers twice.

4. Bake, covered, for 20 minutes. Uncover; bake 20-25 minutes longer or until bubbly and cheese is melted. Let stand 10 minutes before serving.

CREAMY TUNA-NOODLE CASSEROLE

Canned tuna is an excellent standby when you need supper on the table in a hurry. You'll love this casserole. It's packed with peas, peppers and onions. No tuna on hand? Try making it with chicken instead.

—**EDIE DESPAIN** LOGAN, UT

PREP: 20 MIN. • **BAKE:** 25 MIN. • **MAKES:** 6 SERVINGS

- 5 cups uncooked egg noodles
- 1 cup frozen peas
- 1 can (10¾ ounces) reduced-fat reduced-sodium condensed cream of mushroom soup, undiluted
- 1 cup (8 ounces) fat-free sour cream
- ⅔ cup grated Parmesan cheese
- ⅓ cup 2% milk
- ¼ teaspoon salt
- 2 cans (5 ounces each) light tuna in water, drained and flaked
- ¼ cup finely chopped onion
- ¼ cup finely chopped green pepper

TOPPING
- ½ cup soft bread crumbs
- 1 tablespoon butter, melted

1. Preheat oven to 350°. Cook noodles according to package directions for al dente, adding peas during the last minute of cooking; drain.

2. Meanwhile, in a large bowl, combine soup, sour cream, cheese, milk and salt; stir in tuna, onion and pepper. Add noodles and peas; toss to combine.

3. Transfer to an 11x7-in. baking dish coated with cooking spray. In a small bowl, toss bread crumbs with melted butter; sprinkle over top. Bake, uncovered, 25-30 minutes or until the casserole is bubbly.

CHEESE ENCHILADAS

You won't bring home leftovers when you take these easy enchiladas to a potluck. With a homemade sauce and cheesy filling, they always go fast. You can substitute any type of cheese you wish.

—**ASHLEY SCHACKOW** DEFIANCE, OH

PREP: 25 MIN. • **BAKE:** 25 MIN. • **MAKES:** 16 ENCHILADAS

- 2 cans (15 ounces each) tomato sauce
- 1⅓ cups water
- 2 tablespoons chili powder
- 2 garlic cloves, minced
- 1 teaspoon dried oregano
- ½ teaspoon ground cumin
- 16 flour tortillas (8 inches), warmed
- 4 cups (16 ounces) shredded Monterey Jack cheese
- 2½ cups (10 ounces) shredded cheddar cheese, divided
- 2 medium onions, finely chopped
- 1 cup (8 ounces) sour cream
- ¼ cup minced fresh parsley
- ½ teaspoon salt
- ½ teaspoon pepper
  Shredded lettuce, sliced ripe olives and additional sour cream, optional

1. Preheat oven to 350°. In a large saucepan, combine the first six ingredients. Bring to a boil. Reduce heat; simmer, uncovered, for 4-5 minutes or until thickened, stirring occasionally. Spoon 2 tablespoons sauce over each tortilla.

2. In a large bowl, combine the Monterey Jack, 2 cups of the cheddar cheese, onions, sour cream, parsley, salt and pepper. Place about ⅓ cup down the center of each tortilla. Roll up and place seam side down in two greased 13x9-in. baking dishes. Pour remaining sauce over top.

3. Bake, uncovered, 20 minutes. Sprinkle with remaining cheddar cheese. Bake 4-5 minutes longer or until the cheese is melted. If desired, garnish with the lettuce, olives and sour cream.

PIZZA PASTA CASSEROLE

Kids will line up for this zippy pizza-flavored dish. The recipe makes two casseroles, so you can serve one to your family right away and keep the other in the freezer for another night.

—**NANCY SCARLETT** GRAHAM, NC

PREP: 20 MIN. + FREEZING • **BAKE:** 25 MIN.
MAKES: 2 CASSEROLES (8 SERVINGS EACH)

- 2 **pounds ground beef**
- 1 **large onion, chopped**
- 3½ **cups spaghetti sauce**
- 1 **package (16 ounces) spiral pasta, cooked and drained**
- 4 **cups (16 ounces) shredded part-skim mozzarella cheese**
- 8 **ounces sliced pepperoni**

1. Preheat oven to 350°. In a large skillet, cook beef and onion over medium heat until meat is no longer pink; drain. Stir in spaghetti sauce and pasta.
2. Transfer to two greased 13x9-in. baking dishes. Sprinkle with cheese. Arrange pepperoni over the top.
3. Bake, uncovered, 25-30 minutes or until heated through.
FREEZE OPTION *Cool unbaked casseroles; cover and freeze for up to 3 months. To use, partially thaw in refrigerator overnight. Remove from refrigerator 30 minutes before baking. Preheat oven to 350°. Bake as directed, increasing time to 35-40 minutes or until heated through and a thermometer inserted in center reads 165°.*

THE BEST EGGPLANT PARMESAN

Truly delicious! I love eggplant and have many recipes, but this one's my favorite. The cheeses and seasonings make this dish unforgettable.

—**DOTTIE KILPATRICK** WILMINGTON, NC

PREP: 1¼ HOURS • **BAKE:** 35 MIN. + STANDING
MAKES: 2 CASSEROLES (8 SERVINGS EACH)

- 3 **garlic cloves, minced**
- ⅓ **cup olive oil**
- 2 **cans (28 ounces each) crushed tomatoes**
- 1 **cup pitted ripe olives, chopped**
- ¼ **cup thinly sliced fresh basil leaves or 1 tablespoon dried basil**
- 3 **tablespoons capers, drained**
- 1 **teaspoon crushed red pepper flakes**
- ¼ **teaspoon pepper**

EGGPLANT

- 1 **cup all-purpose flour**
- 4 **eggs, beaten**
- 3 **cups dry bread crumbs**
- 1 **tablespoon garlic powder**
- 1 **tablespoon minced fresh oregano or 1 teaspoon dried oregano**
- 4 **small eggplants (about 1 pound each), peeled and cut lengthwise into ½-inch slices**
- 1 **cup olive oil**

CHEESE

- 2 **eggs, beaten**
- 2 **cartons (15 ounces each) ricotta cheese**

- 1¼ **cups shredded Parmesan cheese, divided**
- ½ **cup thinly sliced fresh basil leaves or 2 tablespoons dried basil**
- ½ **teaspoon pepper**
- 8 **cups (32 ounces) shredded part-skim mozzarella cheese**

1. In a Dutch oven over medium heat, cook garlic in oil 1 minute. Stir in the tomatoes, olives, basil, capers, pepper flakes and pepper. Bring to a boil. Reduce heat; simmer, uncovered, 45-60 minutes or until thickened.
2. Meanwhile, for eggplant, place flour and eggs in separate shallow bowls. In another bowl, combine bread crumbs, garlic powder and oregano. Dip the eggplant in flour, eggs, then bread crumb mixture.
3. In a large skillet, cook eggplant in batches in oil 5 minutes on each side or until tender. Drain on paper towels. In a large bowl, mix eggs, ricotta, ½ cup Parmesan cheese, basil and pepper.
4. Preheat oven to 350°. In each of two greased 13x9-in. baking dishes, layer 1½ cups tomato sauce, four eggplant slices, 1 cup ricotta mixture and 2 cups mozzarella cheese. Repeat layers. Sprinkle each with the remaining Parmesan cheese. Bake, uncovered, 35-40 minutes or until bubbly. Let stand 10 minutes before cutting.

> "We loved this. Add sour cream and lettuce on top—it was a hit. Next time would use medium instead of mild can of green chilies and maybe medium instead of mild taco seasoning."
>
> —GSB4728 TASTEOFHOME.COM

COBRE VALLEY CASSEROLE

We live in southeastern Ar[...] of the state known as Cobre Valley[...] is Spanish for copper, which is mined here. Variations of this recipe have been enjoyed in our area for many years.

—**CAROLYN DEMING** MIAMI, AZ

PREP: 15 MIN. • **BAKE:** 30 MIN.
MAKES: 8 SERVINGS

- 1 **pound ground beef**
- 1 **medium onion, chopped**
- 1 **celery rib, chopped**
- 1 **envelope taco seasoning**
- ¼ **cup water**
- 2 **cans (16 ounces each) refried beans**
- 1 **can (4 ounces) chopped green chilies, optional**
- 1 **cup (4 ounces) shredded cheddar cheese**
- 2 **green onions, sliced**
- 1 **large tomato, peeled, seeded and chopped**
- ⅓ **cup sliced ripe olives**
- 1½ **cups crushed tortilla chips**

1. Preheat oven to 350°. In a large skillet, cook the beef, onion and celery over medium heat until meat is no longer pink; drain. Stir in the taco seasoning, water, beans and, if desired, green chilies.

2. Transfer to a greased 11x7-in. baking dish. Bake, uncovered, for 30 minutes or until heated through. Top with the cheese, green onions, tomato, olives and chips.

FREEZE OPTION *Cool unbaked casserole; cover and freeze. To use, partially thaw in refrigerator overnight. Remove from refrigerator 30 minutes before baking. Preheat oven to 350°. Bake casserole as directed, increasing time as necessary to heat through and for a thermometer inserted in center to read 165°. Top as directed.*

TOP TIP

Use the Last Crumb

If your kids leave the broken chips in tortilla or potato chip bags, save them for casserole toppings. They'll add a nice crunch.

SLOW-COOKED LEMON CHICKEN, PAGE 139

SLOW COOKER ENCHILADAS, 137

SLOW COOKER BEEF VEGETABLE STEW, 136

CAROLINA-STYLE PORK BARBECUE, 138

Slow Cooker Dinners

Wishing someone else would cook dinner for a change? Then these recipes are for you. Open a few cans, chop some veggies, maybe brown a little meat—then dump it all into a slow cooker. The prep will take 15 to 20 minutes, and you're done. Just place the lid on the cooker, set the temperature, and hours later come home to the welcome aroma of dinner!

CHICAGO-STYLE BEEF ROLLS

I have fond memories of eating these big, messy sandwiches at a neighbor's house when I was growing up. If there is any extra, the beef can be frozen to use for another meal.
—**TRISHA KRUSE** EAGLE, ID

PREP: 20 MIN. • **COOK:** 8 HOURS • **MAKES:** 16 SERVINGS

- 1 **boneless beef chuck roast (4 to 5 pounds)**
- 1 **tablespoon olive oil**
- 3 **cups beef broth**
- 1 **medium onion, chopped**
- 1 **package Italian salad dressing mix**
- 3 **garlic cloves, minced**
- 1 **tablespoon Italian seasoning**
- ½ **teaspoon crushed red pepper flakes**
- 16 **sourdough rolls, split**
  Sliced pepperoncini and pickled red pepper rings, optional

1. Brown roast in oil on all sides in a large skillet; drain. Transfer beef to a 5-qt. slow cooker. Combine the broth, onion, dressing mix, garlic, Italian seasoning and pepper flakes in a large bowl; pour over roast.

2. Cover and cook on low for 8-10 hours or until tender. Remove meat; cool slightly. Skim fat from cooking juices. Shred beef with two forks and return to slow cooker; heat through. Place ½ cup on each roll, using a slotted spoon. If desired, serve with pepperoncini and pepper rings.

---

⑤ INGREDIENTS

SLOW COOKER TURKEY BREAST

Here's a simple recipe to try when you're craving turkey. It's handy because it uses pantry ingredients.
—**MARIA JUCO** MILWAUKEE, WI

PREP: 10 MIN. • **COOK:** 5 HOURS • **MAKES:** 14 SERVINGS

- 1 **bone-in turkey breast (6 to 7 pounds), skin removed**
- 1 **tablespoon olive oil**
- 1 **teaspoon dried minced garlic**
- 1 **teaspoon seasoned salt**
- 1 **teaspoon paprika**
- 1 **teaspoon Italian seasoning**
- 1 **teaspoon pepper**
- ½ **cup water**

Brush turkey with oil. Combine the garlic, seasoned salt, paprika, Italian seasoning and pepper; rub over turkey. Transfer to a 6-qt. slow cooker; add water. Cover and cook on low for 5-6 hours or until tender.

TOP TIP

Keep the Lid On

Unless the recipe instructs you to stir in or add ingredients, refrain from lifting the lid while the slow cooker is cooking. Every time you lift the lid, steam is lost and you add 15 to 30 minutes to the required cooking time.

SPINACH AND SAUSAGE LASAGNA

Dig in to the rich layers of this hearty lasagna that features plenty of Italian sausage and gooey cheese. No-cook noodles, frozen spinach and jarred spaghetti sauce simplify the prep. But it tastes far from ordinary!

—KATHY MORROW HUBBARD, OH

PREP: 25 MIN. • **COOK:** 3 HOURS • **MAKES:** 8 SERVINGS

- 1 pound bulk Italian sausage
- 1 jar (24 ounces) garden-style spaghetti sauce
- ½ cup water
- 1 teaspoon Italian seasoning
- ½ teaspoon salt
- 1 carton (15 ounces) ricotta cheese
- 1 package (10 ounces) frozen chopped spinach, thawed and squeezed dry
- 2 cups (8 ounces) shredded part-skim mozzarella cheese, divided
- 9 no-cook lasagna noodles
  Grated Parmesan cheese

1. Cook sausage in a large skillet over medium heat until no longer pink; drain. Stir in the spaghetti sauce, water, Italian seasoning and salt. Combine ricotta, spinach and 1 cup mozzarella cheese in a small bowl.

2. Spread 1 cup sauce mixture in a greased oval 5-qt. slow cooker. Layer with three noodles (breaking noodles if necessary to fit), 1¼ cups sauce mixture and half of the cheese mixture. Repeat layers. Layer with remaining noodles and sauce mixture; sprinkle with remaining mozzarella cheese.

3. Cover and cook on low for 3-4 hours or until noodles are tender. Sprinkle servings with Parmesan cheese.

SPICY CHICKEN CHILI

This easy chili is loaded with chicken and beans. The spicy heat can be tamed a bit by cool sour cream.

—FRED LOCKWOOD PLANO, TX

PREP: 25 MIN. • **COOK:** 5 HOURS
MAKES: 10 SERVINGS (3½ QUARTS)

- 4 bone-in chicken breast halves (14 ounces each)
- 2 medium onions, chopped
- 2 medium green peppers, chopped
- 1 cup pickled jalapeno slices
- 1 can (4 ounces) chopped green chilies
- 2 jars (16 ounces each) salsa verde
- 2 cans (15½ ounces each) navy beans, rinsed and drained
- 1 cup (8 ounces) sour cream
- ½ cup minced fresh cilantro
  Optional toppings: shredded Colby-Monterey Jack cheese, sour cream and crushed tortilla chips

1. Place the chicken, onions, peppers, jalapenos and chilies in a 5- or 6-qt. slow cooker. Pour salsa over top. Cover and cook on low for 5-6 hours or until chicken is tender.

2. Remove chicken; cool slightly. Shred chicken with two forks, discarding skin and bones; return meat to slow cooker. Stir in the beans, sour cream and cilantro; heat through. Serve with toppings of your choice.

FREEZE OPTION *Before adding sour cream, cilantro and toppings, cool chili. Freeze chili in freezer containers. To use, partially thaw in refrigerator overnight. Heat through in a saucepan, stirring occasionally and adding a little water if necessary. Stir in the sour cream and cilantro. If desired, serve with toppings.*

NOTE *Wear disposable gloves when cutting hot peppers; the oils can burn skin. Avoid touching your face.*

STEPHANIE'S SLOW COOKER STEW

Start this warming one-pot meal before you head out for the day. By the time you get home, the well-seasoned meat will be tender and mouthwatering.

—STEPHANIE RABBITT-SCHAPP CINCINNATI, OH

PREP: 20 MIN. • **COOK:** 7½ HOURS
MAKES: 5 SERVINGS

- 1 **pound beef stew meat**
- 2 **medium potatoes, peeled and cubed**
- 1 **can (14½ ounces) beef broth**
- 1 **can (11½ ounces) V8 juice**
- 2 **celery ribs, chopped**
- 2 **medium carrots, chopped**
- 1 **medium sweet onion, chopped**
- 3 **bay leaves**
- ½ **teaspoon salt**
- ½ **teaspoon dried thyme**
- ½ **teaspoon chili powder**
- ¼ **teaspoon pepper**
- 2 **tablespoons cornstarch**
- 1 **tablespoon cold water**
- ½ **cup frozen corn**
- ½ **cup frozen peas**

1. In a 3-qt. slow cooker, combine the first 12 ingredients. Cover and cook on low for 7-8 hours or until meat is tender. Discard bay leaves.
2. In a small bowl, combine the cornstarch and water until smooth; stir into stew. Add the corn and peas. Cover and cook on high for 30 minutes or until thickened.

SOY-GINGER CHICKEN

This is the first recipe I ever tried making without a cookbook, and it came out so tender and delicious. Garlic, ginger and spices give the rich sauce plenty of authentic Asian flavor.

—KAEL HARVEY BROOKLYN, NY

PREP: 25 MIN. • **COOK:** 5 HOURS
MAKES: 4 SERVINGS

- 4 **bone-in chicken thighs (about 1½ pounds), skin removed**
- 4 **chicken drumsticks (about 1 pound), skin removed**
- 2 **medium carrots, sliced**
- 4 **green onions, thinly sliced**
- ⅓ **cup soy sauce**
- 2 **tablespoons brown sugar**
- 1 **piece fresh gingerroot (about 2 inches), peeled and thinly sliced**
- 5 **garlic cloves, minced**
- 1 **tablespoon balsamic vinegar**
- 1 **teaspoon ground coriander**
- ½ **teaspoon pepper**
- 1 **tablespoon cornstarch**
- 1 **tablespoon cold water**
  Hot cooked rice and minced fresh cilantro

1. Place chicken, carrots and green onions in a 3-qt. slow cooker. Combine the soy sauce, brown sugar, ginger, garlic, vinegar, coriander and pepper in a small bowl. Pour over top. Cover and cook on low for 5-6 hours or until chicken is tender.
2. Remove chicken to a serving platter; keep warm. Pour juices into a small saucepan. Bring to a boil. Combine cornstarch and water until smooth; gradually stir into pan. Bring to a boil; cook and stir for 1-2 minutes or until thickened. Serve with chicken and rice; sprinkle servings with cilantro.

> "Very, very good... smells wonderful in the house when it's cooking. The flavors all blend beautifully."
>
> **—SGALLIRN**
> TASTEOFHOME.COM

MEXICAN BEEF & BEAN STEW

I like that this stew is quick to toss together. The beans, veggies and spices taste amazing together, and it really warms me up on frosty days.
—**TACY FLEURY** CLINTON, SC

PREP: 20 MIN. • **COOK:** 8 HOURS
MAKES: 10 SERVINGS (2½ QUARTS)

- 1 **cup all-purpose flour**
- ¼ **teaspoon salt**
- ⅛ **teaspoon pepper**
- 1 **pound beef stew meat, cut into 1-inch cubes**
- 2 **tablespoons canola oil**
- 1 **can (16 ounces) kidney beans, rinsed and drained**
- 1 **can (15¼ ounces) whole kernel corn, drained**
- 2 **medium potatoes, cubed**
- 2 **small carrots, sliced**
- 2 **celery ribs, sliced**
- 1 **small onion, chopped**
- 2 **cans (15 ounces each) tomato sauce**
- 1 **cup water**
- 1 **envelope taco seasoning**
- ½ **teaspoon ground cumin**
  Tortilla chips and shredded cheddar cheese

1. Combine the flour, salt and pepper in a large resealable plastic bag. Add beef, a few pieces at a time, and shake to coat.
2. Brown meat in batches in oil in a large skillet; drain. Transfer to a 5-qt. slow cooker. Add the beans, corn, potatoes, carrots, celery and onion.
3. Whisk the tomato sauce, water, taco seasoning and cumin; pour over top. Cover and cook on low for 8-10 hours or until meat is tender. Serve with tortilla chips and cheese.

MACHACA BEEF DIP SANDWICHES

The winning combination of beef, cumin, chili powder and the spicy heat of chipotle peppers makes these sandwiches game-day food all the fans will love!
—**KAROL EZELL** NACOGDOCHES, TX

PREP: 20 MIN. • **COOK:** 8 HOURS
MAKES: 6 SERVINGS

- 1 **boneless beef chuck roast (2 to 3 pounds)**
- 1 **large sweet onion, thinly sliced**
- 1 **can (14½ ounces) reduced-sodium beef broth**
- ½ **cup water**
- 3 **chipotle peppers in adobo sauce, chopped**
- 1 **tablespoon adobo sauce**
- 1 **envelope au jus gravy mix**
- 1 **tablespoon Creole seasoning**
- 1 **tablespoon chili powder**
- 2 **teaspoons ground cumin**
- 6 **French rolls, split**
  Guacamole and salsa, optional

1. Place roast in a 3- to 4-qt. slow cooker; top with onion. Combine the broth, water, chipotle peppers, adobo sauce, gravy mix, Creole seasoning, chili powder and cumin; pour over meat. Cover and cook on low for 8-10 hours or until meat is tender.

2. Remove roast; cool slightly. Skim fat from cooking juices. Shred beef with two forks. Return to slow cooker; heat through. Using a slotted spoon, place meat on rolls. Serve with cooking juices and if desired, guacamole or salsa.
FREEZE OPTION *Freeze individual portions of cooled meat mixture and juices in freezer containers. To use, partially thaw in refrigerator overnight. Heat through in a saucepan, stirring occasionally and adding a little water if necessary. Serve on rolls with guacamole and salsa if desired.*
NOTE *Wear disposable gloves when cutting hot peppers; the oils can burn skin. Avoid touching your face. The following spices may be substituted for 1 tablespoon Creole seasoning: ¾ teaspoon each salt, garlic powder and paprika; and a pinch each of dried thyme, ground cumin and cayenne pepper.*

TOP TIP

Pick the Right Meat for Slow-Cooked Stew

We've seen recipes for 30-minute stews that use sirloin. These fast-dinner recipes don't cook long enough to make a tough cut of meat tender, so sirloin is a good choice. But when braising meat traditionally in a little liquid for hours, the best choice is a less-tender cut from the chuck or round, because a tender cut such as sirloin will become overcooked, tough and chewy during the long cooking time.

HAM WITH CRANBERRY-PINEAPPLE SAUCE

Flag this dish for the times you crave the mouthwatering combo of cranberry, pineapple and stone-ground mustard served with thick slices of smoky boneless ham.
—**CAROLE RESNICK** CLEVELAND, OH

PREP: 15 MIN. • **COOK:** 5 HOURS
MAKES: 20 SERVINGS (4½ CUPS SAUCE)

- 1 fully cooked boneless ham (5 to 6 pounds)
- 12 whole cloves
- 1 can (20 ounces) crushed pineapple, undrained
- 1 can (14 ounces) whole-berry cranberry sauce
- 2 garlic cloves, minced
- 2 tablespoons stone-ground mustard
- ½ teaspoon coarsely ground pepper
- 2 tablespoons cornstarch
- 2 tablespoons cold water

1. Score the ham, making ½-in.-deep diamond shapes; insert a clove in each diamond. Place ham in a 5-qt. slow cooker. In a large bowl, combine the pineapple, cranberry sauce, garlic, mustard and pepper; pour over ham.
2. Cover and cook on low for 5-6 hours or until a thermometer reads 140°. Remove meat to a cutting board and keep warm; remove and discard cloves.
3. Transfer sauce to a small saucepan. Bring to a boil. Combine cornstarch and water until smooth; gradually stir into pan. Bring to a boil; cook and stir 2 minutes or until thickened. Slice ham and serve with sauce.

SLOW COOKER BEEF VEGETABLE STEW

Come home to warm comfort food! The stew is based on my mom's wonderful recipe, though I tweaked it for the slow cooker. Add a sprinkle of Parmesan to each bowl for a nice finishing touch.
—**MARCELLA WEST** WASHBURN, IL

PREP: 20 MIN. • **COOK:** 6½ HOURS • **MAKES:** 8 SERVINGS (3 QUARTS)

- 1½ pounds boneless beef chuck roast, cut into 1-inch cubes
- 3 medium potatoes, peeled and cubed
- 3 cups hot water
- 1½ cups fresh baby carrots
- 1 can (10¾ ounces) condensed tomato soup, undiluted
- 1 medium onion, chopped
- 1 celery rib, chopped
- 2 tablespoons Worcestershire sauce
- 1 tablespoon browning sauce, optional
- 2 teaspoons beef bouillon granules
- 1 garlic clove, minced
- 1 teaspoon sugar
- ¾ teaspoon salt
- ¼ teaspoon pepper
- ¼ cup cornstarch
- ¾ cup cold water
- 2 cups frozen peas, thawed

1. Place the beef, potatoes, hot water, carrots, soup, onion, celery, Worcestershire sauce, browning sauce if desired, bouillon granules, garlic, sugar, salt and pepper in a 5- or 6-qt. slow cooker. Cover and cook on low for 6-8 hours or until meat is tender.
2. Combine cornstarch and cold water in a small bowl until smooth; gradually stir into stew. Stir in peas. Cover and cook on high for 30 minutes or until thickened.

SLOW COOKER ENCHILADAS

When you're craving Southwestern food but don't want to spend time preparing it in the evening, try my recipe. I simply fill the slow cooker in the morning, then come home to a sensational supper.
—MARY LUEBBERT BENTON, KS

PREP: 30 MIN. • **COOK:** 5 HOURS • **MAKES:** 4 SERVINGS

- 1 **pound ground beef**
- 1 **cup chopped onion**
- ½ **cup chopped green pepper**
- 1 **can (16 ounces) pinto or kidney beans, rinsed and drained**
- 1 **can (15 ounces) black beans, rinsed and drained**
- 1 **can (10 ounces) diced tomatoes and green chilies, undrained**
- ⅓ **cup water**
- 1 **teaspoon chili powder**
- ½ **teaspoon ground cumin**
- ½ **teaspoon salt**
- ¼ **teaspoon pepper**
- 1 **cup (4 ounces) shredded sharp cheddar cheese**
- 1 **cup (4 ounces) shredded Monterey Jack cheese**
- 6 **flour tortillas (6 inches)**

1. In a large skillet, cook the beef, onion and green pepper until meat is no longer pink; drain. Add the beans, tomatoes, water and seasonings; bring to a boil. Reduce heat; cover and simmer for 10 minutes. Combine cheeses.
2. In a 5-qt. slow cooker, layer about ¾ cup beef mixture, one tortilla and about ⅓ cup cheese. Repeat layers. Cover and cook on low for 5-7 hours or until heated through.

ASIAN RIBS

My husband adores this dish, and I love how good it makes the house smell. The mild, tangy, salty-sweet sauce with fresh ginger and garlic is delicious with rice or noodles.

—JULIE KO ROGERS, AR

PREP: 15 MIN. • **COOK:** 6 HOURS
MAKES: 6 SERVINGS (ABOUT 4 CUPS SAUCE)

- 6 **pounds pork baby back ribs, cut into serving-size pieces**
- 1⅓ **cups packed brown sugar**
- 1 **cup reduced-sodium soy sauce**
- ¼ **cup rice vinegar**
- ¼ **cup sesame oil**
- ¼ **cup minced fresh gingerroot**
- 6 **garlic cloves, minced**
- 1 **teaspoon crushed red pepper flakes**
- ¼ **cup cornstarch**
- ¼ **cup cold water**
   Thinly sliced green onions and sesame seeds, optional

1. Place ribs in a 6-qt. slow cooker. In a small bowl, combine the brown sugar, soy sauce, vinegar, oil, ginger, garlic and pepper flakes; pour over ribs. Cover and cook on low for 6-7 hours or until meat is tender.
2. Remove the meat to a serving platter; keep warm. Skim fat from cooking juices; transfer to a small saucepan. Bring to a boil.
3. Combine cornstarch and water until smooth. Gradually stir into the pan. Bring to a boil; cook and stir 2 minutes or until thickened. Serve with ribs. If desired, garnish with onions and sesame seeds.

CAROLINA-STYLE PORK BARBECUE

I'm originally from North Carolina, where swine are divine, and this recipe for the slow cooker is one my family adores. My husband swears my authentic Carolina 'cue is the best BBQ he has ever eaten!
—**KATHRYN RANSOM WILLIAMS** SPARKS, NV

PREP: 30 MIN. • **COOK:** 6 HOURS • **MAKES:** 14 SERVINGS

- 1   boneless pork shoulder butt roast (4 to 5 pounds)
- 2   tablespoons brown sugar
- 2   teaspoons salt
- 1   teaspoon paprika
- ½   teaspoon pepper
- 2   medium onions, quartered
- ¾   cup cider vinegar
- 4   teaspoons Worcestershire sauce
- 1   tablespoon sugar
- 1   tablespoon crushed red pepper flakes
- 1   teaspoon garlic salt
- 1   teaspoon ground mustard
- ½   teaspoon cayenne pepper
- 14 hamburger buns, split
- 1¾ pounds deli coleslaw

1. Cut roast into quarters. Mix brown sugar, salt, paprika and pepper; rub over meat. Place meat and onions in a 5-qt. slow cooker.

2. In a small bowl, whisk vinegar, Worcestershire sauce, sugar and seasonings; pour over roast. Cook, covered, on low 6-8 hours or until meat is tender.

3. Remove the roast and cool slightly. Reserve 1½ cups cooking juices; discard remaining juices. Skim fat from reserved juices. Shred pork with two forks. Return pork and reserved juices to slow cooker; heat through. Serve on buns with coleslaw.

GARLIC LOVER'S BEEF STEW

The wine gives a mellow flavor to this stew that has tender pieces of beef and carrots. We like to serve it over mashed potatoes.
—**ALISSA BROWN** FORT WASHINGTON, PA

PREP: 30 MIN. • **COOK:** 8 HOURS • **MAKES:** 10 SERVINGS

- 1   boneless beef chuck roast (3 pounds), cut into 2-inch pieces
- 1¼ teaspoons salt
- ¾   teaspoon coarsely ground pepper
- ½   cup all-purpose flour
- 2   tablespoons olive oil
- 12   garlic cloves, minced
- 1   cup dry red wine or reduced-sodium beef broth
- 2   cans (14½ ounces each) diced tomatoes, undrained
- 1   can (14½ ounces) reduced-sodium beef broth
- 6   medium carrots, thinly sliced
- 2   medium onions, chopped
- 2   tablespoons tomato paste
- 2   teaspoons minced fresh rosemary or ½ teaspoon dried rosemary, crushed
- 2   teaspoons minced fresh thyme or ½ teaspoon dried thyme
- 2   bay leaves
       Dash ground cloves
       Hot mashed potatoes

1. Sprinkle beef with salt, pepper and flour; toss to coat.

2. In a large skillet, heat oil over medium-high heat. Brown beef in batches. Remove with a slotted spoon. Reduce heat to medium. Add garlic; cook and stir 1 minute.

3. Add wine to skillet, stirring to loosen browned bits from pan. Transfer to a 5- or 6-qt. slow cooker. Stir in tomatoes, broth, carrots, onions, tomato paste, rosemary, thyme, bay leaves, cloves and beef.

4. Cook, covered, on low 8-10 hours or until beef is tender. Remove bay leaves. Serve with mashed potatoes.

SLOW-COOKED LEMON CHICKEN

Garlic, oregano and lemon juice give a spark to this main dish. It's easy to fix— just brown the chicken [and] let the slow cooker do the rest. This is definitely good enough [to] serve to company.

—**WALTER POWELL** WILMINGTON, DE

PREP: 20 MIN. • **COOK:** 5¼ HOURS • **MAKES:** 6 SERVINGS

- 6 **bone-in chicken breast halves (12 ounces each), skin removed**
- 1 **teaspoon dried oregano**
- ½ **teaspoon seasoned salt**
- ¼ **teaspoon pepper**
- 2 **tablespoons butter**
- ¼ **cup water**
- 3 **tablespoons lemon juice**
- 2 **garlic cloves, minced**
- 1 **teaspoon chicken bouillon granules**
- 2 **teaspoons minced fresh parsley**
  Hot cooked rice

1. Pat chicken dry with paper towels. Combine the oregano, seasoned salt and pepper; rub over chicken. In a skillet over medium heat, brown the chicken in butter; transfer to a 5-qt. slow cooker. Add water, lemon juice, garlic and bouillon to the skillet; bring to a boil, stirring to loosen browned bits. Pour over chicken.

2. Cover and cook on low for 5-6 hours. Baste chicken with cooking juices. Add parsley. Cover and cook 15-30 minutes longer or until meat juices run clear. If desired, remove chicken to a platter and keep warm; thicken cooking juices. Serve over chicken and rice.

(5) INGREDIENTS

CRANBERRY-DIJON PORK ROAST

Five everyday ingredients are all you need for my sweet and tangy pork roast.

—**MARY-ELLEN STEELE** BRISTOL, CT

PREP: 15 MIN. • **COOK:** 4 HOURS + STANDING • **MAKES:** 6 SERVINGS

- 1 **boneless pork loin roast (2 to 3 pounds)**
- 2 **tablespoons butter**
- 1 **envelope golden onion soup mix**
- 1 **can (14 ounces) whole-berry cranberry sauce**
- 2 **teaspoons Dijon mustard**

1. In a large skillet, brown roast in butter on all sides. Transfer to a 5-qt. slow cooker; sprinkle with soup mix. Add cranberry sauce to skillet, stirring to loosen browned bits from pan. Pour over roast.

2. Cover and cook on low for 4-5 hours or until meat is tender. Remove roast to a serving platter; let stand for 10 minutes before slicing. Stir mustard into cooking juices. Serve with roast.

❝ I made this dish for 15 people, just doubled the recipe. It was fantastic, there was nothing left! The sauce makes the dish! ❞

—**AROBBINS** TASTEOFHOME.COM

GOLDEN HONEY PAN ROLLS, PAGE 143

SOFT BEER PRETZELS, 145

TOMATO-HERB FOCACCIA, 153

BRUNCH CINNAMON ROLLS, 149

Breads & Rolls

A bite of freshly baked bread slathered with melting butter is one of life's simple pleasures. Besides comforting breads and rolls, try a variety of tasty coffee cakes, muffins, sweet rolls and quick breads. For company, serve the impressive Almond Coffee Cake or Swiss & Caraway Flatbreads or, if time is in short supply, dazzle them with Cinnamon Sweet Potato Muffins.

SWISS & CARAWAY FLATBREADS

My mom came across this rustic-looking flatbread recipe many years ago and always made it on Christmas Eve. Now I make it for my own family, especially during the holidays. It's easy to double or cut in half depending on how many you're serving.

—**DIANE BERGER** SEQUIM, WA

PREP: 20 MIN. + RISING • **BAKE:** 10 MIN.
MAKES: 2 LOAVES (16 PIECES EACH)

- 2 loaves (1 pound each) frozen bread dough, thawed
- ¼ cup butter, melted
- ¼ cup canola oil
- 1 tablespoon dried minced onion
- 1 tablespoon Dijon mustard
- 2 teaspoons caraway seeds
- 1 teaspoon Worcestershire sauce
- 1 tablespoon dry sherry, optional
- 2 cups (8 ounces) shredded Swiss cheese

1. On a lightly floured surface, roll each portion of dough into a 15x10-in. rectangle. Transfer to two greased 15x10x1-in. baking pans. Cover with kitchen towels; let rise in a warm place until doubled, about 45 minutes.

2. Preheat oven to 425°. Using fingertips, press several dimples into dough. In a small bowl, whisk melted butter, oil, onion, mustard, caraway seeds, Worcestershire sauce and, if desired, sherry until blended; brush over dough. Sprinkle with cheese. Bake 10-15 minutes or until golden brown. Serve warm.

FREEZE OPTION *Cut cooled flatbreads into pieces. Freeze in resealable plastic freezer bags. To use, reheat flatbreads on an ungreased baking sheet in a preheated 425° oven until warm.*

MORNING MAPLE MUFFINS

Maple combines with a subtle touch of cinnamon and nuts to give these muffins the flavor of a hearty pancake breakfast.

—**ELIZABETH TALBOT** LEXINGTON, KY

START TO FINISH: 30 MIN. • **MAKES:** 16 MUFFINS

- 2 cups all-purpose flour
- ½ cup packed brown sugar
- 2 teaspoons baking powder
- ½ teaspoon salt
- ¾ cup milk
- ½ cup butter, melted
- ½ cup maple syrup
- ¼ cup sour cream
- 1 egg
- ½ teaspoon vanilla extract

TOPPING

- 3 tablespoons all-purpose flour
- 3 tablespoons sugar
- 2 tablespoons chopped nuts
- ½ teaspoon ground cinnamon
- 2 tablespoons cold butter

1. Preheat oven to 400°. In a large bowl, combine flour, brown sugar, baking powder and salt. In another bowl, combine milk, butter, syrup, sour cream, egg and vanilla. Stir into dry ingredients just until moistened.

2. Fill greased or paper-lined muffin cups two-thirds full. For topping, combine flour, sugar, nuts and cinnamon; cut in butter until crumbly. Sprinkle over batter.

3. Bake 16-20 minutes or until a toothpick inserted in center comes out clean. Cool 5 minutes before removing from pans to wire racks. Serve warm.

FREEZE OPTION *Freeze cooled muffins in resealable plastic freezer bags. To use, thaw at room temperature or, if desired, microwave each muffin on high for 20-30 seconds or until heated through.*

GOLDEN HONEY PAN ROLLS

Using your bread machine to make the dough saves about 2 hours compared to the traditional method. The rich buttery taste of the honey-glazed rolls will be popular with your family and friends.
—**SARA WING** PHILADELPHIA, PA

PREP: 35 MIN. + RISING • **BAKE:** 20 MIN. • **MAKES:** 2 DOZEN

- 1 cup warm 2% milk (70° to 80°)
- 1 egg
- 1 egg yolk
- ½ cup canola oil
- 2 tablespoons honey
- 1½ teaspoons salt
- 3½ cups bread flour
- 2¼ teaspoons active dry yeast

GLAZE

- ⅓ cup sugar
- 2 tablespoons butter, melted
- 1 tablespoon honey
- 1 egg white
  Additional honey, optional

1. In bread machine pan, place the first eight ingredients in order suggested by manufacturer. Select dough setting (check the dough after 5 minutes of mixing; add 1 to 2 tablespoons of water or flour if needed.)

2. When cycle is completed, turn dough onto a lightly floured surface. Punch down; cover and let rest for 10 minutes. Divide into 24 pieces; shape each into a ball. Place 12 balls each in two greased 8-in.-square baking pans. Cover the dough and let rise in a warm place until doubled, about 30 minutes. Preheat oven to 350°.

3. For glaze, combine the sugar, butter, honey and egg white; drizzle over dough. Bake 20-25 minutes or until golden brown. Brush with additional honey if desired.

NOTE *We recommend you do not use a bread machine's time-delay feature for this recipe.*

TOP TIP

Measuring Yeast

Envelopes of yeast generally weigh ¼ ounce each and measure approximately 2¼ teaspoons. If your recipe calls for less yeast, just measure the amount called for in your recipe from an individual packet, then fold the packet closed and store remaining yeast in the fridge for next time.

FAST FIX

CINNAMON SWEET POTATO MUFFINS

This is my own recipe, and I make it often. My five grandchildren think these are a delicious treat.

—CHRISTINE JOHNSON RICETOWN, KY

START TO FINISH: 25 MIN.
MAKES: 2 DOZEN

- 2 **cups self-rising flour**
- 2 **cups sugar**
- 2 **teaspoons ground cinnamon**
- 1 **egg**
- 2 **cups cold mashed sweet potatoes (without added butter or milk)**
- 1 **cup canola oil**

GLAZE
- 1 **cup confectioners' sugar**
- 2 **tablespoons plus 1½ teaspoons 2% milk**
- 1½ **teaspoons butter, melted**
- 1 **teaspoon vanilla extract**
- ½ **teaspoon ground cinnamon**

1. Preheat oven to 375°. In a small bowl, combine flour, sugar and cinnamon. In another bowl, whisk egg, sweet potatoes and oil. Stir into dry ingredients just until moistened.
2. Fill greased muffin cups two-thirds full. Bake 15-18 minutes or until a toothpick inserted in muffin comes out clean. Cool 5 minutes before removing from the pans to wire racks.
3. In a small bowl, combine glaze ingredients; drizzle glaze over the warm muffins.

FREEZE OPTION *Freeze unglazed cooled muffins in resealable plastic freezer bags. To use, thaw at room temperature or, if desired, microwave each muffin on high 20-30 seconds or until heated through.*

NOTE *As a substitute for each cup of self-rising flour, place 1½ teaspoons baking powder and ½ teaspoon salt in a measuring cup. Add all-purpose flour to measure 1 cup.*

SOFT BEER PRETZELS

What goes together better than beer and pretzels? Not much that I can think of. That's why I put them together into one delicious recipe. I'm always looking for new ways to combine fun flavors and this pretzel certainly fits the bill.

—ALYSSA WILHITE WHITEHOUSE, TX

PREP: 1 HOUR + RISING • **BAKE:** 10 MIN.
MAKES: 8 PRETZELS

- 1 **bottle (12 ounces) amber beer or nonalcoholic beer**
- 1 **package (¼ ounce) active dry yeast**
- 2 **tablespoons unsalted butter, melted**
- 2 **tablespoons sugar**
- 1½ **teaspoons salt**
- 4 **to 4½ cups all-purpose flour**
- 10 **cups water**
- ⅔ **cup baking soda**

TOPPING

- 1 **egg yolk**
- 1 **tablespoon water**
  Coarse salt

1. In a small saucepan, heat beer to 110°-115°; remove from heat. Stir in yeast until dissolved. In a large bowl, combine butter, sugar, salt, yeast mixture and 3 cups flour; beat on medium speed until smooth. Stir in enough remaining flour to form a soft dough (dough will be sticky).

2. Turn dough onto a floured surface; knead until smooth and elastic, about 6-8 minutes. Place in a greased bowl, turning once to grease the top. Cover with plastic wrap and let rise in a warm place until doubled, about 1 hour.

3. Preheat oven to 425°. Punch the dough down. Turn onto a lightly floured surface; divide and shape into eight balls. Roll each into a 24-in. rope. Curve the ends of each rope to form a circle; twist ends once and lay over the opposite side of circle, pinching ends to seal.

4. In a Dutch oven, bring water and baking soda to a boil. Drop pretzels, two at a time, into boiling water. Cook 30 seconds. Remove with a slotted spoon; drain well on paper towels.

5. Place 2 in. apart on greased baking sheets. In a small bowl, whisk the egg yolk and water; brush over pretzels. Sprinkle with the coarse salt. Bake 10-12 minutes or until golden brown. Remove from the pans to a wire rack to cool.

FREEZE OPTION *Freeze cooled pretzels in resealable plastic freezer bags. To use, thaw at room temperature or, if desired, microwave each pretzel on high 20-30 seconds or until heated through.*

FLUFFY BISCUITS

If you're looking for a flaky basic biscuit, this recipe is the best. These golden-brown rolls bake up tall, light and tender. Their mild flavor tastes even better when the warm biscuits are spread with butter or jam.

—NANCY HORSBURGH EVERETT, ON

START TO FINISH: 30 MIN.
MAKES: 1 DOZEN

- 2 **cups all-purpose flour**
- 4 **teaspoons baking powder**
- 3 **teaspoons sugar**
- ½ **teaspoon salt**
- ½ **cup shortening**
- 1 **egg**
- ⅔ **cup 2% milk**

1. Preheat oven to 450°. In a small bowl, combine the flour, baking powder, sugar and salt. Cut in shortening until the mixture resembles coarse crumbs. Whisk egg and milk; stir into dry ingredients just until moistened.

2. Turn onto a well-floured surface; knead dough 20 times. Roll to ¾-in. thickness; cut with a floured 2½-in. biscuit cutter. Place on a lightly greased baking sheet.

3. Bake 8-10 minutes or until golden brown. Serve warm.

CINNAMON ROLLS

I present these yummy frosted rolls warm from the oven as a Christmas morning treat at our house. Even if you are not accustomed to working with yeast dough, you'll find this dough is easy to handle.
—**JULIE STERCHI** CAMPBELLSVILLE, KY

PREP: 30 MIN. + RISING • **BAKE:** 10 MIN. + COOLING
MAKES: 2 DOZEN

- 5 to 6 cups all-purpose flour
- 1 package yellow cake mix (regular size)
- 2 packages (¼ ounce each) quick-rise yeast
- 2½ cups warm water (120° to 130°)
- ¼ cup butter, melted
- ½ cup sugar
- 1 teaspoon ground cinnamon

FROSTING

- 6 tablespoons butter, softened
- 3 cups confectioners' sugar
- 1½ teaspoons vanilla extract
- 2 to 3 tablespoons 2% milk

1. In a large bowl, combine 4 cups flour, cake mix, yeast and warm water until smooth. Add enough remaining flour to form a soft dough.

2. Turn onto a lightly floured surface; knead until smooth and elastic, about 5 minutes. Place in a greased bowl, turning once to grease top. Cover and let rise until doubled, about 45 minutes.

3. Punch dough down. Turn onto a lightly floured surface; divide in half. Roll each portion into a 14x10-in. rectangle. Brush with butter; sprinkle with sugar and cinnamon.

4. Roll up jelly-roll style, starting with a long side. Cut each roll into 12 slices; place cut side down in two greased 13x9-in. baking pans. Cover and let rise until almost doubled, about 20 minutes. Preheat oven to 400°.

5. Bake 10-15 minutes or until golden brown. Cool for 20 minutes. For frosting, in a large bowl, cream the butter, confectioners' sugar and vanilla and enough milk to achieve desired consistency. Frost warm rolls.

CINNAMON PEACH KUCHEN

With its flaky, buttery crust and sweet peach topping, this is one of my favorites. Use as a coffee cake or dessert and served warm or cold. It's a tried and true recipe from my mother.
—**RACHEL GARCIA** COLORADO SPRINGS, CO

PREP: 25 MIN. • **BAKE:** 45 MIN. + COOLING • **MAKES:** 10 SERVINGS

- 2 cups all-purpose flour
- 2 tablespoons sugar
- ½ teaspoon salt
- ¼ teaspoon baking powder
- ½ cup cold butter, cubed
- 2 cans (15¼ ounces each) peach halves, drained and patted dry
- 1 cup packed brown sugar
- 1 teaspoon ground cinnamon
- 2 egg yolks, lightly beaten
- 1 cup heavy whipping cream

1. Preheat oven to 350°. In a small bowl, combine flour, sugar, salt and baking powder; cut in butter until crumbly. Press onto the bottom and 1½ in. up the sides of a greased 9-in. springform pan.

2. Place pan on a baking sheet. Arrange peach halves, cut side up, in the crust. Combine brown sugar and cinnamon; sprinkle over peaches.

3. Bake 20 minutes. Combine egg yolks and cream; pour over peaches. Bake 25-30 minutes longer or until top is set. Cool on a wire rack. Refrigerate leftovers.

BEERNANA BREAD

Really, it's simple arithmetic. Beer is good. Banana bread is good. Beernana bread is great! Even guys who don't know their way around the kitchen can pull this one off.
—**STEVE CAYFORD** DUBUQUE, IA

PREP: 15 MIN. • **BAKE:** 55 MIN. + COOLING
MAKES: 1 LOAF (16 SLICES)

- 3 cups self-rising flour
- ¾ cup quick-cooking oats
- ½ cup packed brown sugar
- 1½ cups mashed ripe bananas (about 3 medium)
- 1 bottle (12 ounces) wheat beer
- ¼ cup maple syrup
- 2 tablespoons olive oil
- 1 tablespoon sesame seeds
- ¼ teaspoon kosher salt

1. Preheat oven to 375°. In a large bowl, mix flour, oats and brown sugar. In another bowl, mix bananas, beer and maple syrup until blended. Add to flour mixture; stir just until moistened.

2. Transfer to a greased 9x5-in. loaf pan. Drizzle with oil; sprinkle with sesame seeds and salt. Bake 55-60 minutes or until a toothpick inserted in center comes out clean. Cool in pan 10 minutes before removing to wire rack to cool.

FREEZE OPTION *Securely wrap and freeze cooled loaf in foil and place in resealable plastic freezer bag. To use, thaw at room temperature.*

"This recipe is wonderful! The bread is moist and delicious and a welcome change from more traditional banana bread recipes. My husband and I slathered our slices with butter, which was not necessary, but really tasted good!"
—SGRONHOLZ TASTEOFHOME.COM

GARLIC-HERB BRAID

Savory flavors of rosemary, dill, garlic and basil blend beautifully in this homey loaf that goes great with almost any main dish. Get ready for oohs and aahs when you bring this tender and impressive braid to the table!

—TASTE OF HOME TEST KITCHEN

PREP: 20 MIN. + RISING • **BAKE:** 20 MIN. + COOLING
MAKES: 1 LOAF (16 SLICES)

    4 to 4½ cups all-purpose flour
    3 tablespoons sugar
    2 packages (¼ ounce each) quick-rise yeast
    2 teaspoons dried basil
 1¾ teaspoons dill weed
 1½ teaspoons salt
    ¾ teaspoon garlic powder
    ¾ teaspoon dried rosemary, crushed
    ¾ cup 2% milk
    ½ cup water
    ¼ cup butter, cubed
    1 egg
    1 tablespoon butter, melted

1. In a large bowl, combine 1½ cups flour, sugar, yeast and seasonings. In a small saucepan, heat the milk, water and cubed butter to 120°-130°. Add to dry ingredients; beat just until moistened. Add egg; beat until smooth. Stir in enough remaining flour to form a soft dough.
2. Turn onto a floured surface; knead until smooth and elastic, about 4-6 minutes. Cover and let rest 10 minutes.
3. Divide dough into thirds. Shape each into a 15-in. rope. Place ropes on a greased baking sheet and braid; pinch ends to seal and tuck under. Cover and let rise until doubled, about 25 minutes. Preheat oven to 375°.
4. Bake 20-25 minutes or until golden brown. Brush with melted butter. Remove from pan to a wire rack to cool.
FREEZE OPTION *Securely wrap and freeze cooled loaf in heavy-duty foil. To use, thaw at room temperature.*

TOP TIP
About Quick-Rise Yeast

Quick-rise or rapid-rise yeast has two time-saving advantages over active dry yeast: It does not need to be dissolved in water before mixing, and it requires only one rise after shaping. Simply add the dry yeast to the flour mixture. Heat the liquid ingredients to 120°-130° (rather than 110°-115° for dissolving active dry yeast). In place of the first rise, allow the dough to rest for 10 minutes before shaping. The next rise should take about half the time stated in a recipe that calls for active dry yeast.

DOUGHNUT MUFFINS

My mom and I went to a bakery every morning on the way to school and I got to pick out a different treat each day. That's how my affinity for doughnuts began.

—MORGAN BOTWINICK RICHMOND, VA

PREP: 30 MIN. • **BAKE:** 20 MIN. • **MAKES:** 1 DOZEN

    ¾ cup butter, softened
    ⅔ cup packed brown sugar
    ¼ cup sugar
    2 eggs
 1¼ cups 2% milk
    1 teaspoon vanilla extract
    3 cups all-purpose flour
 2½ teaspoons baking powder
    ¾ teaspoon salt
    ½ teaspoon ground nutmeg
    ½ teaspoon ground cinnamon
    ¼ teaspoon baking soda
COATING
    1 cup coarse sugar
    1 tablespoon ground cinnamon
    ⅓ cup butter, melted

1. Preheat oven to 350°. In a large bowl, cream butter and sugars until light and fluffy. Add eggs, one at a time, beating well after each addition. Gradually beat in milk and vanilla. In another bowl, whisk flour, baking powder, salt, nutmeg, cinnamon and baking soda. Add to creamed mixture; stir just until moistened.
2. Fill greased or paper-lined muffin cups. Bake for 18-20 minutes or until a toothpick inserted in center comes out clean. Cool 5 minutes before removing from the pan to a wire rack.
3. Meanwhile, for coating, combine coarse sugar and cinnamon. Dip tops of warm muffins in butter, then coat in cinnamon-sugar.

BRUNCH CINNAMON ROLLS

This family friendly breakfast bun is glazed with maple and vanilla flavors which deliciously accent the cinnamon and nuts.

—**RITA VOGEL** MALCOM, IA

PREP: 30 MIN. • **BAKE:** 20 MIN. • **MAKES:** 1 DOZEN

- ¾ cup 4% small-curd cottage cheese
- ⅓ cup reduced-fat plain yogurt
- ¼ cup sugar
- ¼ cup butter, melted
- 1 teaspoon vanilla extract
- 2 cups all-purpose flour
- 2 teaspoons baking powder
- ¼ teaspoon baking soda
- ½ teaspoon salt

FILLING

- 2 tablespoons butter, melted
- 1 cup chopped pecans
- ⅔ cup packed brown sugar
- 1½ teaspoons ground cinnamon

MAPLE GLAZE

- ⅔ cup confectioners' sugar
- 3 tablespoons maple syrup
- 1 teaspoon vanilla extract

1. Preheat oven to 400°. In a food processor, combine the first five ingredients; cover and process until smooth. Add the flour, baking powder, baking soda and salt; cover and pulse until mixture forms a soft dough.

2. Transfer to a lightly floured surface; knead 4-5 times. Roll into a 15x12-in. rectangle. Brush butter to within ½ in. of edges. Combine the pecans, brown sugar and cinnamon; sprinkle over dough. Roll up jelly-roll style, starting with a long side; pinch seam to seal. Cut into 12 slices. Place cut side down in a greased 9-in. round baking pan.

3. Bake 20-25 minutes or until golden brown. Cool for 5 minutes before inverting onto a serving plate. Combine glaze ingredients; drizzle over rolls. Serve warm.

ALMOND COFFEE CAKE

I've been making this cake for gatherings on cold winter m for years, and the platter goes from full to empty in minutes think it's doubly delicious because of the cream cheese and w chip filling. One piece just leads to another!

—**MARY SHIVERS** ADA, OK

PREP: 35 MIN. + RISING • **BAKE:** 20 MIN. + COOLING
MAKES: 8-10 SERVINGS

- 1 loaf (1 pound) frozen bread dough, thawed
- 1 package (8 ounces) cream cheese, softened
- ¼ cup sugar
- 1 egg
- ½ teaspoon almond extract
- ¾ cup white baking chips
- 1 tablespoon 2% milk

GLAZE

- 1 cup confectioners' sugar
- ¼ teaspoon almond extract
- 1 to 2 tablespoons 2% milk
- ½ cup slivered almonds, toasted

1. On a lightly floured surface, roll dough into a 15x9-in. rectangle. Transfer to a lightly greased baking sheet.

2. In a small bowl, beat cream cheese and sugar until smooth. Beat in egg and extract (filling will be soft). Spread down center of rectangle; sprinkle with chips. On each long side, cut 1-in.-wide strips, about ½ in. from filling.

3. Starting at one end, fold alternating strips at an angle across filling. Seal ends. Cover and let rise in a warm place until doubled, about 1 hour.

4. Preheat oven to 350°. Brush with milk. Bake 20-30 minutes or until golden brown. Cool on a wire rack.

5. For glaze, in a small bowl, combine the confectioners' sugar and extract. Stir in enough milk to achieve desired consistency. Drizzle over the coffee cake. Sprinkle with the almonds.

NEW ORLEANS BEIGNETS

These sweet French doughnuts are square instead of round and have no hole in the middle. They're a traditional part of breakfast in New Orleans.

—BETH DAWSON JACKSON, LA

PREP: 15 MIN. + CHILLING • **COOK:** 5 MIN./BATCH • **MAKES:** 4 DOZEN

  1 **package (¼ ounce) active dry yeast**
  ¼ **cup warm water (110° to 115°)**
  1 **cup evaporated milk**
  ½ **cup canola oil**
  ¼ **cup sugar**
  1 **egg**
  4½ **cups self-rising flour**
      Oil for deep-fat frying
      Confectioners' sugar

1. In a large bowl, dissolve yeast in warm water. Add milk, oil, sugar, egg and 2 cups flour. Beat until smooth. Stir in enough remaining flour to form a soft dough (dough will be sticky). Do not knead. Cover and refrigerate overnight.

2. Punch dough down. Turn onto a floured surface; roll into a 16x12-in. rectangle. Cut into 2-in. squares.

3. In an electric skillet or deep-fat fryer, heat oil to 375°. Fry the squares, a few at a time, until golden brown on both sides. Drain on paper towels. Roll the warm beignets in confectioners' sugar.

NOTE *As a substitute for each cup of self-rising flour, place 1½ teaspoons baking powder and ½ teaspoon salt in a measuring cup. Add all-purpose flour to measure 1 cup.*

BREAKFAST-IN-A-MUFFIN

I can never seem to get out of bed with enough time to make breakfast. My solution is to make these muffins ahead of time and pop them in the microwave for 30 seconds just before I head out the door. That way, I can get breakfast on the go.

—SARA SANDERS FOUNTAIN CITY, IN

PREP: 20 MIN. • **BAKE:** 15 MIN. • **MAKES:** 1 DOZEN

  ⅓ **pound bulk Italian sausage**
  3 **eggs**
  ⅛ **teaspoon seasoned salt**
  ⅛ **teaspoon pepper**
  1 **package (8½ ounces) corn bread/muffin mix**
  ¾ **cup shredded cheddar cheese, divided**

1. Preheat oven to 400°. Line 12 muffin cups with paper liners. In a skillet, cook the sausage over medium heat 4-5 minutes or until no longer pink, breaking into crumbles. Remove to paper towels to drain.

2. In a small bowl, whisk the eggs, seasoned salt and pepper. Pour into the same pan; cook and stir over medium heat until eggs are thickened and no liquid egg remains. Remove from heat.

3. In a large bowl, prepare muffin mix according to package directions. Fold in sausage, scrambled eggs and ½ cup cheese. Fill prepared cups two-thirds full.

4. Bake 10 minutes. Sprinkle with remaining cheese; bake 5 minutes longer or until a toothpick inserted in center comes out clean. Cool 5 minutes before removing from pan. Serve warm.

MAPLE-BACON DOUGHNUT BITES

While these delicious bite-size treats are ready in minutes, they disappear in a flash. And don't relegate the deep-fried goodness to the breakfast nook; I've never had anyone turn these down no matter the time of day.

—**CHELSEA TURNER** LAKE ELSINORE, CA

PREP: 20 MIN. • **COOK:** 5 MIN./BATCH • **MAKES:** ABOUT 2 DOZEN

- 1½ **cups all-purpose flour**
- ½ **cup sugar**
- 2 **teaspoons baking powder**
- ½ **teaspoon salt**
- 1 **egg**
- ½ **cup 2% milk**
- 1 **tablespoon butter, melted**
    Oil for deep-fat frying

GLAZE
- 1 **cup confectioners' sugar**
- 3 **tablespoons maple syrup**
- 1 **tablespoon 2% milk**
- 1 **teaspoon vanilla extract**
- 7 **maple-flavored bacon strips, cooked and crumbled**

1. In a large bowl, whisk flour, sugar, baking powder and salt. In another bowl, whisk egg, milk and melted butter until blended. Add to flour mixture; stir just until moistened.

2. Heat oil to 350° in an electric skillet or deep fryer. Drop tablespoonfuls of batter, a few at a time, into hot oil. Fry 3-4 minutes or until golden brown, turning often. Drain on paper towels.

3. In a small bowl, mix confectioners' sugar, maple syrup, milk and vanilla until smooth. Dip warm doughnuts into glaze; sprinkle tops with bacon.

SWISS BEER BREAD

Unlike other cheese breads I have tried, this one isn't greasy! So, I enjoy making it and serving it. It's great with soup or stew. You'll be amazed how fast it disappears!

—**DEBI WALLACE** CHESTERTOWN, NY

PREP: 15 MIN. • **BAKE:** 50 MIN. + COOLING
MAKES: 1 LOAF (12 SLICES)

- 4 **ounces Jarlsberg or Swiss cheese**
- 3 **cups all-purpose flour**
- 3 **tablespoons sugar**
- 3 **teaspoons baking powder**
- 1½ **teaspoons salt**
- ½ **teaspoon pepper**
- 1 **bottle (12 ounces) beer or nonalcoholic beer**
- 2 **tablespoons butter, melted**

1. Preheat oven to 375°. Divide cheese in half. Cut half of cheese into ¼-in. cubes; shred remaining cheese. In a large bowl, combine the flour, sugar, baking powder, salt and pepper. Stir beer into dry ingredients just until moistened. Fold in cheese.

2. Transfer to a greased 8x4-in. loaf pan. Drizzle with butter. Bake 50-60 minutes or until a toothpick inserted near the center comes out clean. Cool 10 minutes before removing from pan to a wire rack.

❝ Delicious for a quick bread recipe. Was gone in about 15 min. My kids and husband loved it! ❞

—**DONNA.ANDERSON** TASTEOFHOME.COM

JUMBO BLUEBERRY MUFFINS

In Michigan there are lots of blueberries, so I enjoy trying recipes with them, such as a jumbo version of a classic muffin.

—JACKIE HANNAHS CEDAR SPRINGS, MI

PREP: 15 MIN. • **BAKE:** 20 MIN.
MAKES: 8 JUMBO MUFFINS

- ½ **cup butter, softened**
- 1 **cup sugar**
- 2 **eggs**
- ½ **cup buttermilk**
- 1 **teaspoon vanilla extract**
- 2 **cups all-purpose flour**
- 2 **teaspoons baking powder**
- ¼ **teaspoon salt**
- 2 **cups fresh or frozen blueberries**

TOPPING
- 3 **tablespoons sugar**
- ⅛ **teaspoon ground cinnamon**
- ⅛ **teaspoon ground nutmeg**

1. Preheat oven to 400°. In a large bowl, cream butter and sugar until light and fluffy. Add eggs, one at a time, beating well after each addition. Beat in buttermilk and vanilla. In another bowl, whisk flour, baking powder and salt. Add to creamed mixture; stir just until moistened. Fold in blueberries.

2. Fill greased or paper-lined jumbo muffin cups two-thirds full. Mix topping ingredients; sprinkle over tops. Bake 20-25 minutes or until a toothpick inserted in center comes out clean. Cool 5 minutes before removing from pan to a wire rack. Serve warm.

FOR STANDARD-SIZE MUFFINS
Make batter as directed; fill greased or paper-lined standard muffin cups two-thirds full. Bake in a preheated 400° oven for 15-20 minutes or until a toothpick comes out clean. Yield: about 16 standard muffins.

ISLAND BREEZES COFFEE CAKE

Invite sunshine to brunch with a delightful make-ahead bread. You won't believe how simple it is.

—DEBBIE GOFORTH NEWPORT, TN

PREP: 20 MIN. + CHILLING
BAKE: 35 MIN. + COOLING
MAKES: 12 SERVINGS

- ⅔ **cup packed brown sugar**
- ½ **cup flaked coconut, toasted**
- 1 **package (3.4 ounces) cook-and-serve coconut cream pudding mix**
- 20 **frozen bread dough dinner rolls**
- 1 **can (20 ounces) pineapple tidbits, drained**
- 1 **jar (3 ounces) macadamia nuts, coarsely chopped**
- ½ **cup butter, cubed**

1. In a small bowl, combine the brown sugar, coconut and pudding mix. Place 10 rolls in a greased 10-in. fluted tube pan; layer with half the sugar mixture, 1 cup pineapple tidbits, ⅓ cup nuts and ¼ cup butter. Repeat layers. Cover the pan with plastic wrap and refrigerate overnight.

2. Remove pan from refrigerator about 1¾ hours before serving; let rise in a warm place until dough reaches top of pan, about 1 hour.

3. Preheat oven to 350°. Remove the plastic wrap. Bake the coffee cake 35-40 minutes or until golden brown. (Cover loosely with foil if top browns too quickly.) Cool 10 minutes before inverting the coffee cake onto a serving plate; serve warm.

NOTE *To toast coconut, spread in a 15x10x1-in. baking pan. Bake at 350° for 5-10 minutes or until golden brown, stirring frequently.*

TOP TIP

Pull-Apart Breads

Island Breezes Coffee Cake can be cut into slices to serve or each roll may be separately pulled off the loaf. This type of bread is also called monkey bread, bubble load, Hungarian coffee cake and pinch-me cake.

TOMATO-HERB FOCACCIA

With its savory medley of herbs and tomatoes, this rustic bread will liven up any occasion, from a family meal to a game day get-together.

—**JANET MILLER** INDIANAPOLIS, IN

PREP: 30 MIN. + RISING • **BAKE:** 20 MIN.
MAKES: 1 LOAF (12 PIECES)

- 1 **package (¼ ounce) active dry yeast**
- 1 **cup warm water (110° to 115°)**
- 2 **tablespoons olive oil, divided**
- 1½ **teaspoons salt**
- 1 **teaspoon sugar**
- 1 **teaspoon garlic powder**
- 1 **teaspoon each dried oregano, thyme and rosemary, crushed**
- ½ **teaspoon dried basil**
  Dash pepper
- 2 **to 2½ cups all-purpose flour**
- 2 **plum tomatoes, thinly sliced**
- ¼ **cup shredded part-skim mozzarella cheese**
- 1 **tablespoon grated Parmesan cheese**

1. In a large bowl, dissolve yeast in warm water. Add 1 tablespoon oil, salt, sugar, garlic powder, herbs, pepper and 1½ cups flour. Beat until smooth. Stir in enough remaining flour to form a soft dough (dough will be sticky).

2. Turn onto a floured surface; knead until smooth and elastic, about 6-8 minutes. Place in a greased bowl, turning once to grease the top. Cover and let rise in a warm place until doubled, about 1 hour.

3. Punch dough down. Cover and let rest for 10 minutes. Shape into a 13x9-in. rectangle; place on a greased baking sheet. Cover and let rise until doubled, about 30 minutes. Preheat oven to 400°.

4. With fingertips, make several dimples over top of dough. Brush dough with remaining oil; arrange tomatoes over the top. Sprinkle with cheeses. Bake 20-25 minutes or until golden brown. Remove to a wire rack.

FREEZE OPTION *Freeze cooled focaccia squares in freezer containers, separating layers with waxed paper. To use, reheat squares on a baking sheet in a preheated 400° oven until heated through.*

"Made this last month and it's to die for! The flavors were wonderful and the smell was scrumptious! Will make regularly! I made it in the tube pan and it came out perfect!"

—MUFFNETTE TASTEOFHOME.COM

CINNAMON COFFEE CAKE

I love the excellent texture of this old-fashioned streusel-topped coffee cake. It's always a crowd-pleaser. The lovely vanilla flavor is enriched by sour cream may remind you of breakfast at Grandma's!
—**ELEANOR HARRIS** CAPE CORAL, FL

PREP: 20 MIN. • **BAKE:** 1 HOUR + COOLING • **MAKES:** 16-20 SERVINGS

- 1 cup butter, softened
- 2¾ cups sugar, divided
- 4 eggs
- 2 teaspoons vanilla extract
- 3 cups all-purpose flour
- 1 teaspoon baking soda
- 1 teaspoon salt
- 2 cups (16 ounces) sour cream
- 2 tablespoons ground cinnamon
- ½ cup chopped walnuts

1. Preheat oven to 350°. In a large bowl, cream butter and 2 cups sugar until light fluffy. Add eggs, one at a time, beating well after each addition. Beat in vanilla. Combine the flour, baking soda and salt; add alternately with sour cream, beating just enough after each addition to keep batter smooth.

2. Spoon a third of batter into a greased 10-in. tube pan. Combine cinnamon, nuts and remaining sugar; sprinkle a third over batter in pan. Repeat layers two more times. Bake 60-65 minutes or until a toothpick inserted near the center comes out clean. Cool 15 minutes before removing from pan to a wire rack to cool completely.

IRISH SODA BREAD

This is the best Irish soda bread I've ever had. It is lighter and softer than most others I've tried. We like to have slices spread with whipped butter.
—**KERRY AMUNDSON** OCEAN PARK, WA

PREP: 15 MIN. • **BAKE:** 40 MIN. + COOLING
MAKES: 1 LOAF (12 WEDGES)

- 3½ cups all-purpose flour
- ½ cup sugar
- 2 tablespoons caraway seeds
- 2 teaspoons baking powder
- 1 teaspoon salt
- ½ teaspoon baking soda
- 2 eggs
- 2 cups (16 ounces) sour cream
- ¾ cup raisins

1. Preheat oven to 350°. In a large bowl, combine the flour, sugar, caraway seeds, baking powder, salt and baking soda. In a small bowl, whisk eggs and sour cream. Stir into dry ingredients just until moistened. Fold in raisins.

2. Spoon into a greased 9-in. springform pan. Bake 40-45 minutes or until a toothpick inserted near the center comes out clean. Cool on a wire rack 10 minutes before removing sides of pan. Cut into wedges; serve warm.

PUMPKIN CHIP MUFFINS

I started cooking and baking at a young age, just as my sisters and brothers did. Our mother was a very good teacher, and she told us we would have to learn our way around the kitchen. Now, I've let my children know the same thing!
—**CINDY MIDDLETON** CHAMPION, AB

PREP: 10 MIN. • **BAKE:** 15 MIN. + COOLING
MAKES: ABOUT 2 DOZEN MUFFINS

- 4 eggs
- 2 cups sugar
- 1 can (15 ounces) solid-pack pumpkin
- 1½ cups canola oil
- 3 cups all-purpose flour
- 2 teaspoons baking soda
- 1 teaspoon baking powder
- 1 teaspoon ground cinnamon
- 1 teaspoon salt
- 2 cups (12 ounces) semisweet chocolate chips

1. Preheat oven to 400°. In a large bowl, beat the eggs, sugar, pumpkin and oil until smooth. Combine the flour, baking soda, baking powder, cinnamon and salt; gradually add to pumpkin mixture and mix well. Fold in chocolate chips. Fill greased or paper-lined muffin cups three-fourths full.

2. Bake 15-18 minutes or until a toothpick inserted near the center comes out clean. Cool in pan 10 minutes before removing to a wire rack.

TOP TIP

Irish Soda Bread

This classic quick bread from Ireland is so named because it uses baking soda for leavening. Legend has it that people would cut an X into the top of the bread before baking it to ward off evil spirits.

LEMON SUPREME PIE, PAGE 175

RASPBERRY SWIRL CUPCAKES, 178

CRANBERRY-ORANGE TRIFLE, 171

CHOCOLATE HAZELNUT MOUSSE CUPS, 160

Cakes, Pies & Desserts

The promise of a sweet ending to a meal is enough to make anyone clean their plates in anticipation! From decadent Triple Layer Brownie Cake and Coconut-Pecan German Chocolate Pie to old-fashioned Blueberry Cobbler and Maple-Nut Cheesecake, there's a dessert just waiting for you to enjoy in this popular chapter.

RASPBERRY SUGAR CREAM TARTS

These tarts bring back childhood memories of baking with my mom. Perfect for holidays at home, the tarts also make fun hostess gifts.

—CATHY BANKS ENCINITAS, CA

PREP: 30 MIN. • **BAKE:** 15 MIN. + COOLING
MAKES: 3 DOZEN

- ¾ cup unsalted butter, softened
- ½ cup sugar
- 2 egg yolks
- ¾ teaspoon almond or vanilla extract
- ⅛ teaspoon salt
- 1¾ cups all-purpose flour

FILLING
- 3 tablespoons seedless raspberry spreadable fruit
- ¾ cup sugar
- 3 tablespoons all-purpose flour
  Dash salt
- ¾ cup heavy whipping cream
- ⅓ cup half-and-half cream
- ½ teaspoon almond or vanilla extract
  Fresh raspberries, optional

1. Preheat oven to 350°. In a large bowl, cream butter and sugar until light and fluffy. Beat in the egg yolks, extract and salt. Gradually beat in the flour.

2. Shape dough into ¾-in. balls; place in greased mini-muffin cups. Press evenly onto bottoms and up sides of cups. Bake 10-12 minutes or until light brown. Cool in pans on wire racks.

3. Spread ¼ teaspoon spreadable fruit onto the bottom of each crust. In a small bowl, combine sugar, flour and salt. Whisk in the whipping cream, half-and-half and extract just until blended (mixture will be thin). Spoon 2 teaspoons filling into each crust. Bake 12-14 minutes or until filling just begins to bubble.

4. Cool 10 minutes before removing from pans; cool completely on wire racks. If desired, top with raspberries. Refrigerate leftovers.

MRS. THOMPSON'S CARROT CAKE

I received this recipe from the mother of a patient I cared for back in 1972 in St. Paul, Minnesota. It was, and is, the best carrot cake I have ever tasted. It's requested for many family gatherings and celebrations.

—**BECKY WACHOB** KELLY, WY

PREP: 30 MIN. • **BAKE:** 35 MIN.
MAKES: 15 SERVINGS

- 3 **cups shredded carrots**
- 1 **can (20 ounces) crushed pineapple, well-drained**
- 2 **cups sugar**
- 1 **cup canola oil**
- 4 **eggs**
- 2 **cups all-purpose flour**
- 2 **teaspoons baking soda**
- 2 **teaspoons ground cinnamon**

FROSTING
- 1 **package (8 ounces) cream cheese, softened**
- ¼ **cup butter, softened**
- 2 **teaspoons vanilla extract**
- 3¾ **cups confectioners' sugar**

1. Preheat oven to 350°. In a large bowl, beat the first five ingredients until well blended. In another bowl, mix flour, baking soda and cinnamon; gradually beat into carrot mixture.
2. Transfer to a greased 13x9-in. baking pan. Bake 35-40 minutes or until a toothpick inserted in center comes out clean. Cool completely in pan on a wire rack.

3. For frosting, in a large bowl, beat the cream cheese, butter and vanilla until blended. Gradually beat in the confectioners' sugar until smooth. Spread over cake. Cover and refrigerate leftovers.

BLUE-RIBBON APPLE PIE

With its hidden layer of walnuts, this pie is a special one. I won a blue ribbon for it at the local fair, which allowed me to enter it in the state farm show.

—**COLLETTE GAUGLER** FOGELSVILLE, PA

PREP: 45 MIN. • **BAKE:** 55 MIN. + COOLING
MAKES: 8 SERVINGS

    Pastry for double-crust pie (9 inches)

WALNUT LAYER
- ¾ **cup ground walnuts**
- 2 **tablespoons brown sugar**
- 2 **tablespoons lightly beaten egg**
- 1 **tablespoon butter, melted**
- 1 **tablespoon 2% milk**
- ¼ **teaspoon lemon juice**
- ¼ **teaspoon vanilla extract**

FILLING
- 6 **cups sliced peeled tart apples (4-5 medium)**
- 2 **teaspoons lemon juice**
- ½ **teaspoon vanilla extract**
- ¾ **cup sugar**
- 3 **tablespoons all-purpose flour**
- 1¼ **teaspoons ground cinnamon**
- ¼ **teaspoon ground nutmeg**
- ⅛ **teaspoon salt**
- 3 **tablespoons butter, cubed**

TOPPING
- 1 **teaspoon 2% milk**
- 2 **teaspoons sugar**

1. Preheat oven to 375°. On a lightly floured surface, roll one half of pastry dough to a ⅛-in.-thick circle; transfer to a 9-in. pie plate. Trim pastry even with rim.
2. In a small bowl, mix walnut layer ingredients until blended. Spread onto bottom of pastry shell. Chill while preparing filling.
3. For filling, in a large bowl, toss apples with lemon juice and vanilla. In a small bowl, mix the sugar, flour, cinnamon, nutmeg and salt; add to apple mixture and toss to coat.
4. Pour filling over walnut layer; dot with butter. Roll remaining pastry dough to a ⅛-in.-thick circle. Place over filling. Trim, seal and flute edge. Brush top with milk; sprinkle with sugar. Cut slits in pastry.
5. Place pie on a baking sheet. Bake 55-65 minutes or until crust is golden brown and filling is bubbly. Cover edge loosely with foil during the last 10 minutes if needed to prevent overbrowning. Remove foil. Cool on a wire rack.

PASTRY FOR DOUBLE-CRUST PIE (9 INCHES) *Combine 2½ cups all-purpose flour and ½ teaspoon salt; cut in 1 cup shortening until crumbly. Gradually add 4 to 5 tablespoons ice water, tossing with a fork until dough holds together when pressed. Divide dough in half and shape into disks; wrap in plastic wrap and refrigerate 1 hour.*

CHOCOLATE HAZELNUT MOUSSE CUPS

Three of my favorite foods—chocolate, hazelnuts and puff pastry—come together for an impressive dessert. Dress them up with drizzles of melted chocolate and a sprinkle of chopped nuts.
—**ROXANNE CHAN** ALBANY, CA

PREP: 30 MIN. + COOLING • **MAKES:** 6 SERVINGS

- 1 package (10 ounces) frozen puff pastry shells, thawed
- ½ cup heavy whipping cream
- 1 to 2 tablespoons confectioners' sugar
- ¼ teaspoon vanilla extract
- ½ cup mascarpone cheese
- ½ cup Nutella
- ¼ teaspoon ground cinnamon
- 2 tablespoons miniature semisweet chocolate chips
  Additional miniature semisweet chocolate chips, melted, optional
- 2 tablespoons chopped hazelnuts, toasted

1. Bake pastry shells according to package directions. Cool completely.
2. In a small bowl, beat cream until it begins to thicken. Add confectioners' sugar and vanilla; beat until soft peaks form.
3. In another bowl, beat mascarpone cheese, Nutella and cinnamon until blended. Fold in the whipped cream and chocolate chips. Spoon into pastry shells. If desired, drizzle with melted chocolate. Sprinkle with hazelnuts. Refrigerate until serving.

NOTE *To toast nuts, spread in a 15x10x1-in. baking pan. Bake at 350° for 5-10 minutes or until lightly browned, stirring occasionally. Or, spread in a dry nonstick skillet and heat over low heat until lightly browned, stirring occasionally.*

SWEET POTATO ICE CREAM PIE

Not one person has ever guessed that canned sweet potatoes are the secret ingredient in this pie! It's so creamy and delicious, I'm always asked for the recipe when I serve it.
—**SUSAN BAZAN** SEQUIM, WA

PREP: 25 MIN. + FREEZING • **MAKES:** 8 SERVINGS

- 2 cups graham cracker crumbs (about 14 whole crackers)
- 3 tablespoons sugar
- ½ cup butter, melted
- 1 can (15 ounces) sweet potatoes, drained
- ½ cup packed brown sugar
- 2 teaspoons pumpkin pie spice
- 1 teaspoon grated orange peel
- ¼ teaspoon salt
- 4 cups vanilla ice cream, softened
- 1 cup heavy whipping cream
- 3 tablespoons confectioners' sugar
- 1 teaspoon vanilla extract

1. In a small bowl, mix cracker crumbs and sugar; stir in butter. Press onto bottom and up sides of a greased 9-in. deep-dish pie plate. Refrigerate 30 minutes.
2. Place sweet potatoes, brown sugar, pie spice, orange peel and salt in a food processor; process until smooth. Add ice cream; process until blended. Spread evenly into crust. Freeze, covered, 8 hours or overnight.
3. Remove from freezer about 10 minutes before serving. Meanwhile, in a small bowl, beat cream until it begins to thicken. Add confectioners' sugar and vanilla; beat until soft peaks form. Spread over pie.

DUTCH APPLE CAKE

My husband and I came to Canada more than 50 years ago from Holland. This recipe, a family favorite, is one I found in a Dutch cookbook. It frequently goes along with me to potluck suppers.
—**ELIZABETH PETERS** MARTINTOWN, ON

PREP: 15 MIN. + STANDING • **BAKE:** 1½ HOURS + COOLING
MAKES: 10-12 SERVINGS

 3 **medium tart apples, peeled and cut into ¼-inch slices (3 cups)**
 3 **tablespoons plus 1 cup sugar, divided**
 1 **teaspoon ground cinnamon**
 ⅔ **cup butter, softened**
 4 **eggs**
 1 **teaspoon vanilla extract**
 2 **cups all-purpose flour**
 ⅛ **teaspoon salt**

1. In a large bowl, combine the apples, 3 tablespoons sugar and cinnamon; let stand 1 hour.
2. Preheat oven to 300°. In another bowl, cream butter and remaining sugar until light and fluffy. Add eggs, one at a time, beating well after each addition. Add vanilla. Mix flour and salt; gradually add to creamed mixture. Beat until smooth.
3. Transfer to a greased 9x5-in. loaf pan. Push apple slices vertically into batter, placing them close together.
4. Bake 1½ to 1¾ hours or until a toothpick inserted near the center comes out clean. Cool 10 minutes before removing from pan to a wire rack. Serve warm.

⑤ INGREDIENTS
ROOT BEER FLOAT PIE

This is the kind of recipe your kids will look back on and always remember. And the only appliance you need is the refrigerator.
—**CINDY REAMS** PHILIPSBURG, PA

PREP: 15 MIN. + CHILLING • **MAKES:** 8 SERVINGS

 1 **carton (8 ounces) frozen reduced-fat whipped topping, thawed, divided**
 ¾ **cup cold diet root beer**
 ½ **cup fat-free milk**
 1 **package (1 ounce) sugar-free instant vanilla pudding mix**
 1 **graham cracker crust (9 inches)**
    Maraschino cherries, optional

1. Set aside and refrigerate ½ cup whipped topping for garnish. In a large bowl, whisk the root beer, milk and pudding mix 2 minutes. Fold in half of the remaining whipped topping. Spread into graham cracker crust.
2. Spread remaining whipped topping over pie. Refrigerate at least 8 hours or overnight.
3. Dollop reserved whipped topping over each serving and, if desired, top with a maraschino cherry.

STICKY TOFFEE PUDDING WITH BUTTERSCOTCH SAUCE

The classic sticky toffee pudding is a traditional dessert in Britain. With this recipe, you don't have to travel to England to enjoy the cake and its rich butterscotch sauce.

—AGNES WARD STRATFORD, ON

PREP: 30 MIN. + COOLING • **BAKE:** 30 MIN.
MAKES: 15 SERVINGS (2½ CUPS SAUCE)

- 2 **cups coarsely chopped pitted dates (about 12 ounces)**
- 2½ **cups water**
- 2 **teaspoons baking soda**
- 1⅔ **cups sugar**
- ½ **cup butter, softened**
- 4 **eggs**
- 2 **teaspoons vanilla extract**
- 3¼ **cups all-purpose flour**
- 2 **teaspoons baking powder**

BUTTERSCOTCH SAUCE

- 7 **tablespoons butter, cubed**
- 2¼ **cups packed brown sugar**
- 1 **cup half-and-half cream**
- 1 **tablespoon brandy**
- ¼ **teaspoon vanilla extract**
  Whipped cream, optional

1. In a small saucepan, mix dates and water; bring to a boil. Remove from heat; stir in baking soda. Cool to lukewarm.
2. Preheat oven to 350°. In a large bowl, cream sugar and butter until light and fluffy. Add eggs, one at a time, beating well after each addition. Beat in vanilla. In another bowl, mix flour and baking powder; gradually add to creamed mixture. Stir in date mixture.
3. Transfer to a greased 13x9-in. baking pan. Bake 30-40 minutes or until a toothpick inserted in center comes out clean. Cool slightly in pan on a wire rack.
4. Meanwhile, in a small saucepan, melt butter; add brown sugar and cream. Bring to a boil over medium heat, stirring constantly. Remove from heat. Stir in brandy and vanilla. Serve sauce warm with the warm cake. If desired, top with whipped cream.

MAPLE-NUT CHEESECAKE

To vary this delicious cheesecake, add cherries to the top, or swirl raspberry jam throughout before it's baked.

—WENDY PAFFENROTH PINE ISLAND, NY

PREP: 45 MIN. • **BAKE:** 45 MIN. + CHILLING • **MAKES:** 12 SERVINGS

- ¾ **cup graham cracker crumbs**
- ½ **cup finely chopped walnuts**
- 3 **tablespoons sugar**
- ¼ **cup butter, melted**

FILLING

- 4 **packages (8 ounces each) cream cheese, softened**
- ¾ **cup sugar**
- 2 **teaspoons maple flavoring**
- ½ **teaspoon almond extract**
- ⅛ **teaspoon grated lemon peel**
- 3 **eggs, lightly beaten**
  Melted chocolate, optional

1. Preheat oven to 325°. Place a greased 9-in. springform pan on a double thickness of heavy-duty foil (about 18 in. square). Wrap foil securely around pan.
2. In a small bowl, mix the cracker crumbs, walnuts and sugar; stir in butter. Press onto bottom and 1 in. up sides of prepared pan. Place pan on a baking sheet. Bake 10 minutes. Cool on a wire rack.
3. For filling, in a large bowl, beat cream cheese and sugar until smooth. Beat in the maple flavoring, extract and lemon peel. Add eggs; beat on low speed just until blended. Pour into crust. Place springform pan in a larger baking pan; add 1 in. of hot water to larger pan.
4. Bake 45-55 minutes or until center is just set and top appears dull. Remove springform pan from water bath. Cool cheesecake on a wire rack 10 minutes. Loosen sides from pan with a knife; remove foil. Cool 1 hour longer. Refrigerate overnight.
5. Remove rim from pan. If desired, drizzle cheesecake with melted chocolate.

BLUEBERRY COBBLER

With a buttery biscuit topping and warm, thick blueberry filling, this home-style cobbler sure doesn't taste light—but I'm glad it is.
—**MARY RELYEA** CANASTOTA, NY

PREP: 20 MIN. • **BAKE:** 30 MIN. • **MAKES:** 8 SERVINGS

    4 **cups fresh or frozen blueberries, thawed**
    ¾ **cup sugar, divided**
    3 **tablespoons cornstarch**
    2 **tablespoons lemon juice**
    ¼ **teaspoon ground cinnamon**
    ⅛ **teaspoon ground nutmeg**
    1 **cup all-purpose flour**
    2 **teaspoons grated lemon peel**
    ¾ **teaspoon baking powder**
    ¼ **teaspoon salt**
    ¼ **teaspoon baking soda**
    3 **tablespoons cold butter**
    ¾ **cup buttermilk**

1. Preheat oven to 375°. In a large bowl, combine the blueberries, ½ cup sugar, cornstarch, lemon juice, cinnamon and nutmeg. Transfer to a 2-qt. baking dish coated with cooking spray.

2. In a small bowl, combine the flour, lemon peel, baking powder, salt, baking soda and remaining sugar; cut in butter until the mixture resembles coarse crumbs. Stir in the buttermilk just until moistened. Drop by tablespoonfuls onto blueberry mixture.

3. Bake, uncovered, 30-35 minutes or until golden brown. Serve warm.

CHOCOLATE CHUNK PECAN PIE

Our family hosts an annual barn party for our close friends, complete with a pie bake-off. A few years ago, this was the recipe that won first prize!
—**JANICE SCHNEIDER** KANSAS CITY, MO

PREP: 35 MIN. + CHILLING • **BAKE:** 55 MIN. + CHILLING
MAKES: 10 SERVINGS

    1¼ **cups all-purpose flour**
    ⅛ **teaspoon salt**
    1 **package (3 ounces) cold cream cheese, cubed**
    ¼ **cup cold butter, cubed**
    2 **to 3 tablespoons ice water**
FILLING
    ⅓ **cup sugar**
    3 **tablespoons butter**
    2 **cups coarsely chopped semisweet chocolate, divided**
    4 **eggs**
    1 **cup dark corn syrup**
    2 **teaspoons vanilla extract**
       Dash salt
    2½ **cups pecan halves, toasted**

1. In a small bowl, mix flour and salt; cut in cream cheese and butter until crumbly. Gradually add ice water, tossing with a fork until dough holds together when pressed. Shape into a disk; wrap in plastic wrap. Refrigerate 30 minutes or overnight.

2. On a lightly floured surface, roll dough to a ⅛-in.-thick circle; transfer to a 9-in. pie plate. Trim the pastry to ½ in. beyond rim of plate; flute edge. Refrigerate while making filling.

3. Preheat oven to 350°. In a small saucepan, combine sugar, butter and 1 cup chopped chocolate; stir over low heat until smooth. Cool slightly.

4. In a large bowl, whisk eggs, corn syrup, vanilla and salt until blended. Stir in chocolate mixture. Layer pecans and remaining chopped chocolate in pastry shell; pour chocolate mixture over top.

5. Bake 55-60 minutes or until set. Cool 1 hour on a wire rack. Refrigerate 2 hours or until cold.

NOTE *To toast nuts, spread in a 15x10x1-in. baking pan. Bake at 350° for 5-10 minutes or until lightly browned, stirring occasionally. Or, spread in a dry nonstick skillet and heat over low heat until lightly browned, stirring occasionally.*

> **TOP TIP**
> ### Freezing Blueberries
> Place fresh berries on a cookie sheet and put them in the freezer until frozen (about an hour and a half). Then place in freezer bags. The berries won't stick together, so you can pour out any portion you desire.
> —**JOHNNIE B.** BIRMINGHAM, AL

CHOCOLATE PEAR HAZELNUT TART

As a teenage foreign exchange student in the south of France, I was horribly homesick. Then my host family's grandmother arrived and asked if I'd like to help her bake a tart from scratch. I figured it would beat crying into my pillows, so I agreed. Miette, the grandmother, turned my trip around from bad to unforgettable and inspired a lifelong passion for baking. As soon as we started creating this nutty tart, a bond formed that needed no words. Weighing ingredients, roasting nuts, kneading dough... the art of baking transcends language.

—**LEXI MCKEOWN** LOS ANGELES, CA

PREP: 45 MIN. + CHILLING • **BAKE:** 30 MIN. + COOLING
MAKES: 12 SERVINGS

- 1¼ cups all-purpose flour
- ⅓ cup ground hazelnuts
- ¼ cup packed brown sugar
  Dash salt
- ½ cup cold butter, cubed
- 3 to 5 tablespoons ice water

FILLING
- 3 eggs, separated
- ⅓ cup butter, softened
- ⅓ cup packed brown sugar
- 2 tablespoons amaretto or ½ teaspoon almond extract
- 1 cup ground hazelnuts
- 2 tablespoons baking cocoa
- 6 canned pear halves, drained, sliced and patted dry
- 2 tablespoons honey, warmed
  Confectioners' sugar

1. In a small bowl, mix flour, hazelnuts, brown sugar and salt; cut in butter until crumbly. Gradually add ice water, tossing with a fork until dough holds together when pressed. Shape dough into a disk; wrap in plastic wrap. Refrigerate 30 minutes or overnight.

2. Place egg whites in a large bowl; let stand at room temperature 30 minutes. Preheat oven to 400°. On a lightly floured surface, roll dough to a ⅛-in.-thick circle; transfer to a 9-in. fluted tart pan with removable bottom. Trim pastry even with edge. Prick bottom of pastry with a fork. Refrigerate while preparing filling.

3. In a large bowl, cream butter and brown sugar until blended. Beat in egg yolks and amaretto. Beat in hazelnuts and cocoa.

4. With clean beaters, beat egg whites on medium speed until stiff peaks form. Fold a third of the egg whites into hazelnut mixture, then fold in remaining whites. Spread onto bottom of pastry shell. Arrange pears over top.

5. Bake on a lower oven rack 30-35 minutes or until the crust is golden brown. Brush pears with warm honey. Cool on a wire rack. If desired, dust with confectioners' sugar before serving.

CARAMEL APPLE CAKE

When I go to potlucks or family gatherings or on hunting and fishing trips with my husband and son, I bring this cake, which is one of my favorite desserts. The flavorful treat stays moist as long as it lasts, which isn't long!

—**MARILYN PARADIS** WOODBURN, OR

PREP: 30 MIN. • **BAKE:** 1½ HOURS + COOLING • **MAKES:** 16 SERVINGS

- 1½ cups canola oil
- 1½ cups sugar
- ½ cup packed brown sugar
- 3 eggs
- 3 cups all-purpose flour
- 2 teaspoons ground cinnamon
- 1 teaspoon baking soda
- ½ teaspoon salt
- ½ teaspoon ground nutmeg
- 3½ cups diced peeled apples
- 1 cup chopped walnuts
- 2 teaspoons vanilla extract

CARAMEL ICING
- ½ cup packed brown sugar
- ⅓ cup half-and-half cream
- ¼ cup butter, cubed
  Dash salt
- 1 cup confectioners' sugar
  Chopped walnuts, optional

1. Preheat oven to 325°. In a large bowl, combine the oil, sugars and eggs until well blended. Combine the flour, cinnamon, baking soda, salt and nutmeg; gradually add to creamed mixture until blended. Fold in the apples, walnuts and vanilla.

2. Pour into a greased and floured 10-in. fluted tube pan. Bake 1½ hours or until a toothpick inserted near the center comes out clean. Cool in pan 10 minutes before removing to a wire rack to cool completely.

In a small heavy saucepan over medium-low heat, cook and stir brown sugar, cream, butter and salt until sugar is dissolved. Transfer mixture to a small bowl; cool to room temperature. Beat in confectioners' sugar until smooth; drizzle over cake. If desired, sprinkle with walnuts.

MAPLE PEANUT BUTTER PIE

Maple nut goodies have been a favorite candy of mine since I was a child, and I think the flavors taste just as wonderful in a pie! This pie freezes well, too. Just remember to take it out to defrost 30 minutes before serving.
—**CRYSTAL SCHLUETER** NORTHGLENN, CO

PREP: 25 MIN. + CHILLING • **MAKES:** 8 SERVINGS

- 1½ cups crushed cream-filled maple sandwich cookies (about 12 cookies)
- 3 tablespoons butter, melted
- ⅓ cup hot fudge ice cream topping
- 1 package (8 ounces) cream cheese, softened
- 1 cup creamy peanut butter
- 1 teaspoon maple flavoring
- 1¼ cups confectioners' sugar
- 1 carton (8 ounces) frozen whipped topping, thawed
- 1 cup heavy whipping cream
- 2 tablespoons maple syrup
- ¼ cup chocolate-covered peanuts, coarsely chopped

1. In a small bowl, mix crushed cookies and butter. Press onto bottom and up sides of an ungreased 9-in. pie plate. Freeze 5 minutes.
2. In a microwave, warm fudge topping 5-10 seconds or until spreadable; spread over bottom and up sides of crust. In a large bowl, beat cream cheese, peanut butter and flavoring until blended. Gradually beat in confectioners' sugar; fold in whipped topping. Spoon into crust, spreading evenly. Refrigerate 4 hours or until set.
3. In a small bowl, beat cream until it begins to thicken. Add syrup; beat until stiff peaks form. Serve with pie; top with the chopped peanuts.

COCONUT RHUBARB DESSERT

What a treat! Sweetened rhubarb combines with crunchy pecans and flaked coconut, while a cake mix becomes a tender topping.
—**CONNIE KORGER** GREEN BAY, WI

PREP: 25 MIN. • **BAKE:** 25 MIN. • **MAKES:** 12 SERVINGS

- 4 cups sliced fresh or frozen rhubarb
- 1½ cups sugar
- 1½ cups water
- ⅛ teaspoon red food coloring, optional
- 1 package butter pecan cake mix (regular size)
- 1 cup flaked coconut
- ½ cup chopped pecans
- ½ cup butter, melted
  Vanilla ice cream, optional

1. Preheat oven to 350°. In a large saucepan, combine rhubarb, sugar, water and, if desired, food coloring. Cook over medium heat 8-10 minutes or until rhubarb is tender; cool slightly. Transfer to a greased 13x9-in. baking dish; sprinkle with cake mix. Top with coconut and pecans. Drizzle with butter.
2. Bake 25-30 minutes or until a toothpick inserted near the center comes out clean. If desired, serve with ice cream.

BAKED APPLE DUMPLINGS

These versatile dumplings can be made with peaches or mixed berries in place of apples, and drizzled with hot caramel sauce instead of icing. Add vanilla custard or ice cream, and they are the perfect dessert.
—**EVANGELINE BRADFORD** ERLANGER, KY

PREP: 35 MIN. • **BAKE:** 15 MIN. • **MAKES:** 1½ DOZEN

- ½ cup sugar
- 3 tablespoons dry bread crumbs
- 4½ teaspoons ground cinnamon
  Dash ground nutmeg
- 1 package (17.3 ounces) frozen puff pastry, thawed
- 1 egg, beaten
- 2¼ cups chopped peeled tart apples

STREUSEL
- ⅓ cup chopped pecans, toasted
- ⅓ cup packed brown sugar
- ⅓ cup all-purpose flour
- 2 tablespoons plus 1½ teaspoons butter, melted

ICING
- 1 cup confectioners' sugar
- 2 tablespoons 2% milk
- 1 teaspoon vanilla extract

1. Preheat oven to 400°. In a small bowl, combine the sugar, bread crumbs, cinnamon and nutmeg. On a lightly floured surface, roll pastry into two 12-in. squares. Cut each sheet into nine 4-in. squares.
2. Brush squares with egg. Place 1 teaspoon sugar mixture in the center of a square; top with 2 tablespoons chopped apple and 1 teaspoon sugar mixture. Gently bring up corners of pastry to center; pinch edges to seal. Repeat with the remaining pastry, crumb mixture and apples. Place on greased baking sheets.
3. In a small bowl, combine streusel ingredients. Brush remaining egg over dumplings; press streusel over tops.
4. Bake 14-18 minutes or until golden brown. Place pans on wire racks. Mix icing ingredients; drizzle over dumplings.

PISTACHIO PUDDING CAKE

This recipe's been under lock and key for years in our family. It perfect for St. Patrick's Day, and you won't need the luck of the Irish to whip it up!
—**SUZANNE WINKHART** BOLIVAR, OH

PREP: 20 MIN. • **BAKE:** 40 MIN. + COOLING • **MAKES:** 12 SERVINGS

- 1 package yellow cake mix (regular size)
- 1 package (3.4 ounces) instant pistachio pudding mix
- 4 eggs
- 1 cup club soda
- ½ cup canola oil
- ½ cup chopped walnuts

ICING
- 1 cup cold heavy whipping cream
- ¾ cup cold 2% milk
- 1 package (3.4 ounces) instant pistachio pudding mix
- 2 teaspoons confectioners' sugar
- ½ cup chopped walnuts

1. Preheat oven to 350°. In a large bowl, combine the cake mix, pudding mix, eggs, soda and oil; beat on low speed 30 seconds. Beat on medium 2 minutes. Stir in walnuts.
2. Pour into a greased and floured 10-in. fluted tube pan. Bake 40-45 minutes or until a toothpick inserted near the center comes out clean. Cool 10 minutes before removing from pan to a wire rack to cool completely.
3. In a large bowl, beat the cream, milk, pudding mix and confectioners' sugar on high until stiff peaks form. Frost cake. Sprinkle with walnuts. Store in the refrigerator.

...ERINGUE ...KE

...ngel food cake that
...g to a special Easter
... curd filling and
...ringue topping complement the
soft and airy texture.

—SHARON KURTZ EMMAUS, PA

PREP: 40 MIN. + STANDING
BAKE: 35 MIN. + COOLING
MAKES: 14 SERVINGS

- 12 **egg whites**
- 1½ **cups sugar, divided**
- 1 **cup cake flour**
- 2 **teaspoons cream of tartar**
- 1½ **teaspoons vanilla extract**
- ¼ **teaspoon salt**
- 1 **jar (10 ounces) lemon curd**

MERINGUE TOPPING
- 4 **egg whites**
- ¾ **teaspoon cream of tartar**
- ½ **cup sugar**

1. Place egg whites in a large bowl; let stand at room temperature for 30 minutes. Sift ½ cup sugar and flour together twice; set aside.

2. Preheat oven to 350°. Add cream of tartar, vanilla and salt to egg whites; beat on medium speed until soft peaks form. Gradually beat in the remaining sugar, 2 tablespoons at a time, on high until stiff glossy peaks form and sugar is dissolved. Gradually fold in the flour mixture, about ½ cup at a time.

3. Gently spoon the batter into an ungreased 10-in. tube pan. Cut through batter with a knife to remove air pockets. Bake on lowest oven rack 35-40 minutes or until the cake is golden brown and the entire top appears dry. Immediately invert pan; cool completely, about 1 hour.

4. Run a knife around side and center tube of pan. Remove cake; split into two horizontal layers. Place cake bottom on an ovenproof plate. Spread with lemon curd; replace cake top.

5. For meringue, in a small bowl, beat egg whites and cream of tartar on medium until soft peaks form. Gradually beat in sugar, 1 tablespoon at a time, on high until stiff glossy peaks form and sugar is dissolved. Spread over top and sides of cake. Bake at 350° 15-18 minutes or until golden brown. Refrigerate leftovers.

COCONUT-PECAN GERMAN CHOCOLATE PIE

This pie combines the ingredients everyone loves in its classic cake cousin. It's so silky and smooth, you won't be able to put your fork down.

—**ANNA JONES** COPPELL, TX

PREP: 50 MIN. + CHILLING
BAKE: 35 MIN. + CHILLING
MAKES: 8 SERVINGS

- 1¼ cups all-purpose flour
- ¼ teaspoon salt
- 6 tablespoons cold lard
- 3 to 4 tablespoons ice water

FILLING
- 4 ounces German sweet chocolate, chopped
- 2 ounces unsweetened chocolate, chopped
- 1 can (14 ounces) sweetened condensed milk
- 4 egg yolks
- 1 teaspoon vanilla extract
- 1 cup chopped pecans

TOPPING
- ½ cup packed brown sugar
- ½ cup heavy whipping cream
- ¼ cup butter, cubed
- 2 egg yolks
- 1 cup flaked coconut
- 1 teaspoon vanilla extract
- ¼ cup chopped pecans

1. In a small bowl, mix flour and salt; cut in lard until crumbly. Gradually add ice water, tossing with a fork until dough holds together when pressed.

Shape into a disk; wrap in plastic wrap. Refrigerate 30 minutes or overnight.
2. Preheat oven to 400°. On a lightly floured surface, roll the dough to a ⅛-in.-thick circle; transfer to a 9-in. pie plate. Trim pastry to ½ in. beyond rim of plate; flute edge. Line unpricked pastry with a double thickness of foil. Fill with pie weights, dried beans or uncooked rice.
3. Bake 11-13 minutes or until bottom is lightly browned. Remove foil and weights; bake 6-8 minutes longer or until light brown. Cool on a wire rack. Reduce oven setting to 350°.
4. In a microwave, melt chocolates in a large bowl; stir until smooth. Cool slightly. Whisk in milk, egg yolks and vanilla; stir in pecans. Pour into crust. Bake 16-19 minutes or until set. Cool 1 hour on a wire rack.
5. Meanwhile, in a small heavy saucepan, combine the brown sugar, cream and butter. Bring to a boil over medium heat, stirring to dissolve sugar. Remove from heat.
6. In a small bowl, whisk a small amount of hot mixture into egg yolks; return all to pan, whisking constantly. Cook 2-3 minutes or until mixture thickens and a thermometer reads 160°, stirring constantly. Remove from heat. Stir in coconut and vanilla; cool 10 minutes.
7. Pour over the filling; sprinkle with the pecans. Refrigerate the pie 4 hours or until cold.

MINT BROWNIE CUPCAKES

Is it a brownie or is it a cupcake? There's no wrong answer to this question, I tell my first-grade students. I found the recipe when I began teaching more than 30 years ago. My husband and children like this treat, too.

—**CAROL MAERTZ** SPRUCE GROVE, AB

PREP: 25 MIN. • **BAKE:** 15 MIN. + CHILLING
MAKES: 10 CUPCAKES

- ½ cup mint chocolate chips
- ½ cup butter, cubed
- ½ cup sugar
- 2 eggs
- ½ cup all-purpose flour

TOPPING
- 2 cups miniature marshmallows
- ⅓ cup 2% milk
- ½ teaspoon peppermint extract
  Green or red food coloring, optional
- ¾ cup heavy whipping cream, whipped
  Additional chocolate chips, optional

1. Preheat oven to 350°. In a large microwave-safe bowl, melt chips and butter; stir until smooth. Cool slightly; stir in sugar and eggs. Gradually stir flour into chocolate mixture until smooth.
2. Fill paper-lined muffin cups two-thirds full. Bake 15-20 minutes or until a toothpick inserted near the center comes out clean. Remove from pan to a wire rack to cool.
3. In a large saucepan, cook and stir marshmallows and milk over low heat until smooth. Remove from heat; stir in extract and, if desired, food coloring.
4. Transfer to a bowl; refrigerate for 15 minutes or until cooled. Fold in whipped cream. Spread over the cupcakes. Refrigerate at least 1 hour. Sprinkle with additional chocolate chips if desired. Store in refrigerator.
NOTE *If mint chocolate chips are not available, place 2 cups (12 ounces) semisweet chocolate chips and ¼ teaspoon peppermint extract in a plastic bag; seal and toss to coat. Allow chips to stand 24-48 hours.*

BANANAS & CREAM POUND CAKE

This dessert got me a date with my future husband. At a church event, he loved it so much, he asked for another piece. The rest, as they say, is history!

—COURTNEY MECKLEY CARTERSVILLE, GA

PREP: 20 MIN. • **BAKE:** 40 MIN. + CHILLING • **MAKES:** 15 SERVINGS

- ½ cup butter, softened
- 1½ cups sugar
- 3 eggs
- 1 teaspoon vanilla extract
- 1½ cups all-purpose flour
- ¼ teaspoon salt
- ⅛ teaspoon baking soda
- ½ cup buttermilk

LAYERS

- 2 cups 2% milk
- 1 package (3.4 ounces) instant French vanilla pudding mix
- 1 package (8 ounces) cream cheese, softened
- ½ cup sweetened condensed milk
- 1 package (12 ounces) frozen whipped topping, thawed, divided
- 5 medium ripe bananas

1. Preheat oven to 325°. In a large bowl, cream butter and sugar until light and fluffy. Add eggs, one at a time, beating well after each addition. Beat in vanilla. In another bowl, mix the flour, salt and baking soda; add to the creamed mixture alternately with buttermilk, beating after each addition just until combined.

2. Transfer to a greased and floured 9x5-in. loaf pan. Bake 40-45 minutes or until a toothpick inserted in center comes out clean. Cool in pan 10 minutes before removing to a wire rack to cool completely.

3. In a small bowl, whisk the milk and pudding mix for 2 minutes. Let stand 2 minutes. Meanwhile, in a large bowl, beat cream cheese and condensed milk until smooth; fold in pudding. Fold in 3½ cups whipped topping.

4. Cut cake into eight slices; arrange on the bottom of an ungreased 13x9-in. dish, trimming to fit as necessary. Slice bananas; arrange over cake. Spread pudding mixture over top. Cover and refrigerate 3 hours. Serve with remaining whipped topping.

CHOCOLATE COOKIE CHEESECAKE

Both cheesecake lovers and chocolate fans go wild when I present this rich dessert sprinkled with cream-filled cookies.

—LISA M VARNER EL PASO, TX

PREP: 30 MIN. • **BAKE:** 50 MIN. + CHILLING • **MAKES:** 12 SERVINGS

- 1½ cups cream-filled chocolate sandwich cookie crumbs (about 16 cookies)
- 3 tablespoons butter, melted
- 4 packages (8 ounces each) cream cheese, softened
- 1 cup sugar
- 1½ cups semisweet chocolate chips, melted and cooled
- 3 teaspoons vanilla extract
- 4 eggs, lightly beaten
- 20 chocolate cream-filled chocolate sandwich cookies, coarsely chopped

1. In a small bowl, combine cookie crumbs and butter. Press onto bottom of a greased 9-in. springform pan. Refrigerate crust while preparing filling.

2. Preheat oven to 325°. In a large bowl, beat cream cheese and sugar until smooth. Beat in chocolate and vanilla. Add eggs; beat on low speed just until combined. Fold in half the chopped cookies. Pour over crust. Sprinkle with remaining cookies. Place pan on a baking sheet.

3. Bake 50-60 minutes or until center is almost set and top appears dull. Cool on a wire rack 10 minutes. Carefully run a knife around edge of pan to loosen; cool 1 hour longer. Refrigerate overnight. Remove side of pan.

❝I made this once for a party and one asked, 'Did you get this from Cheesecake Factory?'❞

—YM_RODRIGUEZ TASTEOFHOME.COM

CRANBERRY-ORANGE TRIFLE

I make this showstopper for many occasions, slightly changing or adding ingredients. I sometimes add toasted coconut.

—RAYMONDE BOURGEOIS SWASTIKA, ON

PREP: 45 MIN. • **COOK:** 15 MIN. + CHILLING
MAKES: 16 SERVINGS (1 CUP EACH)

- 2 packages (12 ounces each) fresh or frozen cranberries
- 1½ cups water
- 1⅓ cups sugar
- 2 teaspoons minced fresh gingerroot
- 4 teaspoons grated orange peel

CUSTARD
- 1 cup sugar
- 2 tablespoons cornstarch
- ¼ teaspoon salt
- 3 cups 2% milk
- 6 egg yolks
- 2 teaspoons vanilla extract

TRIFLE
- 1 loaf (16 ounces) frozen pound cake, thawed and cut into 1-inch cubes
- ¼ cup orange liqueur
- ½ cup slivered almonds, toasted
  Sweetened whipped cream and orange sections

1. In a large saucepan, combine the first five ingredients; bring to a boil, stirring to dissolve sugar. Reduce heat to medium; cook, uncovered, until the berries pop and the mixture is thickened, about 15 minutes. Remove from heat; cool completely.

2. For custard, in a large saucepan, mix sugar, cornstarch and salt. Whisk in milk. Cook and stir over medium-high heat until thickened and bubbly. Reduce heat to low; cook and stir 2 minutes longer. Remove from heat.

3. In a small bowl, whisk a small amount of hot milk mixture into egg yolks; return all to the pan, whisking constantly. Bring to a gentle boil; cook and stir 2 minutes. Immediately transfer to a clean bowl; stir in vanilla. Cool 30 minutes. Press waxed paper onto surface of filling; refrigerate until cold, about 1 hour.

4. To assemble, place half of the cake on the bottom of a 4-qt. trifle bowl or glass bowl; drizzle with 2 tablespoons orange liqueur. Layer with half of the cranberry mixture, ¼ cup almonds and half of the custard. Repeat layers. Refrigerate, covered, until serving. Top with the whipped cream and orange sections.

NOTE *To toast nuts, spread in a 15x10x1-in. baking pan. Bake at 350° for 5-10 minutes or until lightly browned, stirring occasionally. Or, spread in a dry nonstick skillet and heat over low heat until lightly browned, stirring occasionally.*

⑤ INGREDIENTS

APPLE-CINNAMON MINI PIES

One night while snacking on applesauce, I came up with the idea for these little pies with a simple, quick applesauce filling. What's better than a pie that you can hold in your hand to eat?

—KANDY BINGHAM GREEN RIVER, WY

PREP: 20 MIN. • **BAKE:** 15 MIN. • **MAKES:** 1 DOZEN

- 1 package (14.1 ounces) refrigerated pie pastry
- ½ cup chunky applesauce
- 3 teaspoons cinnamon sugar, divided
- 2 tablespoons butter, cut into 12 pieces
- 1 tablespoon 2% milk, divided

1. Preheat oven to 350°. On a lightly floured surface, unroll pastry sheets. Using a floured 3½-in. round cookie cutter, cut six circles from each sheet.

2. In a small bowl, mix applesauce with 1½ teaspoons cinnamon sugar. Place 2 teaspoons applesauce mixture on one half of each circle; dot with butter. Moisten pastry edges with some of the milk. Fold pastry over filling; press edges with a fork to seal.

3. Transfer to ungreased baking sheets. Brush tops with remaining milk; sprinkle with remaining cinnamon sugar. Bake 12-15 minutes or until golden brown. Remove from pans to wire racks. Serve warm or at room temperature.

BUTTERSCOTCH-PECAN BREAD PUDDING

Bread pudding fans are sure to love this rich and delectable version from the slow cooker. Complete each serving with whipped cream and butterscotch ice cream topping.
—LISA M VARNER EL PASO, TX

PREP: 15 MIN. • **COOK:** 3 HOURS • **MAKES:** 8 SERVINGS

- 9 cups cubed day-old white bread (about 8 slices)
- ½ cup chopped pecans
- ½ cup butterscotch chips
- 4 eggs
- 2 cups half-and-half cream
- ½ cup packed brown sugar
- ½ cup butter, melted
- 1 teaspoon vanilla extract
  Whipped cream and butterscotch ice cream topping

1. Place bread, pecans and butterscotch chips in a greased 4-qt. slow cooker. In a large bowl, whisk eggs, cream, brown sugar, melted butter and vanilla until blended. Pour over bread mixture; stir gently to combine.
2. Cook, covered, on low 3-4 hours or until a knife inserted in center comes out clean. Serve warm with whipped cream and butterscotch topping.

GRANDMA'S TANDY KAKE

My grandmother made this for all our family gatherings. Everyone loves it, and now I make it for every party we attend or host.
—JOHN MORGAN LEBANON, PA

PREP: 20 MIN. • **BAKE:** 20 MIN. + CHILLING • **MAKES:** 24 SERVINGS

- 4 eggs
- 2 cups sugar
- 1 cup 2% milk
- 1 teaspoon vanilla extract
- 2 cups all-purpose flour
- 1 teaspoon baking powder
- ¼ teaspoon salt
- 1¾ cups creamy peanut butter
- 5 milk chocolate candy bars (1.55 ounces each), chopped
- 2 tablespoons butter

1. Preheat oven to 350°. In a large bowl, beat eggs and sugar until thick and lemon-colored. Beat in milk and vanilla. In another bowl, combine flour, baking powder and salt; gradually add to egg mixture and mix well.
2. Spread into a greased 15x10x1-in. baking pan. Bake 20-25 minutes or until lightly browned. Cool 15 minutes on a wire rack. Spread peanut butter over top; cool completely.
3. In a double boiler or metal bowl over simmering water, melt chocolate and butter; stir until smooth. Gently spread over peanut butter. Refrigerate 30 minutes or until firm.

TRIPLE LAYER BROWNIE CAKE

A little of this rich brownie cake goes a long way, so you'll have plenty to share with grateful family members and friends. It's a sure way to satisfy a chocolate lover's craving.
—BARBARA DEAN LITTLETON, CO

PREP: 30 MIN. + CHILLING • **BAKE:** 25 MIN. + COOLING
MAKES: 16-20 SERVINGS

- 1½ cups butter
- 6 ounces unsweetened chocolate, chopped
- 3 cups sugar
- 5 eggs
- 1½ teaspoons vanilla extract
- 1½ cups all-purpose flour
- ¾ teaspoon salt

FROSTING
- 16 ounces semisweet chocolate, chopped
- 3 cups heavy whipping cream
- ½ cup sugar, optional
- 2 milk chocolate candy bars (1.55 ounces each), shaved

1. Preheat oven to 350°. In a large microwave-safe bowl, melt the butter and chocolate; stir until smooth. Stir in sugar. Add eggs, one at a time, beating well after each addition. Stir in vanilla, flour and salt.
2. Pour into three greased and floured 9-in. round baking pans. Bake 23-25 minutes or until a toothpick inserted near the center comes out clean. Cool 10 minutes; remove from pan to a wire rack to cool completely.
3. For frosting, melt chocolate in a heavy saucepan over medium heat. Gradually stir in cream and, if desired, sugar until well blended. Heat to a gentle boil; boil and stir for 1 minute. Remove from heat; transfer to a large bowl. Refrigerate 2-3 hours or until mixture reaches a puddinglike consistency, stirring a few times.
4. Beat until soft peaks form. Immediately spread between layers and over top and sides of cake. Sprinkle with shaved chocolate. Store in the refrigerator.

WHITE CHOCOLATE COCONUT CAKE

The white "snowball" look makes this cute cake the perfect choice for a Christmas celebration or other wintertime party.

—GRETA KIRBY CARTHAGE, TN

PREP: 25 MIN. + CHILLING • **BAKE:** 25 MIN. + COOLING
MAKES: 12 SERVINGS

- 1 package white cake mix (regular size)
- 1 cup water
- 1 can (15 ounces) cream of coconut, divided
- 3 egg whites
- 1 can (5 ounces) evaporated milk
- ⅔ cup white baking chips
- 2 ounces cream cheese, softened
- 1 cup heavy whipping cream, divided
- 3½ cups flaked coconut, divided
- 2 teaspoons vanilla extract, divided
- ¼ cup sugar

1. Preheat oven to 350°. In a large bowl, combine cake mix, water, ¾ cup cream of coconut and egg whites; beat on low speed 30 seconds. Beat on medium 2 minutes.

2. Pour into three greased and floured 9-in. round baking pans. Bake 22-26 minutes or until a toothpick inserted near the center comes out clean. Cool 10 minutes before removing from pans to wire racks to cool completely.

3. For filling, in a small saucepan, combine the evaporated milk, chips, cream cheese, 3 tablespoons heavy cream and remaining cream of coconut; cook and stir over low heat until chips are melted.

4. Remove from heat; stir in 1½ cups coconut and 1 teaspoon vanilla. Transfer to a large bowl. Cover and refrigerate until mixture reaches spreading consistency, stirring occasionally.

5. For frosting, in a large bowl, beat remaining cream until it begins to thicken. Add sugar and remaining vanilla; beat until stiff peaks form.

6. Place bottom cake layer on a serving plate; spread with half of the filling. Repeat layers. Top with remaining cake layer. Frost top and sides of cake; sprinkle with remaining coconut. Refrigerate leftovers.

GINGERED ALMOND TRUFFLE TART

Fresh ginger complements the chocolate truffle filling in this elegant, almost sinful tart. Small servings are best!

—JANICE ELDER CHARLOTTE, NC

PREP: 30 MIN. + CHILLING • **BAKE:** 15 MIN. + COOLING
MAKES: 16 SERVINGS

- 1 cup heavy whipping cream
- 2 tablespoons minced fresh gingerroot
- 1 cup all-purpose flour
- ½ cup chopped almonds
- ½ cup confectioners' sugar
- ⅓ cup baking cocoa
- 6 tablespoons cold butter, cubed
- ½ cup amaretto, divided
- 8 ounces bittersweet chocolate, chopped
- ½ cup butter, softened

1. Preheat oven to 350°. In a small heavy saucepan, heat cream and ginger until bubbles form around sides of pan. Remove from heat.

2. Place flour, almonds, confectioners' sugar and cocoa in a food processor; pulse until blended. Add cold butter; pulse until butter is the size of peas. While pulsing, add ¼ cup amaretto to form moist crumbs. Press onto bottom and up sides of an ungreased 9-in. fluted tart pan with removable bottom. Bake 13-16 minutes or until set. Cool on a wire rack.

3. Place chocolate in a small bowl. Bring gingered cream just to a boil. Strain through a fine-mesh strainer over chocolate; discard ginger. Stir chocolate mixture with a whisk until smooth; stir in softened butter and remaining amaretto until blended. Pour into cooled crust. Refrigerate, covered, at least 2 hours or until set.

FROZEN GRASSHOPPER PIE

When I first spread my cream pie wings, this seemed the right recipe for a house of chocolate lovers, and I guessed correctly. It's more of an adult New Year's Eve pie, but some have made it for Christmas dessert. However, you should serve it after the kids have gone to bed!

—LORRAINE CALAND SHUNIAH, ON

PREP: 20 MIN. + CHILLING • **COOK:** 15 MIN. + FREEZING
MAKES: 8 SERVINGS

1¼ cups chocolate wafer crumbs (about 22 wafers)
¼ cup sugar
¼ cup butter, melted
FILLING
1 package (10 ounces) miniature marshmallows
⅓ cup 2% milk
¼ cup creme de menthe
2 tablespoons creme de cacao
¼ teaspoon peppermint extract, optional
2 cups heavy whipping cream
Maraschino cherries and additional whipped cream, optional

1. In a small bowl, mix wafer crumbs and sugar; stir in the butter. Press onto bottom and up sides of a greased 9-in. pie plate. Refrigerate 30 minutes.
2. Meanwhile, in a large saucepan, combine marshmallows and milk; cook and stir over medium-low heat 12-14 minutes or until mixture is smooth. Remove from heat. Cool to room temperature, stirring occasionally. Stir in liqueurs and, if desired, extract.
3. In a large bowl, beat cream until soft peaks form; fold in marshmallow mixture. Transfer to the crust. Freeze 6 hours or until firm. If desired, top with cherries and additional whipped cream just before serving.

LEMON SUPREME PIE

The combination of the cream cheese topping and tart lemon filling is wonderful.

—JANA BECKMAN WAMEGO, KS

PREP: 25 MIN. + CHILLING • **BAKE:** 15 MIN. + CHILLING
MAKES: 6-8 SERVINGS

Frozen deep-dish pie shell
LEMON FILLING
1¼ cups sugar, divided
6 tablespoons cornstarch
½ teaspoon salt
1¼ cups water
2 tablespoons butter
2 teaspoons grated lemon peel
4 to 5 drops yellow food coloring, optional
½ cup lemon juice
CREAM CHEESE FILLING
2 packages (one 8 ounces, one 3 ounces) cream cheese, softened
¾ cup confectioners' sugar
1½ cups whipped topping
1 tablespoon lemon juice

1. Preheat oven to 450°. Line unpricked pie shell with a double thickness of heavy-duty foil. Bake 8 minutes. Remove foil; bake 5 minutes longer. Cool on a wire rack.
2. For lemon filling, combine ¾ cup sugar, cornstarch and salt. Stir in water until smooth. Bring to a boil over medium-high heat. Reduce heat; add the remaining sugar. Cook and stir 2 minutes or until thickened and bubbly. Remove from heat; stir in butter, lemon peel and, if desired, food coloring. Gently stir in lemon juice. Cool to room temperature, about 1 hour.
3. For cream cheese filling, beat the cream cheese and sugar in a large bowl until smooth. Fold in whipped topping and lemon juice. Refrigerate ½ cup for garnish. Spread the remaining cream cheese mixture into pie shell; top with lemon filling. Refrigerate overnight.
4. Place reserved cream cheese mixture in a pastry bag with a #21 star tip; pipe stars onto pie. Store in the refrigerator.

HONEY NUT & CREAM CHEESE BAKLAVA

I love serving desserts that look as if you spent hours in the kitchen when, in reality, they're actually quite easy to make. This is one of those recipes; it takes only half an hour of hands-on time.

—CHERYL SNAVELY HAGERSTOWN, MD

PREP: 30 MIN. • **BAKE:** 35 MIN. + COOLING
MAKES: 3 DOZEN

Butter-flavored cooking spray
½ cup spreadable honey nut cream cheese
1¼ cups sugar, divided
3 cups chopped walnuts
1 package (16 ounces, 14x9-inch sheets) frozen phyllo dough, thawed
1 cup water
½ cup honey

1. Preheat oven to 350°. Coat a 13x9-in. baking pan with cooking spray. In a large bowl, mix the cream cheese and ¼ cup sugar until blended. Stir in walnuts.

2. Unroll phyllo dough; trim to fit into pan. Layer 20 sheets of phyllo in prepared pan, spritzing each with cooking spray. Keep remaining phyllo covered with plastic wrap and a damp towel to prevent it from drying out.

3. Spread with half of the walnut mixture. Layer with five more phyllo sheets, spritzing each with cooking spray. Spread the remaining walnut mixture over phyllo. Top with the remaining phyllo sheets, spritzing each with cooking spray.

4. Cut into 1½-in. diamonds. Bake 35-40 minutes or until golden brown. Meanwhile, in a saucepan, bring water, honey and remaining sugar to a boil, stirring to dissolve sugar. Reduce heat; simmer, uncovered, 10 minutes. Pour over warm baklava.

5. Cool baklava completely in pan on a wire rack. Cover and refrigerate until serving.

MANGO PIE WITH COCONUT CRUST

This was the first pie I created myself. Mangoes are one of my favorite fruits, and they deserve to be represented in a pie. Of course, everything is better with coconut.

—JENNIFER WORRELL NILES, IL

PREP: 50 MIN. + CHILLING
BAKE: 45 MIN. + COOLING
MAKES: 8 SERVINGS

2½ cups all-purpose flour
½ teaspoon salt
⅔ cup cold butter, cubed
⅔ to ¾ cup ice water
5 cups sliced peeled mangoes (about 4 large)
2 tablespoons dark rum or orange juice
⅓ cup sugar
2 tablespoons quick-cooking tapioca
¾ teaspoon ground ginger
¼ teaspoon ground cardamom
Dash white pepper
⅛ teaspoon salt
⅓ cup flaked coconut, toasted

1. In a large bowl, mix flour and salt; cut in butter until crumbly. Gradually add ice water, tossing with a fork until dough holds together when pressed. Divide dough in half. Shape each into a disk; wrap in plastic wrap. Refrigerate 30 minutes or overnight.

2. Preheat oven to 400°. In a large bowl, toss mangoes with rum. In a small bowl, mix sugar, tapioca, spices and salt. Gently stir into fruit mixture; let stand 15 minutes.

3. Sprinkle the coconut on a lightly floured surface. Place one half of dough on coconut; roll dough to a ⅛-in.-thick circle. Transfer to a 9-in. pie plate, coconut side down. Trim pastry even with rim. Add filling.

4. Roll remaining dough to a ⅛-in.-thick circle; cut into ½-in.-wide strips. Arrange over filling in a lattice pattern. Trim and seal strips to edge of bottom pastry; flute edge.

5. Bake 45-50 minutes or until crust is golden brown and filling is bubbly. Cover edge loosely with foil during the last 15 minutes if needed to prevent overbrowning. Remove foil. Cool on a wire rack.

NOTE *To toast coconut, spread in a 15x10x1-in. baking pan. Bake at 350° for 5-10 minutes or until golden brown, stirring frequently.*

CARAMEL APPLE CUPCAKES

Take these extra-special cupcakes to your next event and watch how quickly they disappear! Kids will go for the fun appearance and tasty toppings, while adults will appreciate the tender spiced cake underneath.

—DIANE HALFERTY CORPUS CHRISTI, TX

PREP: 25 MIN. • **BAKE:** 20 MIN. + COOLING
MAKES: 1 DOZEN

- 1 package spice or carrot cake mix (regular size)
- 2 cups chopped peeled tart apples
- 20 caramels
- 3 tablespoons 2% milk
- 1 cup finely chopped pecans, toasted
- 12 wooden pop sticks

1. Preheat oven to 350°. Prepare cake batter according to package directions; fold in apples.

2. Fill 12 greased or paper-lined jumbo muffin cups three-fourths full. Bake 20 minutes or until a toothpick inserted near center comes out clean. Cool 10 minutes before removing from pans to wire racks to cool completely.

3. In a small saucepan, cook caramels and milk over low heat until smooth. Spread over cupcakes. Sprinkle with pecans. Insert a wooden stick into the center of each cupcake.

TOP TIP

Chopping Before or After Measuring

Chopping an ingredient before or after measuring it can make a difference in the outcome of the recipe. Here's a tip to help you decide when to do your chopping. If the word "chopped" comes before the ingredient when listed in a recipe, then chop the ingredient before measuring. If the word "chopped" comes after the ingredient, then chop after measuring.

CRANBERRY-ORANGE CRUMB TART

After my sister took the family to the local cranberry festival, my mom bet me that I couldn't make a holiday pie out of cranberries and oranges. Considering that the pie was gone before the holidays arrived, I think I won!

—**HEATHER CUNNINGHAM** WHITMAN, MA

PREP: 35 MIN. + STANDING • **BAKE:** 10 MIN. + COOLING
MAKES: 12 SERVINGS

- 2 **cups crushed cinnamon graham crackers (about 14 whole crackers), divided**
- ½ **cup sugar, divided**
- 6 **tablespoons butter, melted**

TOPPING
- ¼ **cup all-purpose flour**
- ¼ **cup packed brown sugar**
- ¼ **cup cold butter, cubed**

FILLING
- 1 **large navel orange**
- 1 **cup sugar**
- 3 **tablespoons quick-cooking tapioca**
- ¼ **teaspoon baking soda**
- ¼ **teaspoon ground cinnamon**
- ⅛ **teaspoon ground allspice**
- 4 **cups fresh or frozen cranberries, thawed**
- 2 **tablespoons brandy or cranberry juice**

1. Preheat oven to 375°. In a small bowl, mix 1¾ cups crushed crackers and ¼ cup sugar; stir in melted butter. Press onto bottom and up sides of an ungreased 11-in. fluted tart pan with removable bottom. Bake 7-8 minutes or until edges are lightly browned. Cool on a wire rack.

2. For topping, in a small bowl, mix flour, brown sugar, and remaining crushed crackers and sugar; cut in cold butter until crumbly. Refrigerate while preparing filling.

3. Finely grate enough orange peel to measure 1 tablespoon. Cut a thin slice from top and bottom of orange; stand orange upright on a cutting board. Cut off peel and outer membrane, starting from the top. Holding orange over a bowl to catch juices, remove orange sections by cutting along membrane. Squeeze membrane to reserve additional juice.

4. In a large saucepan, mix sugar, tapioca, baking soda, cinnamon and allspice. Add cranberries, brandy, grated peel and reserved juice; toss to coat. Let stand 15 minutes. Preheat oven to 425°.

5. Bring cranberry mixture to a full boil, stirring constantly. Add orange sections; heat through. Pour into crust; sprinkle with topping. Bake 10-15 minutes or until topping is golden brown. Cool on a wire rack.

RASPBERRY SWIRL CUPCAKES

When I was a teenager growing up on a farm and practicing my baking skills, I turned to this cupcake recipe time and again.

—**CHRISTINE SOHM** NEWTON, ON

PREP: 20 MIN. • **BAKE:** 20 MIN. + COOLING • **MAKES:** 2 DOZEN

- 1 **package white cake mix (regular size)**
- ¼ **cup raspberry pie filling**
- ½ **cup shortening**
- ⅓ **cup 2% milk**
- 1 **teaspoon vanilla extract**
- ¼ **teaspoon salt**
- 3 **cups confectioners' sugar**
  Fresh raspberries and decorative sprinkles, optional

1. Preheat oven to 350°. Prepare cake batter mix according to package directions for cupcakes. Fill paper-lined muffin cups two-thirds full. Drop ½ teaspoon of pie filling in the center of each; cut through batter with a knife to swirl.

2. Bake 20-25 minutes or until a toothpick inserted near center comes out clean. Cool 10 minutes before removing from pans to wire racks to cool completely.

3. In a large bowl, beat shortening until fluffy. Add the milk, vanilla, salt; gradually add confectioners' sugar; beat until smooth. Frost cupcakes. If desired, garnish with raspberries and sprinkles.

PUMPKIN CAKE ROLL

You'll feel smart to keep this one in the freezer for a quick dessert for family or unexpected guests, to take to a gathering or to give as a yummy gift.

—ERICA BERCHTOLD FREEPORT, IL

PREP: 30 MIN. • **BAKE:** 15 MIN. + FREEZING • **MAKES:** 10 SERVINGS

- 3 **eggs, separated**
- 1 **cup sugar, divided**
- ⅔ **cup canned pumpkin**
- ¾ **cup all-purpose flour**
- 1 **teaspoon baking soda**
- ½ **teaspoon ground cinnamon**
- ⅛ **teaspoon salt**

FILLING

- 1 **package (8 ounces) cream cheese, softened**
- 2 **tablespoons butter, softened**
- 1 **cup confectioners' sugar**
- ¾ **teaspoon vanilla extract**

   Additional confectioners' sugar, optional

1. Preheat oven to 375°. Line a 15x10x1-in. baking pan with waxed paper; grease the paper and set aside. In a large bowl, beat egg yolks on high speed until thick and lemon-colored. Gradually add ½ cup sugar and the pumpkin, beating on high until sugar is almost dissolved.

2. In a small bowl, beat egg whites until soft peaks form. Gradually add remaining sugar, beating until stiff peaks form. Fold into egg yolk mixture. Combine flour, baking soda, cinnamon and salt; gently fold into pumpkin mixture. Spread into prepared pan.

3. Bake 12-15 minutes or until cake springs back when lightly touched. Cool 5 minutes. Turn cake onto a kitchen towel dusted with confectioners' sugar. Gently peel off waxed paper. Roll up cake in the towel jelly-roll style, starting with a short side. Cool completely on a wire rack.

4. In a small bowl, beat cream cheese, butter, confectioners' sugar and vanilla until smooth. Unroll cake; spread filling evenly to within ½ in. of edges. Roll up again. Cover and freeze until firm. May be frozen up to 3 months. Remove from the freezer 15 minutes before cutting. If desired, dust with confectioners' sugar.

CHOCOLATE & PEANUT BUTTER PUDDING PIE WITH BANANAS

I created this pie in tribute to Elvis, who was my favorite entertainer, and to Hershey, Pennsylvania, my hometown.

—PENNY HAWKINS MEBANE, NC

PREP: 25 MIN. + CHILLING • **BAKE:** 10 MIN. • **MAKES:** 8 SERVINGS

- 1 **cup chocolate wafer crumbs (about 20 wafers)**
- ¼ **cup butter, melted**
- 2 **medium firm bananas**
- ¾ **cup creamy peanut butter**
- 2 **ounces semisweet chocolate, chopped**
- 2 **cups cold 2% milk**
- 2 **packages (3.4 ounces each) instant vanilla pudding mix**
- 2 **cups whipped topping, divided**
- 2 **tablespoons chopped salted peanuts**

   Peanut butter cups, optional

1. Preheat oven to 350°. In a small bowl, mix wafer crumbs and butter; press onto the bottom and up the sides of an ungreased 9-in. pie plate. Bake 8-10 minutes or until set. Cool completely on a wire rack.

2. Slice bananas; arrange on bottom of crust. In a microwave-safe bowl, combine peanut butter and chocolate; microwave on high 1 to 1½ minutes or until blended and smooth, stirring every 30 seconds. Spoon over bananas.

3. In a large bowl, whisk milk and pudding mix 2 minutes. Let stand 2 minutes or until soft-set. Fold in 1 cup whipped topping; spread over chocolate mixture. Pipe remaining whipped topping over edge. Refrigerate, covered, at least 3 hours.

4. Sprinkle with peanuts just before serving. If desired, serve with cut-up peanut butter cups.

" I made this for a Thanksgiving gathering and it was gone in minutes. "

—BRICKERAMY TASTEOFHOME.COM

SPECIAL-OCCASION CHOCOLATE CAKE

This recipe won the grand championship at the Alaska State Fair, and with one bite, you'll see why! The decadent chocolate cake boasts a luscious ganache filling and fudge buttercream frosting.

—CINDI DECLUE ANCHORAGE, AK

PREP: 40 MIN. + CHILLING • **BAKE:** 25 MIN. + COOLING
MAKES: 12 SERVINGS

- 1 cup baking cocoa
- 2 cups boiling water
- 1 cup butter, softened
- 2¼ cups sugar
- 4 eggs
- 1½ teaspoons vanilla extract
- 2¾ cups all-purpose flour
- 2 teaspoons baking soda
- ½ teaspoon baking powder
- ½ teaspoon salt

GANACHE
- 10 ounces semisweet chocolate, chopped
- 1 cup heavy whipping cream
- 2 tablespoons sugar

FROSTING
- 1 cup butter, softened
- 4 cups confectioners' sugar
- ½ cup baking cocoa
- ¼ cup 2% milk
- 2 teaspoons vanilla extract

GARNISH
- ¾ cup sliced almonds, toasted

1. Preheat oven to 350°. In a bowl, combine cocoa and water; set aside. In a large bowl, cream butter and sugar until light and fluffy. Add eggs, one at a time, beating well after each addition. Beat in vanilla. Combine the flour, baking soda, baking powder and salt; add to creamed mixture alternately with cocoa mixture, beating well after each addition.

2. Pour into three greased and floured 9-in. round baking pans. Bake 25-30 minutes or until a toothpick inserted near the center comes out clean. Cool 10 minutes before removing from pans to wire racks to cool completely.

3. For ganache, place chocolate in a small bowl. In a small heavy saucepan over low heat, bring cream and sugar to a boil. Pour over chocolate; whisk gently until smooth. Refrigerate 35-45 minutes or until ganache begins to thicken, stirring occasionally.

4. For frosting, in a large bowl, beat butter until fluffy. Add the confectioners' sugar, cocoa, milk and vanilla; beat until smooth.

5. Place one cake layer on a serving plate; spread with 1 cup frosting. Top with second layer and 1 cup ganache; sprinkle with ½ cup almonds. Top with third layer; frost top and sides of cake. Warm ganache until pourable; pour over cake, allowing some to drape down the sides. Sprinkle with remaining almonds. Refrigerate until serving.

FRESH BLUEBERRY PIE

Because blueberries are readily available in Michigan, I've been making this dessert for decades. In fact, the state is the leader in blueberry production. Nothing says summer like a piece of fresh blueberry pie!

—LINDA KERNAN MASON, MI

PREP: 15 MIN. + COOLING • **MAKES:** 8 SERVINGS

- ¾ cup sugar
- 3 tablespoons cornstarch
- ⅛ teaspoon salt
- ¼ cup cold water
- 5 cups fresh blueberries, divided
- 1 tablespoon butter
- 1 tablespoon lemon juice
- 1 pastry shell (9 inches), baked

1. In a saucepan over medium heat, combine sugar, cornstarch, salt and water until smooth. Add 3 cups blueberries. Bring to a boil; cook and stir 2 minutes or until thickened and bubbly.

2. Remove from heat. Add butter, lemon juice and remaining berries; stir until butter is melted. Cool. Pour into pastry shell. Refrigerate until serving.

TOP TIP

Buying Fresh Blueberries

Look for fresh blueberries that are firm, dry, plump, smooth-skinned and relatively free of leaves and stems. Berries should be deep purple-blue to blue-black; reddish berries aren't ripe but may be used in cooking.

AMISH SUGAR COOKIES, PAGE 201

CHERRY BARS, 198

CARDAMOM-BLACKBERRY LINZER COOKIES, 190

MARVELOUS MAPLE FUDGE, 190

Cookies & Candies

Where do you stand in the debate....crisp and crunchy or soft and chewy? Or are you happy with any cookie as long as it is chocolate? No matter your cookie of choice, you'll find the perfect treat here. Besides cookies, be sure to try chocolaty brownies, delicious bars or rich candies, too!

AUTUMN LEAF CUTOUTS

Turn classic cookies into a platter of autumn leaves with cookie cutters. Make them in solid colors, or combine pieces of tinted dough for a multicolored effect.
—DARLENE BRENDEN SALEM, OR

PREP: 25 MIN. + CHILLING • **BAKE:** 15 MIN./BATCH + COOLING
MAKES: 4 DOZEN

- 2 **cups butter, softened**
- 1½ **cups sugar**
- 2 **eggs**
- 2 **teaspoons vanilla extract**
- 5½ **cups all-purpose flour**
- ½ **teaspoon baking soda**
- ½ **teaspoon salt**
  Red, green, orange and yellow paste food coloring
- 1⅓ **cups confectioners' sugar**
- 5 **to 7 teaspoons warm water**
- 1 **tablespoon meringue powder**
- ¼ **teaspoon almond extract**
- 2 **tablespoons coarse sugar**

1. In a large bowl, cream butter and sugar until light and fluffy. Beat in eggs and vanilla. In another bowl, whisk flour, baking soda and salt; gradually beat into creamed mixture.
2. Divide dough into four portions; tint one red, one green, one orange and one yellow. Shape each into a disk; wrap in plastic wrap. Chill 30 minutes or until firm enough to roll.
3. Preheat oven to 350°. On a lightly floured surface, roll each portion of dough to ¼-in. thickness. Cut with a floured 3-in. leaf-shaped cookie cutter. Place 2 in. apart on greased baking sheets.
4. Bake 14-17 minutes or until edges are golden brown. Remove from pans to wire racks to cool completely.
5. Meanwhile, in a large bowl, combine confectioners' sugar, water, meringue powder and almond extract; beat on low speed just until blended. Pipe or drizzle on cookies as desired. Sprinkle with coarse sugar. Let stand until set. Store in an airtight container.

BITE-SIZE CINNAMON ROLL COOKIES

If you love a cinnamon roll and a good spiced cookie, this bite-sized version combines the best of both. Genius!
—JASMINE SHETH NEW YORK, NY

PREP: 1 HOUR + CHILLING • **BAKE:** 10 MIN./BATCH
MAKES: 6 DOZEN

- ½ **cup packed brown sugar**
- 4 **teaspoons ground cinnamon**
- 1¼ **cups butter, softened**
- 4 **ounces cream cheese, softened**
- 1½ **cups sugar**
- 2 **eggs**
- 2 **teaspoons vanilla extract**
- 2 **teaspoons grated orange peel**
- 4¼ **cups all-purpose flour**
- 1 **teaspoon baking powder**
- 1 **teaspoon active dry yeast**
- ½ **teaspoon salt**

GLAZE
- 1 **cup confectioners' sugar**
- 2 **tablespoons 2% milk**
- 1 **teaspoon vanilla extract**

1. In a small bowl, mix brown sugar and cinnamon until blended. In a large bowl, cream butter, cream cheese and sugar until light and fluffy. Beat in eggs, vanilla and orange peel. In another bowl, whisk flour, baking powder, yeast and salt; gradually beat into creamed mixture.
2. Divide dough into four portions. On a lightly floured surface, roll each into an 8x6-in. rectangle; sprinkle with about 2 tablespoons brown sugar mixture. Roll up tightly jelly-roll style, starting with a long side. Wrap in plastic wrap. Refrigerate 1 hour or until firm.
3. Preheat oven to 350°. Cut dough crosswise into ⅜-in. slices. Place 1 in. apart on greased baking sheets. Bake 8-10 minutes or until bottoms are light brown. Remove from pans to wire racks to cool completely.
4. In a small bowl, whisk the glaze ingredients. Dip the tops of the cookies in glaze. Let stand until set. Store cookies in an airtight container.

ULTIMATE DOUBLE CHOCOLATE BROWNIES

These decadent brownies may be from scratch, but they only take 15 minutes to mix together! Loaded with nuts and chocolate chunks, the sweet treats can't be beat.

—**CAROL PREWETT** CHEYENNE, WY

PREP: 15 MIN. • **BAKE:** 35 MIN. • **MAKES:** 3 DOZEN

- ¾ cup baking cocoa
- ½ teaspoon baking soda
- ⅔ cup butter, melted, divided
- ½ cup boiling water
- 2 cups sugar
- 2 eggs
- 1 teaspoon vanilla extract
- 1⅓ cups all-purpose flour
- ¼ teaspoon salt
- ½ cup coarsely chopped pecans
- 2 cups (12 ounces) semisweet chocolate chunks

1. Preheat oven to 350°. In a bowl, mix cocoa and baking soda; blend ⅓ cup melted butter. Add boiling water; stir until well blended. Stir in sugar, eggs, vanilla and remaining butter. Add flour and salt. Stir in pecans and chocolate chunks.

2. Pour into a greased 13x9-in. baking pan. Bake for 35-40 minutes or until brownies begin to pull away from sides of pan. Cool.

(5) INGREDIENTS
APPLE KUCHEN BARS

My family's bar recipe is about comfort and simplicity. My mom made them, and now I bake them in my own kitchen. I make double batches to pass on the love!

—**ELIZABETH MONFORT** CELINA, OH

PREP: 35 MIN. • **BAKE:** 1 HOUR + COOLING • **MAKES:** 2 DOZEN

- 3 cups all-purpose flour, divided
- ¼ teaspoon salt
- 1½ cups cold butter, divided
- 4 to 5 tablespoons ice water
- 8 cups thinly sliced peeled tart apples (about 8 medium)
- 2 cups sugar, divided
- 2 teaspoons ground cinnamon

1. Preheat oven to 350°. Place 2 cups flour and salt in a food processor; pulse until blended. Add 1 cup butter; pulse until butter is the size of peas. While pulsing, add just enough ice water to form moist crumbs. Press mixture into a greased 13x9-in. baking pan. Bake 20-25 minutes or until edges are lightly browned. Cool on a wire rack.

2. In a large bowl, combine the apples, 1 cup sugar and cinnamon; toss to coat. Spoon over crust. Place remaining flour, butter and sugar in food processor; pulse until coarse crumbs form. Sprinkle over apples. Bake 60-70 minutes or until golden brown and apples are tender. Cool completely on a wire rack. Cut into bars.

TOP TIP

Cutting Brownies and Bars

If you have trouble cutting bars of equal size, try using a dough scraper, a stainless-steel utensil with a short rectangular blade. Press the blade down into the bars to cut; don't drag it through. You'll have dessert bars with straight, clean edges in just a few seconds!

CARAMEL SNICKERDOODLE BARS

What did I do when I couldn't decide between two of my favorite desserts? Combined them! This snickerdoodle-blondie hybrid is even better with my other favorite ingredient—caramel.

—NIKI PLOURDE GARDNER, MA

PREP: 30 MIN. • **BAKE:** 25 MIN. + CHILLING . • **MAKES:** 4 DOZEN

- 1 cup butter, softened
- 2 cups packed brown sugar
- 2 eggs
- 2 teaspoons vanilla extract
- 2½ cups all-purpose flour
- 2 teaspoons baking powder
- 1 teaspoon salt
- ¼ cup sugar
- 3 teaspoons ground cinnamon
- 2 cans (13.4 ounces each) dulce de leche
- 12 ounces white baking chocolate, chopped
- ⅓ cup heavy whipping cream
- 1 tablespoon light corn syrup

1. Preheat oven to 350°. Line a 13x9-in. baking pan with parchment paper, letting ends extend over sides by 1 inch.
2. In a large bowl, cream butter and brown sugar until light and fluffy. Beat in eggs and vanilla. In another bowl, whisk flour, baking powder and salt; gradually beat into creamed mixture. Spread onto bottom of prepared pan.
3. In a small bowl, mix sugar and cinnamon; sprinkle 2 tablespoons mixture over batter. Bake 25-30 minutes or until edges are light brown. Cool completely in pan on a wire rack.
4. Spread dulce de leche over crust. In a small saucepan, combine white baking chocolate, cream and corn syrup; cook and stir over low heat until smooth. Cool slightly. Spread over dulce de leche. Sprinkle with remaining cinnamon-sugar. Refrigerate, covered, at least 1 hour.
5. Lifting with parchment paper, remove from pan. Cut into bars. Refrigerate leftovers.

NOTE *This recipe was tested with Nestle La Lechera dulce de leche; look for it in the international foods section. If using Eagle Brand dulce de leche (caramel flavored sauce), thicken according to package directions before using.*

ORANGE & LEMON WAFER COOKIES

These light citrus cookies go well with a cup of coffee or tea after a heavy holiday meal.

—PATRICIA SWART GALLOWAY, NJ

PREP: 25 MIN. • **BAKE:** 10 MIN./BATCH
MAKES: ABOUT 4 DOZEN

- ½ cup unsalted butter, softened
- ¾ cup sugar
- 1 egg
- 2 teaspoons grated orange peel
- 1 teaspoon grated lemon peel
- 1 teaspoon vanilla extract
- 1 teaspoon orange extract
- 1 cup all-purpose flour
- 5 teaspoons cornstarch
- ¼ teaspoon baking soda
- ¼ teaspoon salt
  Thin orange or lemon peel strips, optional

1. Preheat oven to 350°. In a large bowl, cream butter and sugar until light and fluffy. Beat in egg, orange peel, lemon peel and extracts. In another bowl, mix flour, cornstarch, baking soda and salt; gradually beat into creamed mixture.
2. Drop by rounded teaspoonfuls 2 in. apart onto parchment paper-lined baking sheets. If desired, top with orange peel strips.
3. Bake 6-8 minutes or until edges are golden brown. Remove from pans to wire racks to cool.

CARAMEL-CHOCOLATE CHIP SANDWICH COOKIES

Here are cookies that are cakelike rather than crisp or chewy. They make a nice change from other chocolate chip cookies. I've been known to add a little peanut butter to the filling, too.

—**LAUREN REIFF** EAST EARL, PA

PREP: 30 MIN. • **BAKE:** 10 MIN./BATCH + COOLING
MAKES: 2½ DOZEN

- ½ cup butter, softened
- 1 cup packed brown sugar
- 2 eggs
- ¼ cup honey
- 1 teaspoon vanilla extract
- 2¾ cups all-purpose flour
- 1 teaspoon baking soda
- 1 teaspoon baking powder
- ½ teaspoon salt
- 1½ cups semisweet chocolate chips

FILLING

- 6 tablespoons butter, cubed
- ¾ cup packed brown sugar
- 3 tablespoons 2% milk
- 1⅓ to 1½ cups confectioners' sugar

1. Preheat oven to 350°. In a large bowl, cream butter and sugar until light and fluffy. Beat in eggs, then honey and vanilla. In another bowl, whisk flour, baking soda, baking powder and salt; gradually beat into creamed mixture. Stir in chocolate chips.

2. Drop by tablespoonfuls 2 in. apart onto ungreased baking sheets. Bake 8-10 minutes or until golden brown. Remove from pans to wire racks to cool completely.

3. For filling, in a small saucepan, melt butter over medium heat. Stir in brown sugar and milk; bring to a boil. Reduce heat to low; cook and stir until sugar is dissolved. Remove from heat; cool to room temperature.

4. Beat in enough confectioners' sugar to reach desired consistency. Spread 1½ teaspoons filling onto bottoms of half of the cookies; cover with remaining cookies.

TURTLE COOKIE CUPS

The gooey caramel pairs wonderfully with crunchy pecans. For a twist, replace the semisweet chips with white chocolate chips in the cups and drizzle with melted white chocolate.

—**HEATHER KING** FROSTBURG, MD

PREP: 35 MIN. + STANDING • **BAKE:** 10 MIN./BATCH + COOLING
MAKES: 4 DOZEN

- 1 cup butter, softened
- 1 cup packed brown sugar
- ½ cup sugar
- 2 eggs
- 1 teaspoon vanilla extract
- 2½ cups all-purpose flour
- 1 teaspoon baking soda
- ½ teaspoon salt
- 1¼ cups semisweet chocolate chips, divided
- ½ cup chopped pecans
- 1 cup Kraft caramel bits
- 3 tablespoons heavy whipping cream
- 48 pecan halves (about ¾ cup)

1. Preheat oven to 375°. In a large bowl, cream butter and sugars until light and fluffy. Beat in eggs and vanilla. In another bowl, whisk flour, baking soda and salt; gradually beat into creamed mixture.

2. Shape dough into 1-in. balls; place in greased mini-muffin cups. Press evenly onto bottoms and up the sides of cups. Bake 9-11 minutes or until edges are golden brown. With the back of measuring teaspoon, make an indentation in each cup. Immediately sprinkle with ¾ cup chocolate chips and chopped pecans. Cool in pans 10 minutes. Remove to wire racks to cool.

3. Meanwhile, in a small saucepan, melt caramel bits with cream; stir until smooth. Spoon into cups. Top each with a pecan half. In a microwave, melt remaining chocolate chips; stir until smooth. Drizzle over pecans.

GLUTEN-FREE PEANUT BUTTER KISS COOKIES

Serve these chocolate-topped cookies, and everyone will want to kiss the cook! For a change of pace, use chunky peanut butter instead of the creamy variety.
—CANADA60 TASTEOFHOME.COM

PREP: 20 MIN. + CHILLING
BAKE: 10 MIN./BATCH • **MAKES:** 4 DOZEN

- ¼ cup butter-flavored shortening
- 1¼ cups packed brown sugar
- ¾ cup creamy peanut butter
- 1 egg
- ¼ cup unsweetened applesauce
- 3 teaspoons vanilla extract
- 1 cup white rice flour
- ½ cup potato starch
- ¼ cup tapioca flour
- 1 teaspoon baking powder
- ¾ teaspoon baking soda
- ¼ teaspoon salt
- 48 milk chocolate kisses, unwrapped

1. In a large bowl, beat shortening, brown sugar and peanut butter until blended. Beat in egg, applesauce and vanilla (mixture will appear curdled). In another bowl, whisk rice flour, potato starch, tapioca flour, baking powder, baking soda and salt; gradually beat into creamed mixture. Refrigerate, covered, 1 hour.

2. Preheat oven to 375°. Shape dough into forty-eight 1-in. balls; place 2 in. apart on ungreased baking sheets. Bake 9-11 minutes or until slightly cracked. Immediately press a chocolate kiss into center of each cookie. Cool on pans 2 minutes. Remove to wire racks to cool.

NOTE *Read all ingredient labels for possible gluten content prior to use. Ingredient formulas can change, and production facilities vary among brands. If you're concerned that your brand may contain gluten, contact the company.*

LIME & GIN COCONUT MACAROONS

I took these lime and coconut macaroons to our annual cookie exchange, where we name a queen. I won the crown!
—**MILISSA KIRKPATRICK** ANGEL FIRE, NM

PREP: 20 MIN.
BAKE: 15 MIN./BATCH + COOLING
MAKES: 2½ DOZEN

- 4 **egg whites**
- ⅔ **cup sugar**
- 3 **tablespoons gin**
- 1½ **teaspoons grated lime peel**
- ¼ **teaspoon salt**
- ¼ **teaspoon almond extract**
- 1 **package (14 ounces) flaked coconut**
- ½ **cup all-purpose flour**
- 8 **ounces white baking chocolate, melted**

1. Preheat oven to 350°. In a small bowl, whisk the first six ingredients until blended. In a large bowl, toss coconut with flour; stir in egg white mixture.
2. Drop by tablespoonfuls 2 in. apart onto greased baking sheets. Bake for 15-18 minutes or until tops are light brown. Remove from pans to wire racks to cool completely.
3. Dip bottoms of macaroons into melted chocolate, allowing excess to drip off. Place on waxed paper; let stand until set. Store in an airtight container.

CREAMY CARAMELS

The recipe for these soft, buttery caramels was printed in a local newspaper several years ago and I have been making them ever since. They beat the store-bought version hands-down!
—**MARCIE WOLFE** WILLIAMSBURG, VA

PREP: 10 MIN. • **COOK:** 30 MIN. + COOLING
MAKES: 2½ POUNDS

- 1 **teaspoon plus 1 cup butter, divided**
- 1 **cup sugar**
- 1 **cup dark corn syrup**
- 1 **can (14 ounces) sweetened condensed milk**
- 1 **teaspoon vanilla extract**

1. Line an 8-in.-square pan with foil; grease the foil with 1 teaspoon butter and set aside.
2. In a large heavy saucepan, combine the sugar, corn syrup and remaining butter; bring to a boil over medium heat, stirring constantly. Boil slowly for 4 minutes without stirring.
3. Remove from heat; stir in milk. Reduce heat to medium-low and cook until a candy thermometer reads 238° (soft-ball stage), stirring constantly. Remove from heat; stir in vanilla.
4. Pour into prepared pan (do not scrape saucepan). Cool. Using foil, lift candy out of pan. Discard the foil; cut the candy into 1-in. squares. Wrap individually in waxed paper; twist ends.
NOTE *We recommend that you test your candy thermometer before each use by bringing water to a boil; the thermometer should read 212°. Adjust your recipe temperature up or down based on the test.*

PEPPERMINT PATTY SANDWICH COOKIES

These cookies are a hit with kids and adults at my annual party. For extra flair, mix food coloring or crushed candy canes into the filling.
—**AMY MARTIN** VANCOUVER, WA

PREP: 30 MIN.
BAKE: 10 MIN./BATCH + COOLING
MAKES: 3 DOZEN

- 2 **packages devil's food cake mix (regular size)**
- 4 **eggs**
- ⅔ **cup canola oil**
  Granulated sugar
- 1 **package (8 ounces) cream cheese, softened**
- ½ **cup butter, softened**
- 1 **teaspoon peppermint extract**
- 4 **cups confectioners' sugar**

1. Preheat oven to 350°. In a large bowl, combine cake mixes, eggs and oil; beat until well blended. Shape into 1-in. balls; place 2 in. apart on greased baking sheets. Flatten with bottom of a glass dipped in granulated sugar.
2. Bake cookies 7-9 minutes or until the tops are cracked. Cool 2 minutes before removing cookies to wire racks to cool completely.
3. In a large bowl, beat cream cheese, butter and extract until blended. Gradually beat in confectioners' sugar until smooth.
4. Spread filling on bottoms of half of the cookies; cover with remaining cookies. Store in an airtight container in the refrigerator.

MARVELOUS MAPLE FUDGE

Since this delicious, easy recipe makes a lot, it is ideal for potlucks, large family gatherings or bake sales. Line your pan with foil to remove the fudge in a snap.
—**JEANNIE GALLANT** CHARLOTTETOWN, PEI

PREP: 10 MIN. • **COOK:** 20 MIN. + COOLING
MAKES: 1¾ POUNDS (64 PIECES)

- 1 teaspoon plus 1 cup butter, divided
- 2 cups packed brown sugar
- 1 can (5 ounces) evaporated milk
- 1 teaspoon maple flavoring
- ½ teaspoon vanilla extract
- ⅛ teaspoon salt
- 2 cups confectioners' sugar

1. Line an 8-in.-square pan with foil; grease the foil with 1 teaspoon butter.
2. Cube remaining butter. In a large saucepan, combine cubed butter, brown sugar and milk. Bring to a full boil over medium heat, stirring constantly. Cook 10 minutes, stirring frequently. Remove from heat.
3. Stir in the maple flavoring, vanilla and salt. Add the confectioners' sugar; beat on medium speed 2 minutes or until smooth. Immediately spread fudge into prepared pan. Cool completely.
4. Using foil, lift fudge out of pan. Remove foil; cut into 1-in. squares. Store in an airtight container.

TOP TIP

Tender Cutouts

Use a light touch when handling the dough for cutout cookies; overhandling will cause the cookies to be tough. The dough will be easier to handle and roll out if it is refrigerated first. This is especially true if it was made with butter versus shortening. Lightly dust the rolling pin and work surface with flour to prevent sticking. Working too much extra flour into the dough will also result in tough cookies.

⑤ INGREDIENTS

COLORFUL CANDY BAR COOKIES

No one will guess these sweet treats with the candy bar center start with store-bought dough. Roll them or just dip the tops in colored sugar. Instead of using miniature candy bars, slice regular size Snickers candy bars into 1-inch pieces for the centers.
—*TASTE OF HOME* TEST KITCHEN

PREP: 35 MIN. • **BAKE:** 10 MIN. • **MAKES:** 2 DOZEN

- ½ tube refrigerated sugar cookie dough, softened
- ¼ cup all-purpose flour
- 24 miniature Snickers candy bars
    Red and green colored sugar

1. Preheat oven to 350°. In a small bowl, beat cookie dough and flour until combined. Shape 1½ teaspoonfuls of dough around each candy bar. Roll in colored sugar.
2. Place 2 in. apart on parchment paper-lined baking sheets. Bake 10-12 minutes or until edges are golden brown. Remove to wire racks.

CARDAMOM-BLACKBERRY LINZER COOKIES

Deeply spiced cardamom is the perfect match for the jam of your choice in this family-favorite sweet treat.
—**CHRISTIANNA GOZZI** ASTORIA, NY

PREP: 50 MIN. + CHILLING • **BAKE:** 10 MIN./BATCH + COOLING
MAKES: ABOUT 2 DOZEN

- 2 cups all-purpose flour
- 1 cup salted roasted almonds
- 2 to 3 teaspoons ground cardamom
- ¼ teaspoon salt
- 1 cup unsalted butter, softened
- ½ cup plus 1 teaspoon sugar, divided
- 1 egg
- 1 jar (10 ounces) seedless blackberry spreadable fruit
- 1 tablespoon lemon juice
- 3 tablespoons confectioners' sugar

1. In a food processor, combine ½ cup flour and almonds; pulse until almonds are finely ground. Add cardamom, salt and remaining flour; pulse until combined.
2. In a large bowl, cream butter and ½ cup sugar until light and fluffy. Beat in egg. Gradually beat in flour mixture. Divide dough in half. Shape each into a disk; wrap in plastic wrap. Refrigerate 1 hour or until firm enough to roll.
3. Preheat oven to 350°. On a lightly floured surface, roll each portion to ⅛-in. thickness. Cut with a floured 2-in. round cookie cutter. Using a floured 1-in. round cookie cutter, cut out the centers of half of the cookies. Place solid and window cookies 1 in. apart on greased baking sheets.
4. Bake 10-12 minutes or until light brown. Remove from pans to wire racks to cool completely.
5. In a small bowl, mix spreadable fruit, lemon juice and remaining sugar. Spread filling on bottoms of solid cookies; top with window cookies. Dust with confectioners' sugar.

PEANUT BUTTER & BACON BLONDIES

The most unusual bar cookie recipe I have is also a favorite. Use store-bought bacon bits to save time.
—**JANIE COLLE** HUTCHINSON, KS

PREP: 20 MIN. • **BAKE:** 25 MIN. + COOLING • **MAKES:** 2 DOZEN

- 2 **cups packed brown sugar**
- 1 **cup butter, melted**
- 2 **eggs**
- 2 **teaspoons vanilla extract**
- 2 **cups all-purpose flour**
- 1 **teaspoon baking powder**
- ¼ **teaspoon baking soda**
  Dash salt
- 8 **bacon strips, cooked and crumbled**

FROSTING

- 1 **cup creamy peanut butter**
- ½ **cup butter, softened**
- 2 **cups confectioners' sugar**
- 1 **teaspoon vanilla extract**
- 3 **to 4 tablespoons 2% milk**
- 6 **bacon strips, cooked and crumbled**

1. Preheat oven to 350°. Line a 13x9-in. pan with parchment paper, letting ends extend up sides; grease paper.
2. In a bowl, beat brown sugar and butter until blended. Beat in eggs and vanilla. Mix flour, baking powder, baking soda and salt; gradually beat into sugar mixture. Fold in bacon.
3. Spread into prepared pan. Bake 25-30 minutes or until a toothpick inserted in center comes out clean (do not overbake). Cool completely in pan on a wire rack. Lifting with parchment paper, remove from pan.

4. For frosting, in a large bowl, beat peanut butter and butter until blended. Gradually beat in confectioners' sugar, vanilla and enough milk to reach desired consistency. Frost blondies; sprinkle with bacon. Cut into bars. Store in the refrigerator.

CASHEW CRUNCH

Folks can't stop eating this buttery, brittle-like candy. Try using almonds or your favorite nut in place of the cashews.
—**KIM CROFT** SAN DIEGO, CA

PREP: 10 MIN. • **COOK:** 20 MIN. + COOLING • **MAKES:** 1¼ POUNDS

- 2 **teaspoons plus 10 tablespoons butter, divided**
- ½ **cup sugar**
- ¼ **cup brown sugar**
- 1 **tablespoon light corn syrup**
- ¾ **teaspoon cayenne pepper**
- ¼ **teaspoon salt**
- 2 **cups salted cashews**

1. Line a 15x10x1-in. pan with foil and grease the foil with 2 teaspoons butter; set aside. In a large heavy saucepan, combine the sugar, brown sugar, corn syrup, cayenne, salt and remaining butter. Cook and stir until sugar is dissolved.
2. Add cashews and bring to a boil; cook and stir until a candy thermometer reads 280° (soft-crack stage), about 6 minutes. Immediately pour into prepared pan; spread with a metal spatula. Cool completely. Break into pieces. Store in an airtight container.
NOTE *We recommend that you test your candy thermometer before each use by bringing water to a boil; the thermometer should read 212°. Adjust your recipe temperature up or down based on the test.*

QUADRUPLE CHOCOLATE CHUNK COOKIES

Of all the recipes in my repertoire, my Quadruple Chocolate Chunk Cookies stood the best shot of winning a cookie contest that I entered. Really, when your cookies feature Oreos, candy bars and all the other goodies, you're nearly guaranteed a winner.

—JEFF KING DULUTH, MN

PREP: 25 MIN. • **BAKE:** 10 MIN./BATCH • **MAKES:** 8 DOZEN

- 1 cup butter, softened
- 1 cup sugar
- 1 cup packed brown sugar
- 2 eggs
- 2 teaspoons vanilla extract
- 2½ cups all-purpose flour
- ¾ cup Dutch-processed cocoa
- 1 teaspoon baking soda
- ¼ teaspoon salt
- 1 cup white baking chips, chopped
- 1 cup semisweet chocolate chips, chopped
- 1 cup chopped Oreo cookies (about 10 cookies)
- 1 Hershey's cookies and cream candy bar (1.55 ounces), chopped

1. Preheat oven to 375°. In a large bowl, cream butter, sugar and brown sugar until light and fluffy. Beat in eggs and vanilla. In another bowl, whisk the flour, cocoa, baking soda and salt; gradually beat into creamed mixture. Stir in the remaining ingredients.

2. Drop by tablespoonfuls 2 in. apart onto greased baking sheets. Bake 6-8 minutes or until set. Cool on pans 1 minute. Remove to wire racks to cool completely. Store cookies in an airtight container.

OAT PEANUT BUTTER BARS

These bars can be dressed up for festive occasions by substituting colored icing for the peanut butter frosting. Drizzle them with pastel colors for Easter...red, white and blue for the Fourth of July...and chocolate for Halloween.

—PATRICIA STAUDT MARBLE ROCK, IA

PREP: 15 MIN. • **BAKE:** 20 MIN. + COOLING • **MAKES:** 3-4 DOZEN

- ½ cup butter, softened
- ½ cup sugar
- ½ cup packed brown sugar
- ½ cup creamy peanut butter
- 1 egg
- 1 teaspoon vanilla extract
- 1 cup all-purpose flour
- ½ cup quick-cooking oats
- 1 teaspoon baking soda
- ¼ teaspoon salt
- 1 cup (6 ounces) semisweet chocolate chips

ICING
- ½ cup confectioners' sugar
- 2 tablespoons creamy peanut butter
- 2 tablespoons milk

1. Preheat oven to 350°. In a large bowl, cream butter, sugars and peanut butter until light and fluffy. Beat in egg and vanilla. Mix flour, oats, baking soda and salt; gradually beat into creamed mixture and mix well. Spread into a greased 13x9-in. baking pan. Sprinkle with chocolate chips.

2. Bake 20-25 minutes or until lightly browned. Cool on a wire rack 10 minutes.

3. Combine icing ingredients; drizzle over the top. Cool completely. Cut into bars.

FOLDED HAZELNUT COOKIES

We made these cookies when my boys were small. The boys were covered in flour, with aprons wrapped around them and Nutella on their faces.

—PAULA MARCHESI LENHARTSVILLE, PA

PREP: 30 MIN. • **BAKE:** 10 MIN./BATCH • **MAKES:** ABOUT 2 DOZEN

- 1 tablespoon finely chopped hazelnuts
- 1 tablespoon sugar
- 1½ cups all-purpose flour
- ½ cup confectioners' sugar
- ¼ cup cornstarch
- ¾ cup cold butter, cubed
- 2 tablespoons Nutella
- 1 egg, lightly beaten

1. Preheat oven to 350°. In a small bowl, mix hazelnuts and sugar. In a large bowl, whisk flour, confectioners' sugar and cornstarch. Cut in butter until crumbly. Transfer to a clean work surface. Knead gently until mixture forms a smooth dough, about 2 minutes (dough will be crumbly but will come together).
2. Divide dough in half. On a lightly floured surface, roll each portion to ⅛-in. thickness. Cut with a floured 2-in. round cookie cutter. Place ¼ teaspoon Nutella in center. Fold dough partially in half, just enough to cover filling.
3. Place 1 in. apart on greased baking sheets. Brush with beaten egg; sprinkle with hazelnut mixture. Bake 10-12 minutes or until bottoms are light brown. Remove from pans to wire racks to cool.

HONEY-PECAN SQUARES

When we left Texas to head north, a neighbor gave me pecans from his trees. I'm happy to send these nutty squares back to him, and he's happy to get them.
—LORRAINE CALAND SHUNIAH, ON

PREP: 15 MIN. • **BAKE:** 30 MIN. • **MAKES:** 2 DOZEN

- 1 cup unsalted butter, softened
- ¾ cup packed dark brown sugar
- ½ teaspoon salt
- 3 cups all-purpose flour

FILLING
- ½ cup unsalted butter, cubed
- ½ cup packed dark brown sugar
- ⅓ cup honey
- 2 tablespoons sugar
- 2 tablespoons heavy whipping cream
- ¼ teaspoon salt
- 2 cups chopped pecans, toasted
- ½ teaspoon maple flavoring or vanilla extract

1. Preheat oven to 350°. Line a 13x9-in. baking pan with parchment paper, letting ends extend up sides of pan. In a large bowl, cream the butter, brown sugar and salt until light and fluffy. Gradually beat in flour. Press into prepared pan. Bake 16-20 minutes or until lightly browned.
2. In a small saucepan, combine the first six filling ingredients; bring to a boil. Cook 1 minute. Remove from heat; stir in pecans and maple flavoring. Pour over crust.
3. Bake 10-15 minutes or until bubbly. Cool in pan on a wire rack. Lifting with parchment paper, transfer to a cutting board; cut into bars.
NOTE *To toast nuts, spread in a 15x10x1-in. baking pan. Bake at 350° for 5-10 minutes or until lightly browned, stirring occasionally. Or, spread in a dry nonstick skillet and heat over low heat until lightly browned, stirring occasionally.*

SNICKERDOODLE BLONDIE BARS
 I whipped up these unique blondies for my boys' football team and was instantly named "the greatest mom."
—**VALONDA SEWARD** COARSEGOLD, CA

PREP: 15 MIN. • **BAKE:** 35 MIN. + COOLING • **MAKES:** 20 SERVINGS

- 1 **cup butter, softened**
- 2 **cups packed brown sugar**
- 2 **eggs**
- 3 **teaspoons vanilla extract**
- 2⅔ **cups all-purpose flour**
- 2 **teaspoons baking powder**
- 1 **teaspoon ground cinnamon**
- ¼ **teaspoon ground nutmeg**
- ½ **teaspoon salt**

TOPPING
- 1½ **teaspoons sugar**
- ½ **teaspoon ground cinnamon**

1. Preheat oven to 350°. In a large bowl, cream butter and brown sugar until fluffy. Beat in eggs and vanilla. Mix flour, baking powder, spices and salt; gradually beat into creamed mixture. Spread into a greased 9-in.-square baking pan.
2. Mix topping ingredients; sprinkle over top. Bake 35-40 minutes or until set and golden brown. Cool in pan on a wire rack. Cut into bars.

❝ I like snickerdoodles, so I thought this recipe looked interesting. Wow...I can't begin to say how good these bars are! They did not disappoint. The flavor is absolutely perfect, and the texture of the bars is tender. This recipe is definitely a keeper. ❞
—**LISAMARIA** TASTEOFHOME.COM

ROOT BEER FLOAT FUDGE
My children have always loved root beer floats so I came up with this fudgy treat just for them. Sweet and creamy with that nostalgic root beer flavor, it's always a best-seller at bake sales.
—**JENNIFER FISHER** AUSTIN, TX

PREP: 15 MIN. • **COOK:** 15 MIN. + CHILLING
MAKES: ABOUT 3 POUNDS

- 1 **teaspoon plus ¾ cup butter, divided**
- 3 **cups sugar**
- 1 **can (5 ounces) evaporated milk**
- 1 **package (10 to 12 ounces) white baking chips**
- 1 **jar (7 ounces) marshmallow creme**
- ½ **teaspoon vanilla extract**
- 2 **teaspoons root beer concentrate**

1. Line a 9-in.-square baking pan with foil; grease foil with 1 teaspoon butter. In a large heavy saucepan, combine sugar, milk and remaining butter. Bring to a rapid boil over medium heat, stirring constantly. Cook and stir 4 minutes.
2. Remove from heat. Stir in baking chips and marshmallow creme until melted. Pour one-third of the mixture into a small bowl; stir in vanilla.
3. To remaining mixture, stir in root beer concentrate; immediately spread into prepared pan. Spread vanilla mixture over top. Refrigerate 1 hour or until firm.
4. Using foil, lift fudge out of pan. Remove foil; cut fudge into 1-in. squares. Store between layers of waxed paper in an airtight container in the refrigerator.
NOTE *This recipe was tested with McCormick root beer concentrate.*

MOCHA MACAROON COOKIES

Here's an updated version of the classic macaroon. With chocolate, coffee and cinnamon, it tastes like a specialty item from a barista. Your java-drinking friends will love it!

—**JEANNE HOLT** MENDOTA HEIGHTS, MN

PREP: 20 MIN.
BAKE: 10 MIN./BATCH + COOLING
MAKES: 4 DOZEN

- 2 **teaspoons instant coffee granules**
- 2 **teaspoons hot water**
- 1 **can (14 ounces) sweetened condensed milk**
- 2 **ounces unsweetened chocolate, melted**
- 1 **teaspoon vanilla extract**
- ¼ **teaspoon ground cinnamon**
- ⅛ **teaspoon salt**
- 1 **package (14 ounces) flaked coconut**
- ⅔ **cup white baking chips, melted Plain or chocolate-covered coffee beans**

1. Preheat oven to 350°. In a large bowl, dissolve coffee granules in hot water. Stir in condensed milk, melted chocolate, vanilla, cinnamon and salt until blended. Stir in coconut. Drop mixture by rounded teaspoonfuls 2 in. apart onto parchment paper-lined baking sheets.
2. Bake 10-12 minutes or until set. Cool on pans 1 minute. Remove from pans to wire racks to cool completely.
3. Drizzle cookies with the melted baking chips. Top with the coffee beans, attaching with melted chips if necessary.

TOP TIP

Softening Flaked Coconut

To soften flaked coconut that's turned hard, soak it in milk 30 minutes. Drain and pat it dry on paper towels before using. The leftover coconut-flavored milk can be used within 5 days in baked goods or blended with fresh fruit for a delightfully tasty beverage.

MAPLE-GLAZED CINNAMON CHIP BARS

Cinnamon chips and a maple glaze add fabulous flavor. When I make these, the kitchen smells like Christmas. The glaze fancies them up a bit.

—**LYNDI PILCH** SPRINGFIELD, MO

PREP: 20 MIN. • **BAKE:** 20 MIN.
MAKES: 2 DOZEN

- 1 **cup butter, softened**
- 2 **cups packed brown sugar**
- 2 **eggs**
- 2 **teaspoons vanilla extract**
- 2⅔ **cups all-purpose flour**
- 2 **teaspoons baking powder**
- 1 **teaspoon salt**
- ¾ **cup cinnamon baking chips**
- 1 **tablespoon cinnamon sugar**
GLAZE
- ½ **cup confectioners' sugar**
- 3 **tablespoons maple syrup**
- ½ **teaspoon vanilla extract**

1. Preheat oven to 350°. In a large bowl, cream butter and brown sugar until well blended. Beat in eggs and vanilla. In another bowl, mix flour, baking powder and salt; gradually beat into the creamed mixture. Stir in the cinnamon chips.
2. Spread into a greased 13x9-in. baking pan. Sprinkle with cinnamon sugar. Bake 20-25 minutes or until golden brown and a toothpick inserted in center comes out clean. Cool completely in pan on a wire rack.
3. In a small bowl, mix all glaze ingredients until smooth; drizzle over the top. Cut into bars. Store in an airtight container.

BLACK & WHITE CEREAL TREATS

When my daughter was just 7 years old, she had the brilliant idea of adding Oreo cookies to cereal treats. Now 24, she still asks for them on occasion.

—**TAMMY PHOENIX** AVA, IL

PREP: 10 MIN. • **COOK:** 10 MIN. + COOLING
MAKES: 2 DOZEN

- ¼ **cup butter, cubed**
- 8 **cups miniature marshmallows**
- 6 **cups Rice Krispies**
- 2½ **cups chopped double-stuffed Oreo cookies (about 16), divided**
- 1⅓ **cups white baking chips, melted**

1. In a Dutch oven, melt butter over medium heat. Add marshmallows; cook and stir until melted. Remove from heat. Stir in cereal and 2 cups Oreos. Press into a greased 13x9-in. baking pan.
2. Spread melted baking chips over top; sprinkle with remaining Oreos, pressing gently to adhere. Cool to room temperature. Cut into bars.

> ❝This was so easy and so delicious. I've actually made these quite a few times now. I added cranberries and coconut, and they were very good, too.❞
>
> —KEL DEHNERT TASTEOFHOME.COM

LIME SHORTBREAD WITH DRIED CHERRIES

This fresh, sweet-tart cookie also works with dried cranberries and orange zest. I freeze the dough for up to a month.

—**ABIGAIL BOSTWICK** TOMAHAWK, WI

PREP: 25 MIN. + CHILLING
BAKE: 10 MIN./BATCH
MAKES: ABOUT 4½ DOZEN

- 1 **cup butter, softened**
- ¾ **cup confectioners' sugar**
- 1 **tablespoon grated lime peel**
- 2 **teaspoons vanilla extract**
- ½ **teaspoon almond extract**
- 2 **cups all-purpose flour**
- ¼ **teaspoon baking powder**
- ⅛ **teaspoon salt**
- ½ **cup chopped dried cherries**

1. In a large bowl, cream butter and confectioners' sugar until blended. Beat in lime peel and extracts. In another bowl, mix flour, baking powder and salt; gradually beat into creamed mixture. Stir in cherries.

2. Divide dough in half; shape each into a 7-in.-long roll. Wrap in plastic wrap; refrigerate 3-4 hours or until dough is firm.

3. Preheat oven to 350°. Unwrap and cut dough crosswise into ¼-in. slices. Place 2 in. apart on ungreased baking sheets. Bake 9-11 minutes or until edges are golden brown. Remove from pans to wire racks to cool.

FREEZE OPTION *Place wrapped logs in resealable plastic freezer bag; freeze. To use, unwrap frozen logs and cut into slices. If necessary, let dough stand a few minutes at room temperature before cutting. Bake as directed.*

TOP TIP

Slicing Refrigerator Cookies

To make refrigerator cookie dough easier to slice, use finely chopped nuts and fruits in the dough. Large pieces will cause the dough to crumble when sliced. Cut the dough with a thin, sharp knife for smooth, clean and even slices.

CHERRY BARS

Whip up a pan of these festive bars in just 20 minutes with pantry staples. They're destined to become a holiday classic for your family.

—**JANE KAMP** GRAND RAPIDS, MI

PREP: 20 MIN. • **BAKE:** 30 MIN. + COOLING
MAKES: 5 DOZEN

- 1 **cup butter, softened**
- 2 **cups sugar**
- 1 **teaspoon salt**
- 4 **eggs**
- 1 **teaspoon vanilla extract**
- ¼ **teaspoon almond extract**
- 3 **cups all-purpose flour**
- 2 **cans (21 ounces each) cherry pie filling**

GLAZE

- 1 **cup confectioners' sugar**
- ½ **teaspoon vanilla extract**
- ½ **teaspoon almond extract**
- 2 **to 3 tablespoons milk**

1. Preheat oven to 350°. In a large bowl, cream butter, sugar and salt until light and fluffy. Add eggs, one at a time, beating well after each addition. Beat in extracts. Gradually add flour.

2. Spread 3 cups batter into a greased 15x10x1-in. baking pan. Spread with pie filling. Drop remaining batter by teaspoonfuls over filling. Bake 30-35 minutes or until golden brown. Cool completely in pan on a wire rack.

3. In a small bowl, mix confectioners' sugar, extracts and enough milk to reach desired consistency. Drizzle over top.

TOP TIP

How to Soften Butter

The easiest way to soften butter is to let it sit out at room temperature for about 30 minutes. A knife should glide through the butter without any resistance. Another method is to put the butter in the microwave at 70 percent power for a few seconds. Watch it carefully. If it is heated for too long, the butter will melt and will not be suitable for creaming.

PECAN PIE THUMBPRINTS

A good buttery dough and nutty filling take time to make, but the results are worth it. After munching on a few, you'll agree, I'm sure.

—PEGGY KEY GRANT, AL

PREP: 30 MIN. + CHILLING • **BAKE:** 10 MIN./BATCH
MAKES: 4½ DOZEN

- 1 cup butter, softened
- ½ cup sugar
- 2 eggs, separated
- ½ cup dark corn syrup
- 2½ cups all-purpose flour

FILLING

- ¼ cup plus 2 tablespoons confectioners' sugar
- 3 tablespoons butter
- 2 tablespoons dark corn syrup
- ¼ cup plus 2 tablespoons finely chopped pecans

1. In a large bowl, cream butter and sugar until light and fluffy. Beat in egg yolks and corn syrup. Gradually beat in flour. Refrigerate, covered, 30 minutes or until firm enough to roll.

2. For filling, in a small saucepan, combine confectioners' sugar, butter and corn syrup. Bring to a boil over medium heat, stirring occasionally. Remove from heat; stir in pecans. Remove from pan; refrigerate 30 minutes or until cold.

3. Preheat oven to 375°. Shape dough into 1-in. balls; place 2 in. apart on parchment paper-lined baking sheets. In a small bowl, whisk egg whites; brush over tops.

4. Bake 5 minutes. Remove from oven. Gently press an indentation in center of each cookie with the end of a wooden spoon handle. Fill each with a scant ½ teaspoon pecan mixture. Bake 4-5 minutes or until edges are light brown.

5. Cool on pans 5 minutes. Remove to wire racks to cool.

(5) INGREDIENTS
PEANUT BUTTER FUDGE

My sister shared the recipe for this unbelievably easy confection. I prefer using creamy peanut butter, but the chunky style works just as well.

—MRS. KENNETH RUMMEL LINGLESTOWN, PA

PREP: 15 MIN. + CHILLING • **MAKES:** 3-4 DOZEN

- 2 cups sugar
- ½ cup milk
- 1⅓ cups peanut butter
- 1 jar (7 ounces) marshmallow creme

In a saucepan, bring sugar and milk to a boil; boil 3 minutes. Add peanut butter and marshmallow creme; mix well. Quickly pour into a buttered 8-in.-square pan; chill until set. Cut into squares.

CHEWY GOOD OATMEAL COOKIES

Here's a great oatmeal cookie with all my favorite extras: dried cherries, white chocolate chips and macadamia nuts.

—SANDY HARZ GRAND HAVEN, MI

PREP: 20 MIN. • **BAKE:** 10 MIN./BATCH • **MAKES:** 3½ DOZEN

- 1 cup butter, softened
- 1 cup packed brown sugar
- ½ cup sugar
- 2 eggs
- 1 tablespoon honey
- 2 teaspoons vanilla extract
- 2½ cups quick-cooking oats
- 1½ cups all-purpose flour
- 1 teaspoon baking soda
- ½ teaspoon salt
- ½ teaspoon ground cinnamon
- 1⅓ cups dried cherries
- 1 cup white baking chips
- 1 cup (4 ounces) chopped macadamia nuts

1. Preheat oven to 350°. In a large bowl, cream butter and sugars until light and fluffy. Beat in the eggs, honey and vanilla. In another bowl, mix the oats, flour, baking soda, salt and cinnamon; gradually beat into creamed mixture. Stir in the remaining ingredients.

2. Drop dough by rounded tablespoonfuls 2 in. apart onto greased baking sheets. Bake 10-12 minutes or until golden brown. Cool on pan 2 minutes; remove to wire racks to cool.

CHOCOLATE-DIPPED SPUMONI COOKIES

I combined my favorite cookie and ice cream into one dessert. With so many delicious flavors going on, it's hard to eat just one.
—**ERICA INGRAM** LAKEWOOD, OH

PREP: 20 MIN. • **BAKE:** 10 MIN./BATCH + COOLING
MAKES: ABOUT 6 DOZEN

- 1 cup butter, softened
- ¾ cup sugar
- ¾ cup packed brown sugar
- 2 eggs
- 1 tablespoon vanilla extract
- 2½ cups all-purpose flour
- ½ cup Dutch-processed cocoa
- 1 teaspoon baking soda
- ½ teaspoon salt
- 1⅓ cups finely chopped pistachios, divided
- 1⅓ cups finely chopped dried cherries, divided
- 1¾ cups semisweet chocolate chips
- 1 tablespoon shortening

1. Preheat oven to 350°. In a large bowl, cream butter and sugars until light and fluffy. Beat in eggs and vanilla. In another bowl, whisk flour, cocoa, baking soda and salt; gradually beat into creamed mixture. Stir in 1 cup each pistachios and cherries.

2. Drop by tablespoonfuls 2 in. apart onto ungreased baking sheets. Bake 10-12 minutes or until set. Cool on pans for 2 minutes. Remove to wire racks to cool completely.

3. In a microwave, melt the chocolate chips and shortening; stir until smooth. Dip each cookie halfway into chocolate, allowing excess to drip off; sprinkle with the remaining pistachios and cherries. Place the cookies on waxed paper; let stand until set.

THICK SUGAR COOKIES

Thicker than the norm, this sugar cookie is like one you might find at a good bakery. My children often request these for their birthdays and are always happy to help decorate.
—**HEATHER BIEDLER** MARTINSBURG, WV

PREP: 25 MIN. + CHILLING • **BAKE:** 10 MIN./BATCH + COOLING
MAKES: ABOUT 3 DOZEN

- 1 cup butter, softened
- 1 cup sugar
- 2 eggs
- 3 egg yolks
- 1½ teaspoons vanilla extract
- ¾ teaspoon almond extract
- 3½ cups all-purpose flour
- 1½ teaspoons baking powder
- ¼ teaspoon salt

FROSTING
- 4 cups confectioners' sugar
- ½ cup butter, softened
- ½ cup shortening
- 1 teaspoon vanilla extract
- ½ teaspoon almond extract
- 2 to 3 tablespoons 2% milk
  Assorted colored nonpareils, optional

1. In a large bowl, cream butter and sugar until light and fluffy. Beat in eggs, egg yolks and extracts. In another bowl, whisk flour, baking powder and salt; gradually beat into creamed mixture. Shape into a disk; wrap in plastic wrap. Refrigerate 1 hour or until firm enough to roll.

2. Preheat oven to 375°. On a lightly floured surface, roll dough to ½-in. thickness. Cut with a floured 2-in. cookie cutter. Place 1 in. apart on ungreased baking sheets.

3. Bake 10-12 minutes or until edges begin to brown. Cool on pans 5 minutes. Remove to wire racks to cool completely.

4. For frosting, in a large bowl, beat confectioners' sugar, butter, shortening, extracts and enough milk to reach desired consistency. Spread over cookies. If desired, sprinkle with nonpareils.

CHOCOLATE-COVERED ALMOND BUTTER BRICKLE

I love this soft brickle because the texture is different, and the flavors remind me of one of my favorite candy bars.

—**JOANN BELACK** BRADENTON, FL

PREP: 10 MIN. • **COOK:** 20 MIN. + CHILLING
MAKES: ABOUT 1¾ POUNDS

- 1½ teaspoons plus 2 tablespoons unsalted butter, divided
- 1 cup crunchy almond butter
- ½ teaspoon baking soda
- 1 teaspoon plus 2 tablespoons water, divided
- ¾ cup sugar
- ¾ cup light corn syrup
- 1 teaspoon almond extract
- 1 cup 60% cacao bittersweet chocolate baking chips
- ⅓ cup chopped almonds, toasted
- ¾ cup flaked coconut

1. Grease a 15x10x1-in. pan with 1½ teaspoons butter; set aside. Place almond butter in a microwave-safe bowl; microwave, covered, at 50% power 30-60 seconds or until softened, stirring once. In a small bowl, dissolve baking soda in 1 teaspoon water. Set aside the almond butter and baking soda mixture.

2. In a large heavy saucepan, combine sugar, corn syrup and 2 tablespoons water. Bring to a boil over medium heat, stirring constantly. Using a pastry brush dipped in water, wash down sides of the pan to eliminate sugar crystals. Cook until a candy thermometer reads 240° (soft-ball stage), stirring occasionally, about 10 minutes. Add remaining butter; cook until candy thermometer reads 300° (hard-crack stage), stirring frequently, about 5 minutes longer.

3. Remove from heat; stir in the softened almond butter, almond extract and dissolved baking soda. (Candy will foam.) Immediately pour into prepared pan. Spread to ¼-in. thickness.

4. Sprinkle with chocolate chips; let stand until chocolate begins to melt. Spread evenly; sprinkle with almonds and coconut, pressing slightly to adhere. Cool slightly. Chill 1 hour or until chocolate is set. Break candy into pieces. Store between layers of waxed paper in an airtight container.
NOTE *To toast nuts, spread in a dry nonstick skillet and heat over low heat until lightly browned, stirring occasionally. We recommend that you test your candy thermometer before each use by bringing water to a boil; the thermometer should read 212°. Adjust the recipe temperature up or down based on the test.*

AMISH SUGAR COOKIES

These easy-to-make cookies simply melt in your mouth! I've passed the recipe around to many friends. After I gave the recipe to my sister, she entered the cookies in a local fair and won the "best of show" prize!

—**SYLVIA FORD** KENNETT, MO

PREP: 10 MIN. • **BAKE:** 10 MIN./BATCH • **MAKES:** ABOUT 5 DOZEN

- 1 cup butter, softened
- 1 cup canola oil
- 1 cup sugar
- 1 cup confectioners' sugar
- 2 eggs
- 1 teaspoon vanilla extract
- 4½ cups all-purpose flour
- 1 teaspoon baking soda
- 1 teaspoon cream of tartar

1. Preheat oven to 375°. In a bowl, beat butter, oil and sugars. Beat in eggs until well blended. Beat in vanilla. Mix flour, baking soda and cream of tartar; gradually add to oil mixture.

2. Drop by small teaspoonfuls onto ungreased baking sheets. Bake 8-10 minutes or until lightly browned. Remove to wire racks to cool.

SHORTBREAD LEMON BARS

I've put together two family cookbooks over the years, and this recipe ranks among my favorites. The special lemon bars have a yummy shortbread crust and refreshing flavor. I'm never afraid to make this dessert for guests because I know it will be a hit!

—MARGARET PETERSON FOREST CITY, IA

PREP: 25 MIN. • **BAKE:** 15 MIN. + CHILLING
MAKES: 3 DOZEN

- 1½ cups all-purpose flour
- ½ cup confectioners' sugar
- 1 teaspoon grated lemon peel
- 1 teaspoon grated orange peel
- ¾ cup cold butter, cubed

FILLING

- 4 eggs
- 2 cups sugar
- ⅓ cup lemon juice
- ¼ cup all-purpose flour
- 2 teaspoons grated lemon peel
- 2 teaspoons grated orange peel
- 1 teaspoon baking powder

TOPPING

- 2 cups (16 ounces) sour cream
- ⅓ cup sugar
- ½ teaspoon vanilla extract

1. Preheat oven to 350°. In a food processor, combine the flour, confectioners' sugar, and lemon and orange peel. Add butter; cover and process until mixture forms a ball.

2. Pat dough into a greased 13x9-in. baking pan. Bake for 12-14 minutes or until set and the edges are lightly browned.

3. In a large bowl, mix the filling ingredients. Pour over hot crust. Bake 14-16 minutes or until set and lightly browned.

4. In a small bowl, combine the topping ingredients. Spread over filling.

5. Bake 7-9 minutes longer or until topping is set. Cool on a wire rack. Refrigerate overnight. Cut into bars just before serving. Store in the refrigerator.

SUGAR-CONE CHOCOLATE CHIP COOKIES

If I could make a batch of cookies a day, I'd be in baking heaven. I made these for my boys when they were growing up, and now I treat my grandkids, too.

—PAULA MARCHESI LENHARTSVILLE, PA

PREP: 25 MIN. • **BAKE:** 10 MIN./BATCH • **MAKES:** 6 DOZEN

- 1 cup butter, softened
- ¾ cup sugar
- ¾ cup packed brown sugar
- 2 eggs
- 3 teaspoons vanilla extract
- 2¼ cups all-purpose flour
- 1 teaspoon baking soda
- ½ teaspoon salt
- 2 cups milk chocolate chips
- 2 cups coarsely crushed ice cream sugar cones (about 16)
- 1 cup sprinkles

1. Preheat oven to 375°. In a large bowl, cream butter and sugars until light and fluffy. Beat in eggs and vanilla. In another bowl, whisk flour, baking soda and salt; gradually beat into creamed mixture. Stir in chocolate chips, crushed sugar cones and sprinkles.

2. Drop by tablespoonfuls 2 in. apart onto ungreased baking sheets. Bake 8-10 minutes or until golden brown. Remove from pans to wire racks to cool.

CORNMEAL LIME COOKIES

Here's something a little different for your platter of Christmas sweets. Cornmeal gives these light cookies crunch, and the tart lime glaze tops them off perfectly.

—**WENDY RUSCH** TREGO, WI

PREP: 45 MIN. + FREEZING • **BAKE:** 12 MIN./BATCH
MAKES: 8 DOZEN

- 1 **cup butter, softened**
- ½ **cup sugar**
- ½ **cup packed brown sugar**
- 1 **egg**
- ¼ **cup lime juice**
- 4½ **teaspoons grated lime peel**
- 2 **cups all-purpose flour**
- 1 **cup yellow cornmeal**

GLAZE

- 2 **cups confectioners' sugar**
- 3 **tablespoons lime juice**
  Holiday sprinkles

1. In a large bowl, cream butter and sugars until light and fluffy. Beat in the egg, lime juice and peel. Combine flour and cornmeal; gradually add to creamed mixture and mix well.
2. Shape into two 12-in. rolls; wrap each in plastic wrap. Refrigerate 30 minutes. Shape each roll into a square-shaped log. Freeze 1 hour or until firm.
3. Preheat oven to 350°. Unwrap logs and cut into ⅜-in. slices. Place 1 in. apart on parchment paper-lined baking sheets. Bake 11-14 minutes or until set. Remove to wire racks to cool completely.
4. Combine confectioners' sugar and lime juice; spread over cookies. Decorate with sprinkles. Let stand until set.

CALLAHAN CHRISTMAS WREATHS

When my family asked for good old Norwegian wreath cookies, I studied several recipes for ideas, then added my own touches to create a special version. What a cute addition to a cookie platter!

—**CASSIDY CALLAHAN** FITCHBURG, MA

PREP: 30 MIN. • **BAKE:** 10 MIN./BATCH • **MAKES:** 2½ DOZEN

- ½ **cup butter, softened**
- ½ **cup shortening**
- 1 **cup sugar**
- 2 **eggs**
- 2 **teaspoons grated orange peel**
- ½ **teaspoon almond extract**
- 2½ **cups all-purpose flour**
  Green food coloring
  Red and green candied cherries

1. Preheat oven to 400°. In a large bowl, cream butter, shortening and sugar until light and fluffy. Beat in eggs, orange peel and extract. Gradually beat in flour. Divide dough in half; tint one portion green with food coloring.
2. For each wreath, shape two 6-in. ropes using 2 teaspoons plain dough for one and 2 teaspoons green dough for the other. Place the two ropes side by side; press together lightly, then twist several times. Shape into a circle, pinching ends to seal. Place 2 in. apart on ungreased baking sheets. Repeat with remaining dough.
3. Cut candied cherries into small pieces and place on wreaths to decorate as desired, pressing lightly to adhere. Bake cookies 6-8 minutes or until set and bottoms are light brown. Remove from pans to wire racks to cool. Store in an airtight container.

LEMONY COCONUT FROZEN YOGURT, PAGE 209

EASY & ELEGANT TENDERLOIN ROAST, 219

EASTER BUNNY ROLLS, 207

LEMON-HERB ROASTED TURKEY, 217

Seasonal Specialties

Every season offers family-favorite traditions. Easter brightens up tables with refreshing flavors, like lemon and fresh produce. In summer, we crave grilled foods, juicy sweet fruits and icy cold treats. As the air turns crisp, apples, pears and pumpkins are featured in whimsical dishes for Halloween and Thanksgiving. The winter holidays showcase heartier fare, such as roasts, sides and a variety of scrumptious desserts. With the great sampling of seasonal specialties here, add some new ones to your family celebration.

CHOCOLATE GUINNESS CAKE

One bite and everyone will propose a toast to this moist, chocolaty cake. The cream cheese frosting resembles the foamy head on a pint of Guinness!

—**MARJORIE HENNIG** SEYMOUR, IN

PREP: 25 • **BAKE:** 45 MIN. + COOLING • **MAKES:** 12 SERVINGS

- 1 cup Guinness (dark beer)
- ½ cup butter, cubed
- 2 cups sugar
- ¾ cup baking cocoa
- 2 eggs, beaten
- ⅔ cup sour cream
- 3 teaspoons vanilla extract
- 2 cups all-purpose flour
- 1½ teaspoons baking soda

TOPPING
- 1 package (8 ounces) cream cheese, softened
- 1½ cups confectioners' sugar
- ½ cup heavy whipping cream

1. Preheat oven to 350°. Grease a 9-in. springform pan and line the bottom with parchment paper; set aside.

2. In a small saucepan, heat beer and butter until butter is melted. Remove from heat; whisk in sugar and cocoa until blended. Combine eggs, sour cream and vanilla; whisk into beer mixture. Combine flour and baking soda; whisk into beer mixture until smooth. Pour batter into prepared pan.

3. Bake 45-50 minutes or until a toothpick inserted near the center comes out clean. Cool completely in pan on a wire rack. Remove sides of pan.

4. In a large bowl, beat cream cheese until fluffy. Add confectioners' sugar and cream; beat until smooth (do not overbeat). Remove cake from the pan and place on a platter or cake stand. Ice top of cake so that it resembles a frothy pint of beer. Store in the refrigerator.

WEARING O' GREEN CAKE

When you taste this colorful cake and you'll think you've found the pot o' gold at the end of the rainbow. It's the perfect dessert to round out your St. Patrick's Day meal.

—**MARGE NICOL** SHANNON, IL

PREP: 25 MIN. • **BAKE:** 30 MIN. + COOLING • **MAKES:** 12-15 SERVINGS

- 1 package white cake mix (regular size)
- 2 packages (3 ounces each) lime gelatin
- 1 cup boiling water
- ½ cup cold water

TOPPING
- 1 cup cold milk
- 1 package (3.4 ounces) instant vanilla pudding mix
- 1 carton (8 ounces) frozen whipped topping, thawed
  Green sprinkles

1. Prepare and bake cake according to package directions, using a greased 13x9-in. baking dish. Cool on a wire rack for 1 hour. In a small bowl, dissolve gelatin in boiling water; stir in cold water and set aside.

2. With a meat fork or wooden skewer, poke holes about 2 in. apart into cooled cake. Slowly pour gelatin over cake. Cover and refrigerate.

3. In a large bowl, whisk milk and pudding mix 2 minutes (mixture will be thick). Fold in whipped topping. Spread over cake. Decorate with sprinkles. Store in the refrigerator.

❝ Turned out awesome, super easy to make and a definite make again recipe! So yummy! ❞

—**WENDY HEWITT** TASTEOFHOME.COM

EASTER BUNNY ROLLS

If you're planning an Easter feast, why not hop to it and roll out a bevy of bunnies? They'll multiply quicker than you think!

—**BONNIE MYERS** CALLAWAY, NE

PREP: 30 MIN. + RISING • **BAKE:** 10 MIN.
MAKES: 2 DOZEN

- 1 package (¼ ounce) active dry yeast
- ¼ cup warm water (110° to 115°)
- ¾ cup warm milk (110° to 115°)
- 2 tablespoons sugar
- 2 tablespoons shortening
- 1 egg, beaten
- 2 teaspoons celery seed
- 1 teaspoon rubbed sage
- 1 teaspoon salt
- ½ teaspoon ground nutmeg
- 3 to 3½ cups all-purpose flour
  Melted butter

1. In a bowl, dissolve yeast in water. Add milk, sugar, shortening, egg, celery seed, sage, salt, nutmeg and 2 cups flour; beat until smooth. Add enough remaining flour to form a soft dough. Turn dough onto a floured surface and knead until smooth and elastic; about 6-8 minutes.

2. Place in a greased bowl, turning once to grease top. Cover and let rise in a warm place until doubled, about 1 hour. Punch dough down; let rest 10 minutes.

3. Divide dough into 24 pieces. For each bunny, roll one piece of dough into a 20-in. rope. Cut rope into one 10-in. piece, one 5-in. piece, two 2-in. pieces and one 1-in. piece. Coil 10-in. piece for body; place on a greased baking sheet. Coil 5-in. piece for head; place next to body. Form ears from the 2-in. pieces and tail from the 1-in. piece; add to bunny. Pinch and seal pieces together. Repeat, placing bunnies 2 in. apart on the baking sheet. Cover and let rise until doubled, about 25 minutes.

4. Preheat oven to 375°. Bake 10-12 minutes or until lightly browned. Brush with butter. Cool on wire racks.

PEANUT BUTTER EASTER EGGS

You won't be able to eat just one of these peanut buttery treats. And don't forget to get the kids involved with this simple recipe—it'll be worth the sticky fingers!

—**MARY JOYCE JOHNSON** UPPER DARBY, PA

PREP: 35 MIN. + CHILLING
COOK: 5 MIN. • **MAKES:** 16 EGGS

- ¾ cup creamy peanut butter
- ½ cup butter, softened
- ½ teaspoon vanilla extract
- 2⅓ cups confectioners' sugar
- 1 cup graham cracker crumbs
- 1½ cups dark chocolate chips
- 2 tablespoons shortening
  Confectioners' sugar icing, optional

1. In a large bowl, beat peanut butter, butter and vanilla until blended. Gradually beat in confectioners' sugar and cracker crumbs. Shape mixture into 16 eggs; place on waxed paper-lined baking sheets. Refrigerate 30 minutes or until firm.

2. In a microwave, melt chocolate chips and shortening; stir until smooth. Dip eggs in chocolate mixture; allow excess to drip off. Return eggs to baking sheets. Refrigerate 30 minutes.

3. If desired, decorate eggs with icing. Let stand until set. Store in airtight containers in refrigerator.

CONFECTIONERS' SUGAR ICING *In a bowl, mix 2 cups confectioners' sugar, 4 teaspoons corn syrup, 1 teaspoon almond extract and 1-2 tablespoons milk until smooth. Tint with paste food coloring if desired. Yield: ⅔ cup. To decorate eggs with bunny ears: cut decorative paper into bunny ears. Tape each ear to a toothpick; insert into tops of eggs. Remove ears before eating.*

How to Tell if Yeast Dough Has Doubled in Size

Here's a simple way to determine if yeast dough has risen enough. Press two fingers about 1/2 in. into the dough. If the dents remain, the dough has doubled in size and is ready to be punched down.

FOURTH OF JULY BEAN CASSEROLE

The outstanding barbecue taste of these beans makes them an instant favorite for cookouts all summer and into the fall. It's a popular dish with everyone, even kids. Having beef and bacon in with the beans is so much better than plain pork.
—**DONNA FANCHER** LAWRENCE, IN

PREP: 20 MIN. • **BAKE:** 1 HOUR
MAKES: 12 SERVINGS

- ½ **pound bacon strips, diced**
- ½ **pound ground beef**
- 1 **cup chopped onion**
- 1 **can (28 ounces) pork and beans**
- 1 **can (16 ounces) kidney beans, rinsed and drained**
- 1 **can (15¼ ounces) lima beans**
- ½ **cup barbecue sauce**
- ½ **cup ketchup**
- ½ **cup sugar**
- ½ **cup packed brown sugar**
- 2 **tablespoons prepared mustard**
- 2 **tablespoons molasses**
- 1 **teaspoon salt**
- ½ **teaspoon chili powder**

1. Prheat oven to 350°. In a large skillet, cook bacon, beef and onion until meat is no longer pink; drain.
2. Transfer to a greased 2½-qt. baking dish; add all of the beans and mix well. In a small bowl, combine the remaining ingredients; stir into beef and bean mixture.
3. Cover and bake 45 minutes. Uncover; bake 15 minutes longer.

RED, WHITE AND BLUE CHEESECAKE

I made this creamy cheesecake for a patriotic get-together with friends. Everyone raved about it, especially my friend's 9-year-old grandson. It looks so pretty and is so delicious.
—**CONNIE LAFOND** TROY, NY

PREP: 40 MIN. • **BAKE:** 1¼ HOURS + CHILLING
MAKES: 16 SERVINGS

- 1½ **cups all-purpose flour**
- ⅓ **cup sugar**
- 1 **teaspoon grated lemon peel**
- ¾ **cup cold butter, cubed**
- 2 **egg yolks**
- ½ **teaspoon vanilla extract**

FILLING
- 5 **packages (8 ounces each) cream cheese, softened**
- 1 **cup sugar**
- ¼ **cup half-and-half cream**
- 3 **tablespoons all-purpose flour**
- ½ **teaspoon grated lemon peel**
- ¼ **teaspoon salt**
- ¼ **teaspoon vanilla extract**
- 2 **eggs, lightly beaten**
- 1 **egg yolk**
- 1 **cup crushed strawberries**
- 1 **cup crushed blueberries**
  Fresh mixed berries, optional

1. Preheat oven to 400°. In a large bowl, combine flour, sugar and lemon peel. Cut in butter until crumbly. Whisk egg yolks and vanilla; add to flour mixture, tossing with a fork until dough forms a ball.
2. Press onto bottom and 3 in. up sides of a greased 9-in. springform pan. Place the pan on a baking sheet. Bake 12-15 minutes or until golden brown. Cool on a wire rack.
3. For filling, in a large bowl, beat the cream cheese and sugar until smooth. Beat in cream, flour, lemon peel, salt and vanilla. Add eggs and yolk; beat on low speed just until combined.
4. Divide batter in half. Fold crushed strawberries and crushed blueberries into half of the batter. Pour into crust. Top with remaining batter. Return pan to baking sheet.
5. Bake at 400° for 10 minutes. Reduce oven temperature to 300° bake 60-70 minutes longer or until center is almost set. Cool on a wire rack 10 minutes. Carefully run a knife around edge of pan to loosen; cool 1 hour. Refrigerate overnight. Remove sides of pan.
6. Garnish with fresh mixed berries and currants, if desired.

" Light and refreshing! Perfect ending to a summer meal. We churned ours to the consistency of soft serve and there wasn't any left to freeze so I can't comment on how it keeps. I used fat-free Greek plain yogurt and regular half-and-half to cut the fat content. "

—JADAHH6SHRADER TASTEOFHOME.COM

LEMONY COCONUT FROZEN YOGURT

Whenever I crave something cold to beat the heat, I whip up this yogurt dessert and share it with family. Everyone enjoys the sweet relief!
—**CAITLYN HEINZ** OVID, NY

PREP: 15 MIN. + CHILLING
PROCESS: 15 MIN. • **MAKES:** 1¼ QUARTS

- 4 cups (32 ounces) plain yogurt
- ¾ cup sugar
- ½ cup lemon juice
- 3 tablespoons grated lemon peel
- 1 cup half-and-half cream
- ½ cup flaked coconut, toasted
  Ice cream waffle bowls, optional
  Fresh blueberries and
    raspberries, optional

1. Line a strainer or colander with four layers of cheesecloth or one coffee filter; place over a bowl. Place yogurt in the prepared strainer; refrigerate, covered, 3 hours. Remove yogurt from cheesecloth and place in a large bowl; discard drained liquid.
2. Whisk sugar, lemon juice and lemon peel into yogurt until sugar is dissolved. Stir in cream. Pour into cylinder of ice cream freezer; freeze according to the manufacturer's directions, adding coconut during the last 5 minutes of processing time. If desired, serve in waffle bowls and top with berries.
NOTE *To toast coconut, spread in a 15x10x1-in. baking pan. Bake at 350° for 5-10 minutes or until golden brown, stirring frequently.*

BASIL BURGERS WITH SUN-DRIED TOMATO MAYONNAISE

Basil thrives in my backyard and I am often blessed with a bumper crop. Here's one of my favorite ways to use it. These burgers feature great Italian flavor. And who can resist their gooey, cheesy centers and scrumptious toppings?

—VIRGINIA KOCHIS SPRINGFIELD, VA

PREP: 25 MIN. • **GRILL:** 10 MIN. • **MAKES:** 6 SERVINGS

- ¼ **cup sun-dried tomatoes (not packed in oil)**
- 1 **cup boiling water**
- 1 **cup fat-free mayonnaise**
- 2 **teaspoons Worcestershire sauce**
- ¼ **cup fresh basil leaves, coarsely chopped**
- 2 **teaspoons Italian seasoning**
- 2 **garlic cloves, minced**
- ½ **teaspoon pepper**
- ¼ **teaspoon salt**
- 1½ **pounds lean ground beef (90% lean)**
- ¾ **cup shredded part-skim mozzarella cheese**
- 6 **whole wheat hamburger buns, split**
  Additional fresh basil leaves, optional

1. In a small bowl, combine tomatoes and water. Let stand 5 minutes; drain. In a food processor, combine mayonnaise and tomatoes; cover and process until blended. Refrigerate until serving.

2. In a large bowl, combine the Worcestershire sauce, basil, Italian seasoning, garlic, pepper and salt. Crumble the beef over mixture and mix well. Shape into 12 thin patties. Place 2 tablespoons cheese on six patties; top with the remaining patties and press edges firmly to seal.

3. Moisten a paper towel with cooking oil; using long-handled tongs, rub on grill rack to coat lightly. Grill burgers, covered, over medium heat or broil 4 in. from the heat for 5-7 minutes on each side or until a thermometer reads 160° and juices run clear. Serve on buns with mayonnaise mixture and if desired, additional basil.

⑤ INGREDIENTS

PATRIOTIC POPS

My kids love homemade ice pops, and I love knowing that the ones we make are good for them. We whip up a big batch with multiple flavors so they have many choices, but these patriotic red, white and blue ones are always a favorite!

—SHANNON CARINO FRISCO, TX

PREP: 15 MIN. + FREEZING • **MAKES:** 1 DOZEN

- 1¼ **cups sliced fresh strawberries, divided**
- 1¾ **cups (14 ounces) vanilla yogurt, divided**
- 1¼ **cups fresh or frozen blueberries, divided**
- 12 **freezer pop molds or 12 paper cups (3 ounces each) and wooden pop sticks**

1. In a blender, combine 1 cup strawberries and 2 tablespoons yogurt; cover and process until blended. Transfer to a small bowl. Chop remaining strawberries; stir into strawberry mixture.

2. In same blender, combine 1 cup blueberries and 2 tablespoons yogurt; cover and process until blended. Stir in remaining blueberries.

3. Layer 1 tablespoon strawberry mixture, 2 tablespoons yogurt and 1 tablespoon blueberry mixture in each of the 12 molds or paper cups. Top molds with holders. If using cups, top with foil and insert sticks through foil. Freeze until firm.

" This burger was quick and easy to put together and was loaded with flavor. Definitely a redo! "

—SUSAN'S KITCHEN TASTEOFHOME.COM

DAD'S LEMONY GRILLED CHICKEN

Lemon juice, onions and garlic add tangy flavor to my grilled chicken. Try it and see if it isn't a hit at your next barbecue.
—**MIKE SCHULZ** TAWAS CITY, MI

PREP: 20 MIN. + MARINATING • **GRILL:** 30 MIN. • **MAKES:** 8 SERVINGS

- 1 cup olive oil
- ⅔ cup lemon juice
- 6 garlic cloves, minced
- 1 teaspoon salt
- ½ teaspoon pepper
- 2 medium onions, chopped
- 8 chicken drumsticks (2 pounds)
- 8 bone-in chicken thighs (2 pounds)

1. In a small bowl, whisk the first five ingredients until blended; stir in onions. Pour 1½ cups marinade into a large resealable plastic bag. Add chicken; seal bag and turn to coat. Refrigerate overnight. Cover and refrigerate the remaining marinade.

2. Prepare grill for indirect heat. Drain chicken, discarding marinade in bag. Place chicken on grill rack, skin side up. Grill, covered, over indirect medium heat 15 minutes. Turn; grill 15-20 minutes longer or until a thermometer reads 170°-175°, basting occasionally with reserved marinade.

(5) INGREDIENTS

CREAMY WATERMELON PIE

This simple pie is so refreshing that it never lasts long on warm summer days. Watermelon and a few convenience items make it a delightful dessert that's easy to whip up.
—**VELMA BECK** CARLINVILLE, IL

PREP: 15 MIN. + CHILLING • **MAKES:** 6-8 SERVINGS

- 1 package (3 ounces) watermelon gelatin
- ¼ cup boiling water
- 1 carton (12 ounces) frozen whipped topping, thawed
- 2 cups cubed seeded watermelon
- 1 graham cracker crust (9 inches)

In a large bowl, dissolve gelatin in boiling water. Cool to room temperature. Whisk in whipped topping; fold in the watermelon. Spoon into the crust. Refrigerate 2 hours or until set.

TOP TIP

Setting up a Charcoal Grill for Indirect Heat

Start the grill as you normally would for grilling. Once the coals are hot, position half of the coals on one side of the grill and the other half on the opposite side, leaving the center of the grill empty. Place a foil drip pan in the center and replace the cooking grate. Arrange the meat over the drip pan. Cover and grill according to recipe directions.

TRUFFLE FOOTBALL CUPCAKES

These luscious football truffles combine peanut butter and chocolate deliciously. Use the snappy footballs to top cupcakes for a tailgate party or any gathering to cheer on your favorite team. Or, shape them into balls for a holiday treat tray.

—KIM BARKER RICHMOND, TX

PREP: 25 MIN. + STANDING
MAKES: 3 DOZEN

- 3 ounces white candy coating, coarsely chopped, divided
- ⅔ cup creamy peanut butter
- ½ cup confectioners' sugar
- 3 teaspoons vanilla extract
- ⅔ cup crushed granola cereal with oats and honey
- 6 ounces semisweet chocolate, chopped
- 2 tablespoons shortening
- 2 cans (16 ounces each) vanilla frosting, divided
  Green paste food coloring
- 36 cupcakes of your choice

1. In a microwave, melt white candy coating at 70% power for 1 minute; stir. Microwave at additional 10- to 20-second intervals, stirring until smooth. Stir in peanut butter until smooth. Add the confectioners' sugar, vanilla and cereal. Chill for 2-3 hours or until easy to handle.
2. Shape into 1-in. balls; form each ball into football shape and set aside. In a microwave, melt chocolate and shortening; stir until smooth. Dip footballs in chocolate; allow excess to drip off. Place on a wire rack over waxed paper; let stand until set, about 30 minutes.

3. Pipe frosting laces onto footballs. Tint remaining frosting green. Using a #233 or #234 tip, pipe grass over cupcakes. Just before serving, insert a toothpick into each football, then insert opposite end of toothpick into the cupcakes to position the football.

GINGERBREAD WHOOPIE PIES

These spiced-just-right whoopie pies combine two popular flavors in one fun treat. The moist cookies are rolled in sugar before baking for a bit of crunch.

—JAMIE JONES MADISON, GA

PREP: 25 MIN. + CHILLING
BAKE: 10 MIN./BATCH + COOLING
MAKES: ABOUT 2 DOZEN

- ¾ cup butter, softened
- ¾ cup packed brown sugar
- ½ cup molasses
- 1 egg
- 3 cups all-purpose flour
- 2 teaspoons ground ginger
- 1 teaspoon ground cinnamon
- 1 teaspoon baking soda
- ¼ teaspoon salt
- ½ cup sugar

FILLING
- ¾ cup butter, softened
- ¾ cup marshmallow creme
- 1½ cups confectioners' sugar
- ¾ teaspoon lemon extract

1. In a large bowl, cream butter and brown sugar until light and fluffy. Beat in molasses and egg. Combine flour, ginger, cinnamon, baking soda and salt; gradually add to creamed mixture and mix well. Cover and refrigerate at least 3 hours.
2. Preheat oven to 350°. Shape into 1-in. balls; roll in sugar. Place 3 in. apart on ungreased baking sheets. Flatten to ½-in. thickness with a glass dipped in sugar. Bake 8-10 minutes or until set. Cool 2 minutes before removing from pans to wire racks to cool completely.
3. For filling, in a small bowl, beat butter and marshmallow creme until light and fluffy. Gradually beat in confectioners' sugar and extract.
4. Spread filling on the bottoms of half of the cookies, about 1 tablespoon on each; top with remaining cookies.

HALLOWEEN CANDY BARK

My kids and I wanted to make a treat using the beautiful colors of fall and some candy that's special to Halloween. This bark was the tasty result! Let the kids customize their own bark by using their favorite candies and cookies.

—MARGARET BROTT
COLORADO SPRINGS, CO

PREP: 20 MIN. + STANDING
MAKES: 2¾ POUNDS

- 2 teaspoons butter
- 1½ pounds white candy coating, coarsely chopped
- 2 cups pretzels, coarsely chopped
- 10 Oreo cookies, chopped
- ¾ cup candy corn
- ¾ cup dry roasted peanuts
- ½ cup milk chocolate M&M's
- ½ cup Reese's Pieces

1. Line a 15x10x1-in. baking pan with foil; grease foil with butter. In a microwave, melt candy coating; stir until smooth. Spread into prepared pan. Sprinkle with the remaining ingredients; press into candy coating. Let stand about 1 hour.
2. Break or cut bark into pieces. Store in an airtight container.

---

(5) INGREDIENTS

ALL-DAY APPLE BUTTER

When autumn comes around, I like to make several batches of this simple and delicious apple butter and freeze it in jars. Depending on the sweetness of the apples used, you can adjust the sugar to taste.

—BETTY RUENHOLL SYRACUSE, NE

PREP: 20 MIN. • **COOK:** 11 HOURS
MAKES: 4 PINTS

- 5½ pounds apples, peeled and finely chopped
- 4 cups sugar
- 2 to 3 teaspoons ground cinnamon
- ¼ teaspoon ground cloves
- ¼ teaspoon salt

1. Place apples in a 3-qt. slow cooker. Combine sugar, cinnamon, cloves and salt; pour over apples and mix well. Cover and cook on high 1 hour.
2. Reduce heat to low; cover and cook 9-11 hours or until thickened and dark brown, stirring occasionally (stir more frequently as it thickens to prevent the apple butter from sticking).
3. Uncover and cook on low 1 hour longer. If desired, stir with a wire whisk until smooth. Spoon into freezer containers, leaving ½-in. headspace. Cover and refrigerate or freeze.

---

(5) INGREDIENTS

EYEBALL COOKIES

All eyes will definitely be on these adorable cookies when they're set on a buffet table. I created them for my son's kindergarten class for Halloween.

—SHERRY LEE COLUMBUS, OH

PREP: 25 MIN. + CHILLING
MAKES: 20-25 SERVINGS

- 5 ounces white baking chocolate, chopped, divided
- 20 to 25 vanilla wafers
  Blue paste food coloring
- ½ cup semisweet chocolate chips
  Red liquid food coloring

1. In a microwave, melt 4 ounces of white chocolate; stir until smooth. Dip vanilla wafers in melted chocolate; allow excess to drip off. Place on a waxed paper-lined baking sheet. Chill until set.
2. Melt remaining white chocolate; stir until smooth. Tint blue. Spread a small amount onto the center of each cookie; place a chocolate chip in the center of each cookie.
3. For bloodshot eyes, use a toothpick dipped in red food coloring to draw lines from blue circles to outer edges of wafers. Chill until set. Store in an airtight container.

❝ Little kids loved these at our Halloween party and they were so easy to make with my little helpers. ❞

—GLORY66
TASTEOFHOME.COM

CREEPY SPIDERS

Cake mix gives these chocolate sandwich cookies a head start. You can even have kids help assemble the spiders!

—NELLA PARKER HERSEY, MI

PREP: 30 MIN. • **BAKE:** 10 MIN.
MAKES: ABOUT 2 DOZEN

- 1 **package chocolate fudge cake mix (regular size)**
- ½ **cup butter, melted**
- 1 **egg**
- 1 **can (16 ounces) chocolate frosting**
  Shoestring black licorice, cut into 1½ inch pieces
- ¼ **cup red-hot candies**

1. Preheat oven to 350°. In a large bowl, combine the cake mix, butter and egg (dough will be stiff). Shape into 1-in. balls.

2. Place 2 in. apart on ungreased baking sheets. Bake 10-12 minutes or until set. Cool for 1 minute before removing from pans to wire racks.

3. Spread a heaping teaspoonful of frosting over the bottom of half of the cookies. Place four licorice pieces on each side of cookies for spider legs; top with remaining cookies. For eyes, attach two red-hot candies with frosting to top of spider.

TOP TIP

Make Simple Snacks with Leftover Frosting

If you have a little frosting leftover, you can use it to make the following sweet treats. Spread some frosting over a graham cracker or the flat side of cookie, such as a vanilla wafer or gingersnap. Top with another cracker or cookie. Or, spread frosting on top of an ice cream bar, then top with another bar and cut widthwise in half. Cover each half with whipped topping and freeze. When ready to serve, drizzle each serving with ice cream topping and sprinkle with chopped nuts if desired.

STRAWBERRY GHOSTS

These ghosts are so easy to make and always get such a gleeful reaction. Package them up in small gift boxes to give to the neighborhood kids when they stop by for tick-or-treat.

—NANCY MUELLER
HIGHLANDS RANCH, CO

START TO FINISH: 30 MIN.
MAKES: 2½ DOZEN

- 30 **fresh strawberries**
- 8 **ounces white baking chocolate, chopped**
- 1 **teaspoon shortening**
- ⅛ **teaspoon almond extract**
- ¼ **cup miniature semisweet chocolate chips**

1. Wash strawberries and gently pat with paper towels until completely dry. In a microwave-safe bowl, melt white chocolate and shortening at 50% power; stir until smooth. Stir in the extract.
2. Dip the strawberries in chocolate mixture; place on a waxed paper-lined baking sheet, allowing the excess chocolate to form the ghosts' tails. Immediately press the chocolate chips into coating for eyes. Freeze for 5 minutes.
3. In microwave, melt the remaining chocolate chips; stir until smooth. Dip a toothpick into melted chocolate and draw a mouth on each ghost. Store in the refrigerator.

CHEESENSTEIN

The creamy, fun dip will be the hit of every Halloween party! I've done several variations of this cheese ball. It never fails to get plenty of smiles!
—NILA GRAHL GURNEE, IL

PREP: 45 MIN. + CHILLING • **MAKES:** 3 CUPS

- 2 **packages (8 ounces each) cream cheese, softened**
- ¼ **cup mayonnaise**
- 1 **tablespoon Worcestershire sauce**
- 1 **teaspoon hot pepper sauce**
- 2 **cups (8 ounces) shredded cheddar cheese**
- 6 **bacon strips, cooked and crumbled**
- 3 **green onions, thinly sliced**
- 2 **cartons (4 ounces each) whipped cream cheese**
  Moss-green paste food coloring
- 1 **can (4¼ ounces) chopped ripe olives, drained**
- 2 **pepperoncini**
- 3 **colossal ripe olives**
- 2 **slices peeled parsnip**
  Black decorating gel
- 1 **pretzel rod**
- 1 **small cucumber**
  Assorted fresh vegetables

1. In a large bowl, beat the cream cheese, mayonnaise, Worcestershire sauce and pepper sauce until smooth. Stir in the cheddar cheese, bacon and onions. Shape mixture into a 5x4x3-in. rectangle; wrap in plastic wrap. Refrigerate until chilled.
2. Unwrap rectangle; place on a serving platter with a 3-in. side on top. Tint whipped cream cheese green; spread over top and sides of rectangle.
3. Add chopped ripe olives for hair and pepperoncinis for ears. Cut one colossal olive in half; add parsnip slices and olive halves for eyes. With black decorating gel, pipe the brow, mouth and stitches.
4. Break pretzel rod in half; add a colossal olive to each end. Press into sides of head for bolts. Cut a small piece from end of cucumber for a nose (save remaining cucumber for another use). Serve with vegetables.

TOM TURKEYS

With a little prep work by Mom or Dad, these make a
fun after-dinner craft project for the kids to enjoy.
—*TASTE OF HOME* TEST KITCHEN

PREP: 30 MIN. • **COOK:** 5 MIN. + COOLING • **MAKES:** 26 TURKEYS

- 1 **package (12 ounces) semisweet chocolate chips**
- 1 **package (11 ounces) candy corn**
- 52 **fudge-striped cookies**
- ¼ **cup butter, cubed**
- 4 **cups miniature marshmallows**
- 6 **cups crisp rice cereal**
- 52 **white confetti sprinkles**

1. In a microwave, melt chocolate chips; stir until smooth.
For tails, use a dab of chocolate to attach five candy corns to
the chocolate side of half of the cookies in a fan shape;
refrigerate until set.

2. In a large saucepan, melt butter. Add marshmallows; stir
over low heat until melted. Stir in cereal. Cool 10 minutes.
With buttered hands, form cereal mixture into 1½-in. balls.

3. Remelt chocolate if necessary. Using chocolate, attach the
cereal balls to the chocolate side of the remaining cookies.
Position tails perpendicular to the base cookies; attach with
chocolate. Refrigerate until set.

4. For feet, cut off white tips from 52 candy corns; discard
tips. Attach feet to base cookies with chocolate. Attach one
candy corn to each cereal ball for heads.

5. With a toothpick dipped in chocolate, attach two confetti
sprinkles to each head. Using chocolate, dot each sprinkle
to make pupils. Let turkeys stand until set. Store in an
airtight container.

NEXT DAY TURKEY PRIMAVERA

I make this recipe often around the holidays. It's a wonderful way
to use leftover turkey without feeling like it's a repeat meal. I love
pasta, and the creamy sauce in this primavera is so easy to make.
—**ROBYN HARDISTY** LAKEWOOD, CA

START TO FINISH: 30 MIN. • **MAKES:** 4 SERVINGS

- 1 **cup uncooked penne pasta**
- 8 **fresh asparagus spears, trimmed and cut into 1-inch
  pieces**
- ⅔ **cup julienned carrot**
- 3 **tablespoons butter**
- 4 **large fresh mushrooms, sliced**
- ½ **cup chopped yellow summer squash**
- ½ **cup chopped zucchini**
- 1½ **cups shredded cooked turkey**
- 1 **medium tomato, chopped**
- 1 **envelope Italian salad dressing mix**
- 1 **cup heavy whipping cream**
- ¼ **cup grated Parmesan cheese**

1. Cook pasta according to package directions. Meanwhile,
in a large skillet, saute asparagus and carrot in butter for
3 minutes. Add the mushrooms, yellow squash and zucchini;
saute until crisp-tender.

2. Stir in the turkey, tomato, dressing mix and cream. Bring
to a boil; cook and stir 2 minutes.

3. Drain pasta; add to vegetable mixture and toss to
combine. Sprinkle with cheese and toss again.

CRANBERRY DOUBLE-NUT PIE

Tart cranberries provide a delicious contrast to the rich nut filling. In fact it's so scrumptious, I'll hear groans from my family if they don't see it for dessert during the holidays.
—LILY JULOW LAWRENCEVILLE, GA

PREP: 20 MIN. • **BAKE:** 45 MIN. + COOLING • **MAKES:** 8 SERVINGS

    Pastry for single-crust pie (9 inches)
 3 eggs
 ¾ cup packed brown sugar
 ½ cup light corn syrup
 ⅓ cup butter, melted
 2 tablespoons molasses
 ¼ teaspoon salt
 1½ cups fresh or frozen cranberries, thawed
 ¾ cup coarsely chopped walnuts, toasted
 ¾ cup coarsely chopped pecans, toasted

1. Preheat oven to 350°. On a lightly floured surface, roll pastry dough to a ⅛-in.-thick circle; transfer to a 9-in. pie plate. Trim pastry to ½ in. beyond rim of plate; flute edge.
2. In a large bowl, whisk eggs, brown sugar, corn syrup, butter, molasses and salt; stir in cranberries, walnuts and pecans. Pour into pastry.
3. Bake 45-50 minutes or until set. Cool on a wire rack.

PASTRY FOR SINGLE-CRUST PIE (9 INCHES) *Combine 1¼ cups all-purpose flour and ¼ teaspoon salt; cut in ½ cup cold butter until crumbly. Gradually add 3-5 tablespoons ice water, tossing with a fork until dough holds together when pressed. Wrap in plastic wrap and refrigerate for 1 hour.*
NOTE *To toast nuts, spread in a 15x10x1-in. baking pan. Bake at 350° for 5-10 minutes or until lightly browned, stirring occasionally. Or, spread in a dry nonstick skillet and heat over low heat until lightly browned, stirring occasionally.*

LEMON-HERB ROASTED TURKEY

Lemon and thyme are the predominant flavors in this golden, tender and moist turkey. It's so easy, you just can't go wrong.
—FELECIA SMITH GEORGETOWN, TX

PREP: 30 MIN. • **BAKE:** 2¼ HOURS + STANDING
MAKES: 14-16 SERVINGS

 ½ cup butter, melted
 3 tablespoons lemon juice
 2 teaspoons grated lemon peel
 1 teaspoon minced fresh thyme or ¼ teaspoon dried thyme
 1 turkey (14 to 16 pounds)
 2 teaspoons salt
 2 teaspoons pepper
 1 medium lemon, halved
 1 medium onion, quartered
 14 garlic cloves, peeled
 24 fresh thyme sprigs
 1 tablespoon all-purpose flour
 1 turkey-size oven roasting bag

1. Preheat oven to 350°. In a small bowl, combine the butter, lemon juice, lemon peel and minced thyme. Pat turkey dry. Sprinkle salt and pepper over skin of turkey and inside cavity; brush with butter mixture. Place the lemon, onion, garlic and thyme sprigs inside cavity. Skewer turkey openings; tie drumsticks together.
2. Place flour in oven bag and shake to coat. Place bag in a roasting pan; add turkey to bag, breast side up. Cut six ½-in. slits in top of bag; close bag with tie provided.
3. Bake 2¼ to 2¾ hours or until a thermometer inserted in thigh reads 170° to 175°. Remove turkey to a serving platter and keep warm. Let stand 15 minutes before carving. If desired, thicken pan drippings for gravy.

FREEZE OPTION *Place sliced cooled turkey and turkey parts in freezer containers. Freeze cooled gravy in separate containers. To use, partially thaw turkey and gravy in refrigerator overnight. Heat turkey and gravy in a covered skillet, gently stirring and adding a little broth or water if necessary.*

CINNAMON PUMPKIN PIE

My daughter, Jessica, claims this is the best pumpkin pie she's ever eaten! And the best part for the baker is that it's so easy to do!

—**JACKIE DEIBERT** KLINGERSTOWN, PA

PREP: 10 MIN. • **BAKE:** 55 MIN. + COOLING • **MAKES:** 6 SERVINGS

- 1 cup sugar
- 4 teaspoons cornstarch
- ½ teaspoon salt
- ½ teaspoon ground cinnamon
- 2 eggs, lightly beaten
- 1 can (15 ounces) solid-pack pumpkin
- 1 cup milk
- 1 unbaked pastry shell (9 inches)
  Whipped cream in a can, optional

1. Preheat oven to 400°. In a small bowl, combine the sugar, cornstarch, salt and cinnamon. In a large bowl, combine the eggs, pumpkin and sugar mixture. Gradually stir in milk. Pour into pastry shell.

2. Bake 10 minutes. Reduce oven temperature to 350°; bake 45-50 minutes longer or until a knife inserted near the center comes out clean. Cool on a wire rack. Top with whipped cream if desired. Store in the refrigerator.

66 This was a very simple and easy recipe. The kids loved to help make this pie and they just gobbled it all up! 99

—LOPEZWR1TER TASTEOFHOME.COM

FAVORITE SUGAR COOKIES

Making these sweet treats is a family tradition. I hope you love the recipe as much as we do!

—**JUDITH SCHOLOVICH** WAUKESHA, WI

PREP: 30 MIN. + CHILLING • **BAKE:** 10 MIN./BATCH + COOLING
MAKES: 6-7 DOZEN

- 1 cup butter, softened
- 1 cup confectioners' sugar
- 1 egg
- 1½ teaspoons almond extract
- 1 teaspoon vanilla extract
- 2½ cups all-purpose flour
- 1 teaspoon salt

FROSTING

- 6 tablespoons butter, softened
- 3 cups confectioners' sugar
- 1 teaspoon vanilla extract
- 2 to 4 tablespoons 2% milk
  Food coloring of your choice, optional
  Colored sugar, edible glitter, nonpareils or frosting of your choice, optional

1. In a large bowl, cream butter and confectioners' sugar until light and fluffy. Beat in egg and extracts. Combine flour and salt; add to creamed mixture and mix well. Refrigerate for 1-2 hours.

2. Preheat oven to 375°. On a lightly floured surface, roll the dough to ⅛-in. thickness. Cut with a floured 2½-in. cookie cutters. Place on greased baking sheets. Bake 7-9 minutes or until lightly browned. Remove to wire racks to cool.

3. For frosting, in a small bowl, combine the butter, sugar, vanilla and enough milk to achieve a spreading consistency. If desired, tint with food coloring. Frost the cookies; decorate as desired.

(5) INGREDIENTS

EASY & ELEGANT TENDERLOIN ROAST

I love the simplicity of this recipe. Olive oil, garlic, salt and pepper are rubbed over a tenderloin. After an hour or so in the oven you'll have an impressive main dish to feed a crowd. This leaves you with more time to visit with family and less time fussing in the kitchen.
—**MARY KANDELL** HURON, OH

PREP: 10 MIN. • **BAKE:** 50 MIN. + STANDING • **MAKES:** 12 SERVINGS

- 1 beef tenderloin (5 pounds)
- 2 tablespoons olive oil
- 4 garlic cloves, minced
- 2 teaspoons sea salt
- 1½ teaspoons coarsely ground pepper

1. Preheat oven to 425°. Place roast on a rack in a shallow roasting pan. In a small bowl, mix the oil, garlic, salt and pepper; rub over roast.

2. Roast 50-70 minutes or until meat reaches desired doneness (for medium-rare, a thermometer should read 145°; medium, 160°; well-done, 170°). Remove from oven; tent with foil. Let stand 15 minutes before slicing.

(5) INGREDIENTS

GUMDROP FUDGE

Making candy is one of my favorite things to do during the holidays. This sweet white fudge is as easy to put together as it is beautiful and impressive to serve.
—**JENNIFER SHORT** OMAHA, NE

PREP: 20 MIN. + CHILLING • **MAKES:** ABOUT 3 POUNDS

- 1½ pounds white candy coating, coarsely chopped
- 1 can (14 ounces) sweetened condensed milk
- ⅛ teaspoon salt
- 1½ teaspoons vanilla extract
- 1½ cups chopped gumdrops

1. Line a 9-in.-square pan with foil; set aside. In a heavy saucepan, combine the candy coating, milk and salt. Cook and stir over low heat until candy coating is melted. Remove from heat; stir in vanilla and gumdrops.

2. Spread into prepared pan. Cover and refrigerate until firm. Using foil, remove fudge from the pan; cut into 1-in. squares. Store in an airtight container at room temperature.

CHOCOLATE SNOWBALLS

Here is one of my cherished Christmas cookie recipes. The cookies remind me of the snowballs I'd pack as a child during winters in Wisconsin.
—**DEE DEREZINSKI** WAUKESHA, WI

PREP: 20 MIN. • **BAKE:** 15 MIN./BATCH • **MAKES:** ABOUT 4 DOZEN

- ¾ cup butter, softened
- ½ cup sugar
- 1 egg
- 2 teaspoons vanilla extract
- 2 cups all-purpose flour
- ½ teaspoon salt
- 1 cup chopped nuts
- 1 cup (6 ounces) chocolate chips
  Confectioners' sugar

1. Preheat oven to 350°. In a bowl, cream butter and sugar. Add egg and vanilla; mix well. Combine flour and salt; stir into creamed mixture. Fold in the nuts and chips. Roll into 1-in. balls.

2. Place on ungreased baking sheets. Bake 15-20 minutes. Cool cookies slightly before rolling in confectioners' sugar.

"I just finished making these cookies and they are very good. A great dough for cutout cookies."

—**LYNDATONEY** TASTEOFHOME.COM

CRISP GINGERBREAD CUTOUTS

My grandsons started cooking by helping their grandpa mix waffle and pancake batter. They like to help me with these nicely spiced cookies by decorating them with raisins and candies.

—**SHELIA HANAUER** REIDSVILLE, NC

PREP: 25 MIN. + CHILLING • **BAKE:** 10 MIN./BATCH
MAKES: 4½ DOZEN

- ½ cup shortening
- ½ cup sugar
- ½ cup molasses
- 1 egg
- 2¼ cups all-purpose flour
- 1½ teaspoons ground cinnamon
- 1 teaspoon baking powder
- 1 teaspoon ground ginger
- 1 teaspoon ground cloves
- ½ teaspoon salt
- ½ teaspoon baking soda
- ½ teaspoon ground nutmeg

1. In a large bowl, cream shortening and sugar until light and fluffy. Beat in molasses and egg. Combine dry ingredients; add to creamed mixture and mix well (dough will be soft). Refrigerate, covered, for 1 hour or until easy to handle.
2. Preheat oven to 350°. On a lightly floured surface, roll out to ⅛-in. thickness. Cut with floured 2½-in. cookie cutters and place on greased baking sheets.
3. Bake 8-10 minutes or until the edges are lightly browned. Remove to wire racks to cool.

(5) INGREDIENTS

CHOCOLATE PEPPERMINT BARK

If you don't have time to spare, try this holiday bark. It's a snap to make, so I can focus on my guests instead of the kitchen. No one seems to care that it was effortless on my part—they just keep coming back for more.

—**KESLIE HOUSER** PASCO, WA

PREP: 15 MIN. + CHILLING • **MAKES:** ABOUT 1 POUND

- 6 ounces white baking chocolate, chopped
- 1 cup crushed peppermint or spearmint candies, divided
- 1 cup (6 ounces) semisweet chocolate chips

1. In a microwave, melt white chocolate at 70% power; stir until smooth. Stir in ⅓ cup crushed candies. Repeat with the chocolate chips and an additional ⅓ cup candies. Alternately drop spoonfuls of chocolate and white chocolate mixtures onto a waxed paper-lined baking sheet.
2. Using a metal spatula, cut through the candy to swirl and spread to ¼-in. thickness. Sprinkle with the remaining crushed candies.
3. Refrigerate until firm. Break into pieces. Store between layers of waxed paper in an airtight container.
NOTE *This recipe was tested in a 1,100-watt microwave.*

EGGNOG MINI LOAVES

The seasonal flavors of eggnog, rum extract and nutmeg shine through in these tender golden loaves. They bake up in batches of three so you can keep one and give two away.

—**BEVERLY ELMORE** SPOKANE, MI

PREP: 15 MIN. • **BAKE:** 30 MIN. + COOLING • **MAKES:** 3 LOAVES

- 2¼ cups all-purpose flour
- 2½ teaspoons baking powder
- ½ teaspoon salt
- ½ teaspoon ground cinnamon
- ½ teaspoon ground nutmeg
- 2 eggs
- 1 cup eggnog
- ¾ cup sugar
- ½ cup butter, melted
- 2 teaspoons vanilla extract
- 2 teaspoons rum extract

1. Preheat oven to 350°. In a large bowl, combine the flour, baking powder, salt, cinnamon and nutmeg. In another bowl, beat the eggs, eggnog, sugar, butter and extracts; stir into dry ingredients just until moistened.
2. Pour into three greased 5¾x3x 2-in. loaf pans. Bake 30-35 minutes or until a toothpick inserted near the center comes out clean. Cool 10 minutes before removing from pans to wire racks.
NOTE *This recipe was tested with commercially prepared eggnog.*

SUGARPLUM SPICE BREAD

I make Christmas Eve magical with hot cocoa and toasted slices of this fragrant, fruit-studded bread. My son and I combined several recipes to come up with this winner.
—JACKIE BROWN TULLY, NY

PREP: 30 MIN. + RISING • **BAKE:** 30 MIN. • **MAKES:** 8 MINI LOAVES

- ¾ cup butter, softened
- ¾ cup sugar
- 4 eggs
- 5½ to 6 cups all-purpose flour
- 2 packages (¼ ounce each) quick-rise yeast
- 1½ teaspoons ground cardamom
- 1 teaspoon salt
- ¾ teaspoon ground cinnamon
- ¼ teaspoon ground nutmeg
- 1½ cups milk
- 1 cup diced dried fruit
- ½ cup raisins
- ½ cup golden raisins

FROSTING
- 2 tablespoons butter, softened
- 2 tablespoons shortening
- 2 cups confectioners' sugar
- ½ teaspoon vanilla extract
- 2 to 3 tablespoons milk

1. In a large bowl, cream butter and sugar. Add eggs, one at a time, beating well after each addition. Add 4 cups flour, yeast, cardamom, salt, cinnamon and nutmeg. Heat milk to 120°-130°; add to creamed mixture and beat until moistened. Stir in enough remaining flour to form a firm dough. Turn onto a heavily floured surface. Sprinkle with fruit and raisins; knead until smooth and elastic, about 6-8 minutes. Cover and let rise in a warm place until doubled, about 40 minutes.

2. Punch dough down. Turn onto a lightly floured surface; divided into eight portions. Shape into loaves. Place in eight greased 5x3x2-in. loaf pans. Cover and let rise until doubled, about 30 minutes. Preheat oven to 350°.

3. Bake 30-35 minutes or until golden brown. Remove from pans to wire racks to cool.

4. For frosting, in a small bowl, cream the butter and shortening. Gradually beat in the confectioners' sugar, vanilla and enough milk to achieve spreading consistency. Frost loaves.

WHIPPED SHORTBREAD

This version of shortbread is tender, not too sweet and melts in your mouth. Mostly I make it for the holidays, but I'll also prepare it year-round for wedding showers and afternoon tea parties.
—JANE FICIUR BOW ISLAND, AB

PREP: 50 MIN. • **BAKE:** 20 MIN./BATCH • **MAKES:** 16-18 DOZEN

- 3 cups butter, softened
- 1½ cups confectioners' sugar, sifted
- 4½ cups all-purpose flour
- 1½ cups cornstarch
  Nonpareils and/or halved candied cherries

1. Preheat oven to 300°. In a large bowl, cream butter and confectioners' sugar until light and fluffy. Gradually add flour and cornstarch, beating until well blended.

2. With hands lightly dusted with additional cornstarch, roll dough into 1-in. balls. Place 1 in. apart on ungreased baking sheets. Press lightly with a floured fork. Top with nonpareils or cherry halves.

3. Bake 20-22 minutes or until bottoms are lightly browned. Cool 5 minutes before removing from pans to wire racks.

(5) INGREDIENTS
CREME DE MENTHE CHEESECAKE COOKIES

Stir cream cheese and creme de menthe baking chips into purchased dough for richness and a refreshing hint of mint. For a festive finish, pipe candy-coating trees on top.
—**SHEILA SPORN** HOUSTON, TX

PREP: 15 MIN. • **BAKE:** 15 MIN./BATCH + COOLING
MAKES: 4 DOZEN

- 1 tube (16½ ounces) refrigerated sugar cookie dough
- 6 tablespoons all-purpose flour
- 1 large egg
- 1 package (8 ounces) cream cheese, softened
- 1⅓ cups Andes creme de menthe baking chips
  Green candy coating disks and sprinkles, optional

1. Preheat oven to 350°. In a large bowl, beat cookie dough and flour until blended and dough is softened. Beat in egg. Add cream cheese; beat until smooth. Stir in baking chips. (Dough will be soft.)

2. Drop dough by tablespoonfuls 2 in. apart onto ungreased baking sheets. Bake 11-13 minutes or until bottoms are golden brown. Cool 2 minutes before removing from pans to wire racks to cool completely.

3. If decorating cookies, melt candy coating in a microwave. Cut a small hole in the tip of a pastry bag or in a corner of a food-safe plastic bag; insert a small round pastry tip. Fill bag with melted coating. Pipe designs onto cookies; decorate with sprinkles.

FREEZE OPTION *Freeze undecorated cookies in freezer containers. To use, thaw and decorate as desired.*

SNOWMAN TREATS

My daughter, Hannah, and I came up with this recipe on Christmas Eve when she wanted to make treats for Santa. Building a real snowman is fun, but we think coating one in candy is even cooler!
—**LORI DANIELS** BEVERLY, WV

PREP: 20 MIN. + STANDING • **MAKES:** 17 SERVINGS

- 9 pieces candy corn
- ½ to ¾ cup creamy peanut butter
- 34 round butter-flavored crackers
- 12 ounces white candy coating, coarsely chopped
- 34 miniature chocolate chips
- 34 milk chocolate M&M's
  Licorice pieces or assorted colors of decorating gel

1. Remove yellow ends from candy corn. Cut each candy in half lengthwise; set aside.

2. Spread peanut butter over half of the crackers; top with remaining crackers to make sandwiches.

3. In a microwave, melt candy coating; stir until smooth. Dip sandwiches in chocolate; allow excess to drip off. Place on waxed paper.

4. Immediately position chocolate chips for eyes and mouths and add a reserved candy corn half for nose. For earmuffs, place an M&M on either side of face, connected with a piece of licorice or a strip of decorating gel. Let stand 30 minutes or until set.

FAST FIX ▶

CINNAMON HOT CHOCOLATE MIX

When our children left for college, they each insisted on taking a large container of this cinnamony cocoa mix with them to the dorm. For rich results, all you need to do is add hot milk, stir and enjoy!

—LINDA NILSEN ANOKA, MN

START TO FINISH: 10 MIN.
MAKES: ABOUT 3½ CUPS MIX
(18 SERVINGS)

- 1¾ **cups nonfat dry milk powder**
- 1 **cup confectioners' sugar**
- ½ **cup powdered nondairy creamer**
- ½ **cup baking cocoa**
- ½ **teaspoon ground cinnamon**
- 1 **cup miniature marshmallows**

ADDITIONAL INGREDIENTS

- ¾ **cup hot milk**

In a large bowl, combine milk powder, sugar, creamer, cocoa and cinnamon. Add marshmallows; mix well. Store in an airtight container in a cool dry place up to 3 months.

TO PREPARE 1 SERVING *Dissolve 3 tablespoons of the hot chocolate mix in hot milk.*

CRANBERRY FUDGE

We make several types of fudge for the holidays. This cranberry-nut one makes a delightful addition to our fudge variety.
—**DELIA KENNEDY** DEER PARK, WA

PREP: 20 MIN. + CHILLING
MAKES: 1⅓ POUNDS (81 PIECES)

- 2 cups (12 ounces) semisweet chocolate chips
- ¼ cup light corn syrup
- ½ cup confectioners' sugar
- ¼ cup reduced-fat evaporated milk
- 1 teaspoon vanilla extract
- 1 package (5 ounces) dried cranberries
- ⅓ cup chopped walnuts

1. Line a 9-in. square pan with foil. Coat foil with cooking spray; set aside.
2. In a heavy saucepan, mix chocolate chips and corn syrup. Cook and stir over low heat until smooth. Remove from heat. Stir in the confectioners' sugar, milk and vanilla. Beat with a wooden spoon until thickened and glossy, about 5 minutes. Stir in the cranberries and walnuts. Spread into prepared pan; refrigerate until firm.
3. Using foil, lift fudge out of pan; discard foil. Cut fudge into 1-in. squares. Store in an airtight container in the refrigerator.

❝I love this recipe! I have made it with different kinds of nuts; it is really good with cashews or with black walnuts!❞
—**LADY_V**
TASTEOFHOME.COM

CHRISTMAS WREATH BREAD

The wreath design for this bread gives it such a festive look. I always make extras to give to friends and to sell at holiday bazaars. Everyone looks forward to receiving them.
—**AGNES WARD** STRATFORD, ON

PREP: 30 MIN. + RISING
BAKE: 20 MIN. + COOLING
MAKES: 1 WREATH (16 SLICES)

- 2 packages (¼ ounce each) active dry yeast
- 1½ cups warm water (110° to 115°)
- 6 tablespoons butter
- ⅓ cup nonfat dry milk powder
- ¼ cup sugar
- 1 egg
- ¾ teaspoon salt
- 4½ to 5½ cups all-purpose flour
- 2 tablespoons butter, melted
- ½ cup chopped almonds
- 1½ teaspoons ground cinnamon
- 1 cup confectioners' sugar
- 1 tablespoon water
- ¼ teaspoon almond extract

1. In a large bowl, dissolve yeast in warm water. Add the butter, milk powder, sugar, egg, salt and 3 cups flour. Beat on medium speed for 3 minutes. Stir in enough remaining flour to form a soft dough (dough will be sticky).
2. Turn onto a floured surface; knead dough until smooth and elastic, about 6-8 minutes. Place in a greased bowl, turning once to grease the top. Cover and let rise in a warm place until doubled, about 1 hour.
3. Punch dough down. On a lightly floured surface, roll dough into an 18x12-in. rectangle. Brush with melted butter. Sprinkle with chopped almonds and cinnamon to within ½ in. of edges. Roll up jelly-roll style, starting with a long side; pinch seam to seal.
4. Place seam side down on a greased baking sheet; pinch ends together to form a ring. With scissors, cut from outside edge to two-thirds of the way toward center of ring at 1-in. intervals. Separate strips slightly; twist to allow filling to show. Cover and let rise until doubled, about 45 minutes. Preheat oven to 375°.
5. Bake 20-25 minutes or until golden brown. Mix confectioners' sugar, water and extract; drizzle over warm bread.

GENERAL INDEX

Creamy Blueberry
Gelatin Salad, 78

Basil Burgers with Sun-Dried
Tomato Mayonnaise, 210

Black & White
Cereal Treats, 196

Feta
Bruschetta, 15

Simple Creamy
Chicken Enchiladas, 122

No-Bean Chili, 48
Slow Cooker Enchiladas, 137
Spicy Chicken Chili, 133
Tex-Mex Sloppy Joes, 52

CHOCOLATE

Beverage
Cinnamon Hot Chocolate Mix, 224
Bread
Pumpkin Chip Muffins, 155
Cakes & Cupcakes
Chocolate Guinness Cake, 206
Mint Brownie Cupcakes, 169
Special-Occasion Chocolate Cake, 180
Triple Layer Brownie Cake, 173
Truffle Football Cupcakes, 212
Candies
Chocolate-Covered Almond Butter Brickle, 201
Chocolate Peppermint Bark, 221
Cranberry Fudge, 225
Peanut Butter Easter Eggs, 207
Cookies, Bars & Brownies
Caramel-Chocolate Chip Sandwich Cookies, 187
Chocolate Cookie Cheesecake, 170
Chocolate-Dipped Spumoni Cookies, 200
Chocolate Snowballs, 219
Creepy Spiders, 214
Gluten-Free Peanut Butter Kiss Cookies, 188
Mocha Macaroon Cookies, 196
Oat Peanut Butter Bars, 193
Peppermint Patty Sandwich Cookies, 189
Quadruple Chocolate Chunk Cookies, 193
Sugar-Cone Chocolate Chip Cookies, 202
Tom Turkeys, 216
Turtle Cookie Cups, 187
Ultimate Double Chocolate Brownies, 185
Dessert
Chocolate Hazelnut Mousse Cups, 160
Pancakes
Chocolate Chip Elvis Pancakes, 39
Mini-Chip Cocoa Pancakes, 34
Pies & Tarts
Chocolate & Peanut Butter Pudding Pie with Bananas, 179
Chocolate Chunk Pecan Pie, 163
Chocolate Pear Hazelnut Tart, 164
Coconut-Pecan German Chocolate Pie, 169
Gingered Almond Truffle Tart, 174

COCONUT
Coconut Cashew Crunch, 20
Coconut-Pecan German Chocolate Pie, 169
Coconut Rhubarb Dessert, 166
Island Breezes Coffee Cake, 152
Lemony Coconut Frozen Yogurt, 209
Lime & Gin Coconut Macaroons, 189
Mango Pie with Coconut Crust, 176
Mocha Macaroon Cookies, 196
White Chocolate Coconut Cake, 174

COFFEE CAKES
Almond Coffee Cake, 149
Christmas Wreath Bread, 225
Cinnamon Coffee Cake, 155
Cinnamon Peach Kuchen, 146

Cinnamon Hot Chocolate Mix, 224

Island Breezes Coffee Cake, 152
Swedish Puff Coffee Cake, 31

CONDIMENTS
All-Day Apple Butter, 213
Apple Pie Jam, 70
Carrot Cake Jam, 67
Refrigerator Pickles, 64
Texas Jalapeno Jelly, 81
Triple Cranberry Sauce, 69
Yellow Summer Squash Relish, 83

COOKIES
(ALSO SEE BARS & BROWNIES)

Amish Sugar Cookies, 201
Autumn Leaf Cutouts, 184
Bite-Size Cinnamon Roll Cookies, 184
Callahan Christmas Wreaths, 203
Caramel-Chocolate Chip Sandwich Cookies, 187
Cardamom-Blackberry Linzer Cookies, 190
Chewy Good Oatmeal Cookies, 199
Chocolate-Dipped Spumoni Cookies, 200
Chocolate Snowballs, 219
Colorful Candy Bar Cookies, 190
Cornmeal Lime Cookies, 203
Creepy Spiders, 214
Creme de Menthe Cheesecake Cookies, 223
Crisp Gingerbread Cutouts, 221
Eyeball Cookies, 213
Favorite Sugar Cookies, 218
Folded Hazelnut Cookies, 194
Gingerbread Whoopie Pies, 212
Gluten-Free Peanut Butter Kiss Cookies, 188
Lime & Gin Coconut Macaroons, 189
Lime Shortbread with Dried Cherries, 197
Mocha Macaroon Cookies, 196
Orange & Lemon Wafer Cookies, 186
Pecan Pie Thumbprints, 199
Peppermint Patty Sandwich Cookies, 189
Quadruple Chocolate Chunk Cookies, 193
Sugar-Cone Chocolate Chip Cookies, 202
Thick Sugar Cookies, 200

Tom Turkeys, 216
Turtle Cookie Cups, 187
Whipped Shortbread, 222

CORN
Corn with Cilantro-Lime Butter, 65
Fresh Corn & Tomato Fettuccine, 110
Queso Fundido, 16

CORNMEAL
BBQ Chicken Polenta with Fried Egg, 33
Cornmeal Lime Cookies, 203

CRANBERRIES
Cranberry-Dijon Pork Roast, 139
Cranberry Double-Nut Pie, 217
Cranberry Fudge, 225
Cranberry-Orange Crumb Tart, 178
Cranberry-Orange Trifle, 171
Ham with Cranberry-Pineapple Sauce, 136
Holiday Salsa, 12
Michigan Fruit Baked Oatmeal, 36
Triple Cranberry Sauce, 69

CREAM CHEESE
Almond Coffee Cake, 149
Baked Creamy Spinach Dip, 16
Bananas & Cream Pound Cake, 170
Bite-Size Cinnamon Roll Cookies, 184
Blueberry Cheesecake Flapjacks, 41
Blueberry French Toast, 28
Cheesenstein, 215
Chocolate Chunk Pecan Pie, 163
Chocolate Cookie Cheesecake, 170
Creamy Blueberry Gelatin Salad, 78
Creme de Menthe Cheesecake Cookies, 223
Greek Breadsticks, 20
Holiday Salsa, 12
Honey Nut & Cream Cheese Baklava, 176
Hot Bacon Cheese Dip, 18
Lemon Supreme Pie, 175
Maple-Nut Cheesecake, 162
Mrs. Thompson's Carrot Cake, 159
Peppermint Patty Sandwich Cookies, 189
Pumpkin Cake Roll, 179
Red, White and Blue Cheesecake, 208
Simple Creamy Chicken Enchiladas, 122
Spaghetti Pie Casserole, 122
White Chocolate Coconut Cake, 174

CUCUMBERS
Crisp & Spicy Cucumber Salad, 64
Minty Watermelon-Cucumber Salad, 74
Refrigerator Pickles, 64

CURRY
Curry Chicken, 101
Thai Red Curry Chicken, 105

DELI MEAT
Chipotle Roast Beef Sandwiches, 59
Hero Pasta Salad, 115
Italian Muffuletta, 45
Salami Pasta Salad, 73
Super Italian Chopped Salad, 80

Maple-Bacon Doughnut Bites, 151

Artichoke Tuna Melt, 61

S'mores-Dipped
Apples, 9

Mom's Swedish
Meatballs, 107

Apple Pie Jam, 70

Doughnut Muffins, 148

Creamy Watermelon
Pie, 211

Pizza
Margherita, 93

Sugarplum Spice Bread, 222

Slow-Cooked Lemon Chicken, 139

Red, White and
Blue Cheesecake, 208

Summer Vegetable
Cobbler, 125

ALPHABETICAL INDEX

Corn with Cilantro-Lime Butter, 65

Family-Favorite Fried Chicken, 113

Orange & Lemon Wafer Cookies, 186

Simple Shrimp Pad Thai, 92

White Chocolate Party Mix, 11

Ingredient Substitutions

WHEN YOU NEED:	IN THIS AMOUNT:	SUBSTITUTE:
Baking Powder	1 teaspoon	½ teaspoon cream of tartar plus ¼ teaspoon baking soda
Broth	1 cup	1 cup hot water plus 1 teaspoon bouillon granules or 1 bouillon cube
Buttermilk	1 cup	1 tablespoon lemon juice or white vinegar plus enough milk to measure 1 cup; let stand 5 minutes. Or 1 cup plain yogurt.
Cajun Seasoning	1 teaspoon	¼ teaspoon cayenne pepper, ½ teaspoon dried thyme, ¼ teaspoon dried basil and 1 minced garlic clove
Chocolate	1 ounce	3 tablespoons baking cocoa plus 1 tablespoon shortening or canola oil
Chocolate, Semisweet	1 ounce	1 ounce unsweetened chocolate plus 1 tablespoon sugar, or 3 tablespoons semisweet chocolate chips
Cornstarch	1 tablespoon	2 tablespoons all-purpose flour (for thickening)
Corn Syrup, Dark	1 cup	¾ cup light corn syrup plus ¼ cup molasses
Corn Syrup, Light	1 cup	1 cup sugar plus ¼ cup water
Cracker Crumbs	1 cup	1 cup dry bread crumbs
Cream, Half-and-Half	1 cup	1 tablespoon melted butter plus enough whole milk to measure 1 cup
Egg	1 whole	2 egg whites or 2 egg yolks or ¼ cup egg substitute
Flour, Cake	1 cup	1 cup minus 2 tablespoons (⅞ cup) all-purpose flour
Flour, Self-Rising	1 cup	1½ teaspoons baking powder, ½ teaspoon salt and enough all-purpose flour to measure 1 cup
Garlic, Fresh	1 clove	⅛ teaspoon garlic powder
Gingerroot, Fresh	1 teaspoon	¼ teaspoon ground ginger
Honey	1 cup	1¼ cups sugar plus ¼ cup water
Lemon Juice	1 teaspoon	¼ teaspoon cider vinegar
Lemon Peel	1 teaspoon	½ teaspoon lemon extract
Milk, Whole	1 cup	½ cup evaporated milk plus ½ cup water, or 1 cup water plus ⅓ cup nonfat dry milk powder
Molasses	1 cup	1 cup honey
Mustard, Prepared	1 tablespoon	½ teaspoon ground mustard plus 2 teaspoons cider or white vinegar
Onion	1 small onion (⅓ cup chopped)	1 teaspoon onion powder or 1 tablespoon dried minced onion
Poultry Seasoning	1 teaspoon	¾ teaspoon rubbed sage plus ¼ teaspoon dried thyme
Sour Cream	1 cup	1 cup plain yogurt
Sugar	1 cup	1 cup packed brown sugar or 2 cups sifted confectioners' sugar
Tomato Juice	1 cup	½ cup tomato sauce plus ½ cup water
Tomato Sauce	2 cups	¾ cup tomato paste plus 1 cup water

Get Cooking With a Well-Stocked Kitchen

In a perfect world, you would plan weekly or even monthly menus and have all the ingredients on hand to make each night's dinner. The reality, however, is that you likely haven't thought about dinner until you've walked through the door.

With a reasonably stocked pantry, refrigerator and freezer, you'll still be able to serve a satisfying meal in short order. Consider these tips:

QUICK-COOKING MEATS—such as boneless chicken breasts, chicken thighs, pork tenderloin, pork chops, ground meats, Italian sausage, sirloin and flank steaks, fish fillets and shrimp—should be stocked in the freezer. Wrap them individually (except shrimp), so you can remove only the amount you need. For the quickest defrosting, wrap meats for freezing in small, thin packages.

FROZEN VEGETABLES packaged in plastic bags are a real time-saver. Simply pour out the amount needed. No preparation is required!

PASTAS, RICE, RICE MIXES AND COUSCOUS are great staples to have in the pantry—and they generally have a long shelf life. Remember, thinner pastas, such as angel hair, cook faster than thicker pastas. Fresh (refrigerated) pasta cooks faster than dried.

DAIRY PRODUCTS like milk, sour cream, cheeses (shredded, cubed or crumbled), eggs, yogurt and butter or margarine are perishable, so check the use-by date on the packages and replace as needed.

CONDIMENTS such as ketchup, mustard, mayonnaise, salad dressings, salsa, taco sauce, soy sauce, stir-fry sauce, lemon juice, etc., add flavor to many dishes. Personalize the list to suit your family's needs.

FRESH FRUIT AND VEGETABLES can make a satisfying predinner snack. Oranges and apples are not as perishable as bananas. Ready-to-use salad greens are perfect for an instant salad.

DRIED HERBS, SPICES, VINEGARS and seasoning mixes add lots of flavor and keep for months.

PASTA SAUCES, OLIVES, BEANS, broths, canned tomatoes, canned vegetables, and canned or dried soups are smart to have on hand for a quick meal—and many of these items are common recipe ingredients.

GET YOUR FAMILY INTO THE HABIT of posting a grocery list. When an item is used up or is almost gone, just add it to your list for the next shopping trip. This way you won't run completely out of an item, and you'll also save time when writing your grocery list.

Make the Most of Your Time Every Night

With recipes in hand and your kitchen stocked, you're well on your way to a relaxing family meal. Here are some pointers to help you get dinner on the table fast:

PREHEAT THE OVEN OR GRILL before starting on the recipe.

PULL OUT ALL THE INGREDIENTS, mixing tools and cooking tools before beginning any prep work.

USE CONVENIENCE ITEMS whenever possible, such as prechopped garlic, onion and peppers, shredded or cubed cheese, seasoning mixes, jarred sauces, etc.

MULTITASK! While the meat is simmering for a main dish, toss a salad, cook a side dish or start on dessert.

ENCOURAGE HELPERS. Have younger children set the table. Older ones can help with ingredient preparation or even assemble simple recipes themselves.

TAKE CARE OF TWO MEALS IN ONE NIGHT by planning main dish leftovers or making a double batch of favorite sides.

Tricks to Tame Hunger When It Strikes

Are the kids begging for a before-supper snack? Calm their rumbling tummies with some nutritious, not-too-filling noshes.

START WITH A SMALL TOSSED SALAD. Try a ready-to-serve salad mix and add their favorite salad dressing and a little protein, like cubed cheese or julienned slices of deli meat.

CUT UP AN APPLE and smear a little peanut butter on each slice. Or offer other fruits such as seedless grapes, cantaloupe, oranges or bananas. For variety, give kids a vanilla yogurt or reduced-fat ranch dressing as a dipper for the fruit, or combine a little reduced-fat sour cream with a sprinkling of brown sugar. Too tired to cut up the fruit? A fruit snack cup will do the trick, too.

DURING THE COLD MONTHS, serve up a small mug of soup with a few oyster crackers to hit the spot.

RAW VEGGIES such as carrots, cucumbers, mushrooms, broccoli and cauliflower are tasty treats, especially when served with a little hummus for dipping. Many of these vegetables can be purchased precut.

GIVE KIDS A SMALL SERVING of cheese and crackers. Look for sliced cheese and cut the slices into smaller squares to fit the crackers. Choose a cracker that's made from whole wheat, such as an all-natural, seven-grain cracker.